Praise from Healthcare Professionals

"Dr. Lintala combines 20 years of experience as an autism mom with her vast knowledge of the medical and behavioral problems associated with autism spectrum disorders . . . She has helped countless families affected by autism. I am in awe of what Dr. Lintala has achieved not only with her patients but also with her own sons. . . . Using humor and intellect, she shares straightforward, easy-to-understand strategies that can help ASD children achieve their potential. . . . Her protocols are so straightforward and easy to understand that they are sure to help thousands of children and improve the quality of life of many families affected by autism."

—Elizabeth Mumper, MD, FAAP,
Former Medical Director of the Autism Research Institute

"Dr. Lintala's use of natural therapies and an integrated approach with modern medical treatment has not only allowed her to transform the health of her own sons, but to achieve outstanding results among many of her patients. Too good to be true? Read, learn, and be amazed!"

—Shawn Reeseman, MD

"I had the pleasure to see how my own patients' social, behavior, and learning skills improved under Dr. Lintala's management protocols. Parents were very pleased and happy with the results under her care.

This book will be a great help to not only these parents, bu~   ~rested in learning how to improve the life of children and adults aff~

. . . I hope she'll continue her excellent work for y~

~an)

"After trying these simple protocols, my dau~   ~s better sleep."
~s, MD (Neurologist)

"Dr. Lintala is a dynamic clinician and a passiona~   ~ocate for children with autism spectrum disorders. I have been very impressed with the results of her treatment programs as well as the extent of her knowledge in this area. Parents are always excited by the changes they see in their children's sleep, behavior, and digestive issues after starting her program. Dr. Lintala also helps to coordinate other important services and to help parents access a complete spectrum of care for their ASD children. She is truly an amazing individual!"

—Gary Veronneau, OD, FCOVD

"A must-have for all families who are struggling with autism. By understanding the science behind this condition, we can increase the success rate of our transitioning youth to accomplish meaningful work and independence."

—Jeanette Ratcliffe, West Virginia Division of Rehabilitation Services

"Amidst a sea of confusing opinions, techniques, and advice, this book provides a rare combination of science-based research and practical strategies for helping parents and professionals. . . . [Dr. Janet] possesses a deep understanding of autism that enables her to cut through the misconceptions and deliver common-sense, effective strategies for moving these children toward optimal cognitive, behavioral, and physical health.

As a nutritionally oriented registered nurse who has worked in the field of pediatrics for over 35 years, I have witnessed transformations in children with autism that professionals and parents alike thought impossible. Following the clear, concise approaches outlined in this book gives children the best shot at obtaining their maximum potential."

—Maureen H. McDonnell, BS, RN; Health Editor,
WNC Woman Magazine; Former Medical Coordinator, The Imus
Ranch for Kids with Cancer; President, Health Education Ser-
vices, Wellness Workshops, Inc.; Cofounder, Saving
Our Kids, Healing Our Planet (www.SOKHOP.com)

"The reader will find clear, no-nonsense action plans that will address so many of the issues affecting those with autism and will offer new hope to them and to their families. This book must be read by all who are concerned with and about autism. My admiration for Dr. Lintala and her accomplishments is boundless!"

—James Winterstein, DC, LLD (hc),
President Emeritus, National University of Health Sciences

"This book should be considered a MUST for any parent or health professional dealing with individuals with autism! Dr. Lintala has a unique and powerful perspective: as a parent coping with a child diagnosed with autism and as a physician searching for ways to help him and the hundreds of families she sees at her clinic. She is amazing at walking you through these steps in a precise manner with confidence—and positive results. I am honored and grateful to have learned from her; my practice would not be the same had I not met Dr. Lintala."

—Monika A. Buerger, BA, DC; Owner, Eagle Canyon
Wellness & Sensory Development Center; Founder, Intersect4kids

"Dr. Lintala has done something few have done: she has simplified the complex and enabled the parent, caregiver, educator, and practitioner to use tried and tested methods to achieve results with these very complex children on the autism spectrum. It will be a worthwhile read with many aha moments."

—Louis Sportelli, DC; Chiropractic Practitioner
and grandparent of a boy with autism

"Dr. Lintala's "Un-Prescription" concepts are an invaluable resource in my approach to providing optimal health care to both children and adults on the autism spectrum.

Dr. Lintala's focus on methods that allow the body to recover health and function through its own natural processes is clearly in line with the tenets of Osteopathic Medicine."

—Michael L. Antolini, DO, FAWM, Family Medicine

"I have only seen incredible positive outcomes from Dr. Lintala's Autism Health center. I have cried joyful tears with parents when I've seen the massive improvements in their children. Read Dr. Lintala's book. You just have to experience it to believe it."

—Amy, LPN

"As a frequent presenter in the didactics sessions for medical students and residents on our hospital campus, Dr. Lintala provided an enhanced awareness of the opportunities to improve and maximize the health of patients dealing with challenges on the autism spectrum. Her scientific, evidence-based approach lends ultimate credibility to her recommendations toward caring for patients on the autism spectrum with understanding, professionalism, and respect."

—Heather J. Antolini, Former Director
of Physician Relations, Raleigh General Hospital

"*The Un-Prescription for Autism* is a book that will revolutionize your thinking and your practice when treating children on the autism spectrum with speech and language disorders. The children that we treat who are following Dr. Lintala's action plan come to us ready to attend, learn, and retain their targeted communication goals."

—Vickie Pullins, MA/CCC-S, Speech Pathologist

"This book is packed with tips and real-world success strategies you can start using immediately. . . . *The Un-Prescription for Autism* is a must read for parents, family members, or the lay person wanting simple, practical tips on raising a child on the spectrum."

—Kelli A. White, Ph.D., Instructor of Social Services,
New River Community and Technical College

See even more testimonials from parents, p. 275.

The
Un-Prescription
for Autism

A Natural Approach for a Calmer, Happier, and More Focused Child

Janet Lintala, DC
with Martha W. Murphy

Foreword by Elizabeth Mumper, MD

Illustrations by Jill Seale

AMACOM

American Management Association

New York / Atlanta / Brussels / Chicago / Mexico City / San Francisco
Shanghai / Tokyo / Toronto / Washington, D.C.

Bulk discounts available. For details visit: www.amacombooks.org/go/specialsales
Or contact special sales: Phone: 800-250-5308 • Email: specialsls@amanet.org
View all the AMACOM titles at: www.amacombooks.org
American Management Association: www.amanet.org

This publication is designed to provide accurate and authoritative information in regard to the subject matter covered. It is sold with the understanding that the publisher is not engaged in rendering legal, accounting, or other professional service. If legal advice or other expert assistance is required, the services of a competent professional person should be sought.

The ideas and methods in this book are not intended as a substitute for the consultation or treatment of a qualified health professional, and none of the prescriptions, protocols, chemicals, and supplements detailed in this book should be followed without first consulting a physician or other healthcare professional. The dosages and supplements provided in this book are derived from the author's limited experience with specific patients and should not be taken to apply generally to all individuals. The author specifically disclaims any liability, loss, or risk, personal or otherwise, that is incurred as a consequence, directly or indirectly, of the use and application of any of the contents of this book. All client names and identifying details have been changed to protect confidentiality.

Library of Congress Cataloging-in-Publication Data

Names: Lintala, Janet, author. | Murphy, Martha W., author.
Title: The un-prescription for Autism : a natural approach for a calmer,
   happier, and more focused child / Janet Lintala with Martha W. Murphy ;
   foreword by Elizabeth Mumper ; illustrations by Jill Seale.
Other titles: Unprescription for Autism
Description: New York : AMACOM, American Management Association, [2016] |
   Includes bibliographical references and index.
Identifiers: LCCN 2015038238| ISBN 9780814436639 (paperback) | ISBN
   9780814436646 (ebook)
Subjects: LCSH: Autism spectrum disorders. | Asperger's syndrome. | Autistic
   children. | Asperger's syndrome—Patients—Biography. | Asperger's
   syndrome—Patients —Care.
Classification: LCC RC553.A88 L56 2016 | DDC 616.85/882—dc23 LC record available at
   http://lccn.loc.gov/2015038238

About AMA
American Management Association (www.amanet.org) is a world leader in talent development, advancing the skills of individuals to drive business success. Our mission is to support the goals of individuals and organizations through a complete range of products and services, including classroom and virtual seminars, webcasts, webinars, podcasts, conferences, corporate and government solutions, business books, and research. AMA's approach to improving performance combines experiential learning—learning through doing—with opportunities for ongoing professional growth at every step of one's career journey.

Printing number
10 9 8 7 6 5 4 3 2 1

To Alan, who brings me flowers.

Sometimes the questions are complicated,
and the answers are simple.
Dr. Seuss

CONTENTS

I magine that you are an optimistic young woman whose hard work in college has earned professional credentials that allow you to pursue a fulfilling career. You have married your true love, a newly minted radiologist who just happens to look like Bryan Cranston of *Breaking Bad* fame. The birth of your first child, a boy, brings more joy than you had thought possible. You've got the world on a string.

But as time passes, your long-desired, deeply loved son shows signs of developmental changes: He is lost in throes of pain; he becomes aggressive, hyperactive, and sleepless. He is diagnosed with autism.

What would you do?

That story is Janet Lintala's, a clinician of exceptional insight and intelligence, and she made a deal with God: She promised, *if my son gets healthy and happy again, I will use what I learn to help others.* With over a decade of helping autism spectrum disorder (ASD) children and their families, she has kept that promise. Now, with the publication of this book, Janet Lintala will help countless more families and children.

Dr. Lintala and her husband went to extraordinary measures to improve the health of their son, who is now thriving in college. Dr. Lintala, known as "Dr. Jae" to many of her patients, works in her clinic without a salary, helping parents discover underlying health problems in their children on the autism spectrum and strategically addressing those challenges. Her reward has a value beyond measure as she watches her patients become healthier and happier and their so-called autistic behaviors diminish.

Since 1976, when I entered medical school, the prevalence of autism spectrum disorders has increased by orders of magnitude, from one in 5,000 to one in 50 children in the United States, based on recent data from the Centers for Disease Control and Prevention. We know from careful analysis that the majority of this increase is *not* due simply to better diagnosis or increased recognition. I have felt impatient as environmental factors were overlooked during the search for "the autism gene." Recently, evidence keeps emerging indicating that *many* genes and variables are involved in ASD and that *a broad array of environmental factors* needs to be considered before and after conception and birth.

Neurodevelopmental problems are increasing around the world, and concerned clinicians and parents are scrambling to find solutions. My keen interest in figuring out what is happening to this generation of children has led to invitations to lecture and/or mentor in eighteen countries. It has been an honor and a privilege to meet so many compassionate and extraordinary parents and professionals. But no matter where I go, adequate resources are lacking to respond to the tsunami of affected children and the impact on their families. That lack, and the extraordinary outcomes Dr. Lintala has helped hundreds of patients and their families achieve over the past ten years, is why I am delighted to see her accessible and affordable health support strategies gathered into a book.

Let me make it clear that neither Dr. Lintala nor I are trying to "fix" the Sheldon Coopers of the world who are a little quirky but have good health, a circle of friends, and jobs they do well. We feel called to help the little boys who cannot learn to talk until their metabolic pathways are supported . . . the little girls who suffer from horrible allergies and asthma attacks until their gut microbes and immune systems are balanced . . . the adolescents who have terrible anxiety attacks in social situations . . . and the children who bang their heads and bite their wrists until their inflammatory bowel disease is managed.

We believe that children are complex and wonderful creatures. A systems biology approach—like the one used by Dr. Lintala and other leaders in the field of ASD—that goes beyond "the shin bone is connected to the knee bone" is crucial. We must consider the effects of gut health on brain function, and that metabolic messages from the microbes that colonize us affect our cell functions. Sadly, this multisystem approach does not fit easily into our current paradigm of medical care in which short office visits and treatment of single symptoms are the norm as physicians are pressured to see more patients in less time.

Last, let me make it clear that neither Dr. Lintala nor I are opposed to the rational use of prescription medications. But rather than trying to find a "pill for every ill" or use different treatments for each individual symptom, we constantly seek the *source of a health problem* within the limits of our current knowledge, which is ever evolving.

The Un-Prescription strategy starts with Dr. Lintala's extremely comprehensive questionnaire, designed to provide clinicians and caregivers with insights about what factors may be contributing to the challenges the ASD child faces. Factors in the medical history and symptoms the child may be experiencing serve as clues for the detective work that is required to get to the root causes of what is interfering with the child's health and well-being. You'll find that very questionnaire in this book, allowing you to experience a virtual office visit, including learning why Janet asks the questions she does and what the answers may mean.

As an ASD mom herself, Dr. Lintala knows the value of "different strokes for different folks." Therefore, she has divided many of the clinical strategies into pathways that can be modified for the circumstances of any family—taking into account the severity of the child's challenges, the family's financial resources, access to extended family support, and the levels of household chaos and parental energy. Each set of recommendations can morph, depending on the response of the child or the needs of the family.

By reading this book, you can benefit from the lessons learned the hard way by a dedicated autism mom and savvy clinician. You may be moved to tears as you recognize your child or grandchild in these pages. You may gasp in horror at her description of the "poop piñata" episode or even laugh out loud at her descriptions of the strategies autism parents will resort to in order to maintain a sex life. Above all, what you'll find here are valuable clinical insights that are packaged into doable action plans to *help your child*.

Similar to the way canaries in the coal mine are affected by low levels of toxic gas and warn miners before they are hurt, increasing neurodevelopmental challenges in our current generation of children should serve as a wake-up call for the rest of humanity. My fervent hope is that the protocols described in this book can help the medical, therapeutic, and educational communities respond to those challenges—faced bravely by these children daily—and that our patients can achieve health and happiness along with the opportunity to live a fulfilling life.

Elizabeth Mumper, MD, FAAP
President and CEO, Rimland Center for Integrative Medicine
Former Medical Director, Autism Research Institute

ACKNOWLEDGMENTS

I would like to thank:
- My husband, Alan, for sharing the journey
- Angela Akers, my right-hand woman at the office, for your tireless work and your gift of hilarity
- Her husband, Doug Akers, who takes all the broken things and makes them work
- Patricia Akers, "Nanny Granny" to our boys, for your endless and good-natured help when the boys were young
- Elizabeth Mumper, MD, my mentor and Sherpa
- Betsy Billheimer Atwater, for setting our feet on the right path all those years ago and showing us where to find help
- My parents, Edsel and Mary Alice Lucas, who always gave me room to stretch my wings
- Jaquelyn McCandless, MD, for her book *Children with Starving Brains*
- The Autism Research Institute and the Medical Academy of Pediatric Special Needs for their invaluable clinician training
- Ilene Bucholz at ProThera and Klaire Labs for technical information support on probiotics and enzymes
- Dr. Devin Houston for his encyclopedic knowledge of enzymes
- All of the autism parents at my center for their valuable and keen insights
- My book editor, Martha Murphy; my literary agent, Paula Munier; and Ellen Kadin, executive editor, and the entire team at AMACOM Books

—Janet Lintala, DC

I'm deeply grateful to have crossed paths with Dr. Janet Lintala, which happened at a CME writing conference in Boston, thanks to Julie Silver, MD. Janet's clinical work and family life are enlightening and inspiring; it's been an honor to work with her on this book. Thanks also to Paula Munier, literary agent, for championing the proposal, and to Ellen Kadin at AMACOM for her enthusiasm for this project. I had the good fortune to be born into a family of extraordinarily thoughtful, inquisitive people—particular thanks go to my parents for their example of grace. And to Kevin: Thanks for being there.

—Martha W. Murphy

A Mother's Story

Autism spectrum disorder (ASD): a neurodevelopmental disorder characterized by varying degrees of social, communication, and behavioral difficulties. It may be associated with varying degrees of gastrointestinal, immunological, and neurological dysfunction, as well as chronic inflammation and oxidative stress, disordered methylation chemistry, detoxification impairments, and nutritional deficiencies. Many consider autism to be a neurological difference as a result of normal variation in the human genome, and not a disorder to be treated or cured.

My marriage hasn't been typical from the start—come on, a chiropractor and a medical doctor? My husband thought he was hilarious when he would ask, "At what point in the office visit do you bite the head off the chicken?" Or he would yell "Chiropractors!" as we watched the Undead leaping out of the walls and ceiling of the temple in *Indiana Jones and the Kingdom of the Crystal Skull*. Little did we know how essential our sense of humor and our training in the healing arts would be as we started our family.

When the first of our three sons, Evan, was born, he was remarkably sunny in nature. He didn't have typical sleep patterns, only napping for twenty to thirty minutes out of every ninety minutes, around the clock, seven days a week. When he had a bowel movement (numerous times a day), they were volcanic and projectile, and I could hear the ominous rumbling a few seconds before liftoff.

Language was a gift for Evan, and I always joke that he came out talking. He *never* stopped talking, which is more exhausting than you would think, and he could read by the age of three. But I also began to notice his sunny nature had given way to all-day irritability and whining. He was restless and roamed the house carrying objects from one room and setting them down in another, creating a level of chaos that became overwhelming.

He was bright and precocious, constantly engaged in learning new things and asking questions I couldn't answer, like: "Does Jesus have a penis?" Impulse control was not a strength.

By the age of 5 or 6, his irritability had progressed to entire days punctuated by anger and screaming, and it wasn't unusual for him to flip over an armchair or the couch when he was having a meltdown. If we sent him to his room, he would kick a fresh hole in the drywall in the upstairs hallway each time. Soon, there were dozens of holes lining the hall that led to his bedroom. We could usually tell from the moment he got up if it was going to be a good day or a bad one.

His behavior became so unpredictable, I couldn't take my eyes off him for a minute and had to follow him wherever he wandered. By now, we had three boys, and I had to hire a housekeeper just to get the laundry done and get a meal on the table. Alan was working long hours as a new associate, and my days began to take on a tinge of exhaustion, desperation, and panic. I just wasn't nailing this motherhood thing, and the rolling eyes and condescending remarks from family members, friends, and strangers only confirmed it. Life felt like a test we hadn't studied for.

As Evan got older, my world got smaller. I dropped out of clubs and volunteering and abandoned my passion for horticulture (a hobby that earned me the name "the African violet lady"). I still distinctly remember the time I first thought, "I need to find Janet; I can't find her anymore," and the feeling of desperation that filled me.

My husband and I would split up to care for the boys in a "divide and conquer" fashion on outings and vacations, going as far as to take separate plane flights and sit at different tables in restaurants on the bad days. At one point, we even considered buying the house next to us, as Evan became intolerant of the noise level and bustle of a busy family household.

Autism is isolating. Eventually, Evan became the child who didn't get invited to birthday parties or playdates, and no one wanted him on their team. He was the first one to be yelled at when something went wrong and always the one who got the blame. Our home was filled with yelling and chaos. Strangers would suggest we medicate him or spank him harder. His heart was broken when his best friend wasn't allowed to play with him anymore.

After years of being told Evan was just "all boy," and that his issues were due to our terrible parenting skills, we finally realized he had what was then called Asperger's syndrome. (This term has since been replaced by the umbrella term of autism spectrum disorder, or ASD.) I went through all the stages of denial and grief, not because my son was autistic, but because of the bleak outlook painted by doctors at the time. We were told there was nothing we could do and were offered various medications.

We felt helpless to reach Evan at times. He would be destructive and angry, but later would crawl up on my lap seeking to be comforted. "Why do I do those things?" he would ask. Once in the midst of a colossal meltdown, he reared up momentarily, looked us in the eyes, and clutched at our arms. "Don't give up on me," he shrieked, before sinking back into the violent, bucking meltdown. Alan and I were speechless. Later, he explained that he knew his behavior was so "bad" that he was afraid we would give him away. Eventually, people began to suggest that we would need to put him in an institution if he didn't calm down.

Thanks to a childhood friend who directed us to doctors trained by the Autism Research Institute, we discovered that children on the spectrum aren't mentally ill or inherently violent, that they have underlying gastrointestinal, immunological, and other metabolic dysfunctions that cause many of the problems Evan was experiencing, and that he was in a lot of pain and discomfort. We began to travel to visit famous doctors. I began to attend conferences and clinician training. I ordered so many books from Amazon that I started a Lending Library for other autism parents. I was delighted (and tormented with guilt) when, after a mere three weeks, a special diet cleared up *80 percent* of Evan's angry, violent behaviors. How had we not known he was in *pain* all those years? I couldn't sleep at night, thinking of all the other little boys and girls who were in terrible pain but not receiving any help. I went through several phases, including being a "mother warrior" and looking for a cause and a cure.

We learned that there are medical challenges on the spectrum that are unseen. The DSM-5 (*Diagnostic and Statistical Manual of Mental Disorders*, Fifth Edition) description of autism spectrum disorder is what we know, what we see, what we expect. There is a tendency to think that irritability, gastrointestinal problems, sleep disruption, and difficult behaviors are just part of autism. They are not. They are signs of deeper problems that, when ignored, create difficulties with irritability and mood, behavior, language, cognition, and mental clarity. We learned why everyone with ASD is different and that what's miraculous for one child may not have any effect on mine.

Evan's behavior smoothed out as his health improved. He wasn't irritable or aggressive anymore. He became happier and regained self-control. Best of all, he became a good sleeper.

We are asking individuals on the spectrum to do their best while they feel their worst. Every day they try to power through a fog of underlying health issues while learning social skills, language, communication, and their ABCs. Our management of ASD is directed at the *behaviors* we see, but we are completely missing and leaving unaddressed the silent medical issues that are causing those behaviors. If all behavior is communication, we are missing the message. The behavior is not saying, *Hey, I need a little more risperidone here.* It's saying, "I don't feel very good." The good news: There are simple ways to correct and restore their health. And that opens the door to other developmental progress.

This book is not about treating, curing, or preventing autism. It is about restoring, supporting, and maintaining vibrant health on the autism spectrum. You don't have to change your child, but you should help him feel better so that he can have his best chance of success and independence.

I began to teach and share with other parents what I learned—in local, then state, then national workshops. I took more and more training in the biomedical aspects of ASD. Patients were traveling to my center from twelve states, and I finally realized that, kind of like Forrest Gump, I had developed a straggly band of followers.

I never dreamed that my life's work would be in autism. That table wasn't there on career day at the high school. It feels good to complete the circle and give back to the autism community by writing this book. Here, I'm sharing protocols I have developed that merge the science showing that individuals with ASD may benefit from natural supplements with the mixed results one gets in real life. This approach improves outcomes.

Although these protocols may seem simple, they are the result of years of trial and error at my center, Autism Health, and they are born of a desire for simplicity, safety, and science. While I don't want you to think for one minute this is *all* your child needs, these protocols will address the most basic needs while restoring and supporting vibrant health on the spectrum.

I suggest that you start by reading this book from beginning to end. Then, use it as a resource to dip into as needed. You may find yourself returning to a particular chapter or section again and again. That's okay. Progress doesn't happen in a straight line. I encourage you to write to me and let me know how you're doing. You can reach me via my website, www. LoveAutismHealth.com, or unprescription@gmail.com.

I know how much you want to be able to help your child. I understand—I live!—your hopes and dreams for that child: better language and eye contact, improved mood, mainstream schooling, good social skills, independent living, and so much more. It is my sincere belief that the information in this book can play a vital role in helping your child achieve those dreams by addressing and supporting his or her health challenges first. I hope you find that magical missing piece in these pages.

PART ONE

Why—Learning the Rules

1

The Rules of Tack Sitting

"Tacks" Rules, By Sidney MacDonald Baker, MD

Rule Number One: If you are sitting on a tack it takes a lot of aspirin to make it feel good. The appropriate treatment for tack-sitting is tack removal.

Rule Number Two: If you are sitting on two tacks, removing one does not produce a 50% improvement. Chronic illness is, or becomes, multifactorial.

"May I be blunt? You have a thirteen-year-old daughter who weighs forty-eight pounds. She's less than five feet tall, and you keep an appetite suppressant patch on her from morning till night. I think she's starving." Ava was on her first visit to my office and quietly played with a game on her iPad the entire time.

Her parents wore stunned expressions. "What do you mean, an 'appetite suppressant patch'? It's for behavior and she's worn it for years," they say.

Ava is on the autism spectrum, and had the typical trio of problems I see in my patients: chronic constipation, disrupted sleep patterns, and irritability. Apparently Ava behaved quite differently—lots of hitting and biting—when she wasn't wearing this ADHD stimulant-type patch. Her doctor prescribed it to control aggression and irritability, without delving deeper to find out why her behavior was so difficult, and told the parents to keep it on from the moment she woke up to right before she went to sleep at night.

Three months later, Ava's parents returned to my office for a follow-up visit. "I took the patch off over the school break and she ate from morning until night," her mother reported. Ava had gained fifteen pounds and grown an inch since her first visit. The school nurse takes the patch off at lunch time now, and Ava is eating and growing normally again.

In 2007, the American Academy of Pediatrics (AAP) encouraged pediatricians to assess and treat underlying medical conditions before prescribing medications for difficult behaviors in ASD and went as far as to state, "Medications have not been proven to correct the core deficits of ASDs and are not the primary treatment."[1] AAP went on to say, "In some cases, medical factors may cause or exacerbate maladaptive behaviors, and recognition and treatment of medical conditions may eliminate the need for psychopharmacologic agents."[2] I thought this would change the way children on the spectrum are assessed and overmedicated. It did not. The conventional medical approach to children with ASD continues to match prescriptions to behaviors.

For many years, the public seemed superficially aware of gastrointestinal (GI) troubles on the spectrum, although these children have so many issues that it got lost in the noise. Then, in January 2010, a stunning consensus report[3] headed by Dr. Timothy Buie of Massachusetts General, the teaching hospital for Harvard University, brought these issues into better focus and connected the dots between gastrointestinal issues, disrupted sleep patterns, and difficult behaviors such as irritability, self-injuring, and aggression. I thought it would dramatically change the way children and adults with ASD are evaluated and overmedicated. It did not.

I think it's time we change the way conventional medicine looks at and treats children with ASD.

What You See Isn't What You Get

The DSM-5 description of ASD[4] is what we see, what we know, and what we expect when it comes to autism spectrum disorder, as in Figure 1-1.

Typically, when a child is diagnosed with ASD, we launch into intense therapies and classroom supports designed to address the deficits described in the DSM-5. Rigorous demands are placed on the child as we try to improve communication, social skills, behavior, and learning, to name a few. A lot of time, effort, and expense are put into improving function, and the child is working harder than anyone else.

What the DSM-5 doesn't indicate is that the child may actually be staggering under a silent burden of health challenges, such as those in Figure 1-2.

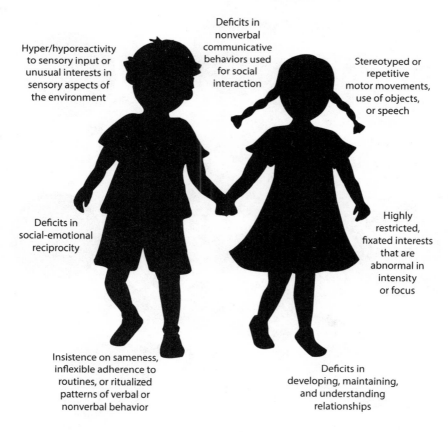

This is what you see:
Autism spectrum disorder as described in the DSM-5

Deficits in nonverbal communicative behaviors used for social interaction

Hyper/hyporeactivity to sensory input or unusual interests in sensory aspects of the environment

Stereotyped or repetitive motor movements, use of objects, or speech

Deficits in social-emotional reciprocity

Highly restricted, fixated interests that are abnormal in intensity or focus

Insistence on sameness, inflexible adherence to routines, or ritualized patterns of verbal or nonverbal behavior

Deficits in developing, maintaining, and understanding relationships

Figure 1-1

These health issues may dramatically affect your child's brain, mood, language, energy level, and ability to learn. Our current conventional approach is focused on medicating behaviors caused by these medical issues into submission (while still leaving the tack in the child's hind end!). In reality, we have suppressed the symptoms, while leaving the original underlying health challenges simmering beneath the surface.

Meanwhile, we continue placing demands on the child in the classroom and in therapy sessions. Interventions, therapies, and behavior programs cannot possibly be at their maximum potential for success when the child they are aimed at is powering through a haze of discomfort and dysfunction. We are asking these children to *do their best while they feel their worst.*

This is what you get:
The invisible health challenges of ASD

Figure 1-2

The children are struggling through their day in a fog of unaddressed health issues. (See Figure 1-3) The perfect storm continues to build, as the medications used to control behavior and mood often amplify and exacerbate these underlying health conditions.[5]

The invisible challenges that children with ASD may have to power through each day

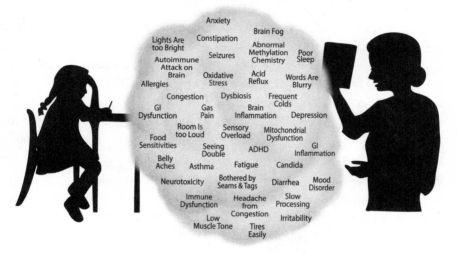

Figure 1-3

No wonder skilled therapists and teachers feel they can't get through to them. One speech pathologist describes it "as if the child with ASD is in a locked room, and I'm standing outside yelling through a locked door."

Did you know that when your child's health is properly supported, these issues can often be minimized, allowing for better focus and function? What am I saying? I'm saying your child will still be autistic but may eat, sleep, and play better, be in a better mood, and have better speech and social skills when these health issues are properly addressed. With some simple natural support strategies, ASD children may catch fewer colds and see their allergies calm down. Every child responds differently, but wouldn't you love for yours to just have a good day most of the time?

I often hear autism parents say their child doesn't need to be "fixed." They accept him just as he is. I get that—I'm an autism mom and I *love* my son just as he is—but this host of physical and medical issues, which can affect everything from language, eye contact, and social skills to sleep, constipation, irritability, and aggression, shouldn't be part of who *any* child is. Accepting your child for who he is doesn't mean you have to accept poor health and impaired function as part of the package. Pulling out these tacks will let his true personality shine through and give him his best chance of success with therapies, school, and life. We need to support vibrant health in these children so that they can be who they are meant to be.

And that's what this book will help you do. We'll explore these underlying health challenges and some simple ways to support balance and healing for your child. Your child must feel his best to do his best.

Would you love to try therapies and programs available for autism, but your child can't even get invited to a birthday party right now? With a calmer child whose gastrointestinal dysfunction, immune dysfunction, and sleep deprivation have been addressed, families can access services and begin therapies they never would have been able to before. The tremendous hope and joy this new reality brings to parents is something I have experienced firsthand and see time and time again at my center.

The medical model in our country is based on very brief visits, at which well-meaning doctors who are pressured for time tend to offer a prescription or even a supplement that "matches" any behaviors or symptoms you might mention during your allotted time (see Table 1-1).

Prescriptions and medications are useful tools (after all, this is not the *Anti*-Prescription you're reading!), but now that you've gotten the Mira-LAX, clonidine, and risperidone, you're probably finding they aren't the

The ASD matching game

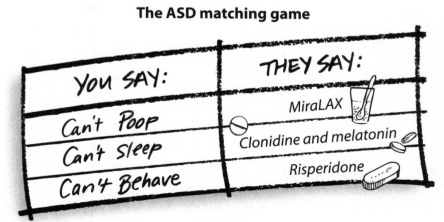

You SAY:	THEY SAY:
Can't Poop	MiraLAX
Can't Sleep	Clonidine and melatonin
Can't Behave	Risperidone

Table 1-1

complete answer you were hoping for. They seemed to help at first with the constipation, lack of sleep, and irritability. They gave you a brief honeymoon period and, after a while, seemed to lose effectiveness. Then the dosages had to be increased, right?

The trouble is, these behaviors and symptoms—can't poop, can't sleep, can't behave—are signs of deeper internal problems that these medications do not address. I've seen parents put young children on enough melatonin to put down a horse in an attempt to keep them asleep all night! But no one is asking *why* they can't sleep soundly. Doctors are putting two- and three-year-olds on risperidone! But no one is asking *why* they are so irritable and restless. Although clinicians and researchers have found many of those answers, sadly, conventional medical approaches do not reflect that yet. You need a plan that addresses the source, not the symptom.

These helpful medications and supplements may be employed as temporary "bandages" without your realizing there is more that could be done to bring real relief. And while they may be helpful on a short-term basis, our parent radar is telling us that they aren't the complete answer. Check Table 1-2 and see if your child is using any "bandages" before we get started:

Tools that act as temporary bandages

Bandages for Constipation and Reflux	Bandages for Poor Sleep Patterns	Bandages for Irritability and Aggression
MiraLAX	*Clonidine*	*Risperidone*
Pedia-Lax	*Antihistamines*	*Abilify*
Stool softeners	*Benzodiazepines*	*Benzodiazepines*
Enemas	*Antipsychotics*	*Antipsychotics*
Prevacid	*Antihypertensives*	*Antihypertensives*
Nexium	*Antidepressants*	*Antidepressants*
Prune juice	*Melatonin, essential oils*	*Stimulant medications and patches*
Toilets with larger openings	*GABA*	
Mattress wedge	*Epsom salt baths*	

Table 1-2

Let's continue to explore the health challenges of autism spectrum disorder—how they affect the brain, behavior, and speech—and discover the areas where *your* child might benefit from the tools you'll find in this book.

My New Patient Questionnaire

The New Patient Questionnaire may at first seem overly long, but it is designed to shine a light on things other doctors may not even notice (but I'll bet you have!) that are vital to figuring out how to help your child. This questionnaire, which I use at my office, not only reveals areas of concern that can be addressed, but also helps build a custom Action Plan and team of experts for your child. It will show us when a referral is appropriate for therapy, a psychological evaluation, a developmental optometry evaluation, a sensory program, a behavioral program, and so on. If indicated, lab tests may need to be ordered. The plan will include everything you need to know to maintain the gains, too, so you can say good-bye to the two-steps forward, one-step backward dance you have probably been practicing.

So what are some of the signs and symptoms that may indicate health problems in your child? Who makes a good candidate for the Un-Prescription Action Plan? Let's start by stepping back and taking a really good look with new eyes at your son or daughter.

Here's a clinical snapshot of common characteristics I see in about three out of four of my patients. Children with some or most of the characteristics are usually the most dramatic responders at my center. If your child has these characteristics, sit up and take notice. Better yet, take *action!*

Common Characteristics

- ☐ Pale, pasty skin
- ☐ Deep, dark under-eye circles
- ☐ Puffiness under the lower eyelids
- ☐ Frequent colds
- ☐ Runny nose

☐ The "allergic salute"—that frequent vertical hand swipe at a runny nose that can create a horizontal crease across the tip of the nose

☐ A sleepy, foggy, or tired look

☐ Acting wired but tired

☐ Eczema

☐ Rashes on face, bottom, arms, legs, back

☐ Red ring around his bottom

☐ Poor eye contact

☐ Chewing on clothing

If you checked off some of these, your child may have GI challenges that could benefit from proper support. This could eliminate pain and discomfort that is causing challenging behaviors and sleep disruption. And there is a good chance he may respond with improved alertness and eye contact, and better immune response, language, and imagination, because as you'll see, the brain is downstream from the gut in a number of ways.[6] In other words, some pollution is being made in the gut that affects brain function. It's not news anymore that ASD children have gastrointestinal issues. Doctors are relying on MiraLAX, clonidine, and risperidone to fill the gap, but your child needs more.

Medications

Next, let's sneak a peek at the medication log, because it will tell me right away many of the things your child is struggling with. See Table 1-3.

Which medications and supplements does *your* child take, and what does that tell us about him or her? Are you just going to accept those issues as "who your child is," or would you like to look deeper?

If you need an *official* diagnosis to obtain an Individualized Education Plan (IEP), Supplemental Security Income (SSI), or another source of aid or support, or just to satisfy personal curiosity, I suggest you take your child to a psychologist who specializes in comprehensive psychological testing.

Translating the medication log

If the medication log says:	Your child probably has:	Conclusions/ Recommendations:
Prevacid, Nexium	Reflux	*Reflux may lead to pain, irritability, night awakenings, aggression, self-injuring*
MiraLAX	Constipation	*Constipation may lead to discomfort, reflux, GI inflammation, and irritability*
Clonidine, melatonin	Poor sleep patterns	*Poor sleep leads to fatigue, irritability, and impaired attention and learning*
Risperidone, Abilify	Aggression, irritability, screaming, crying, difficult behaviors	*These difficult behaviors are likely due to GI pain and discomfort, not autistic or psychotic behaviors*
Singulair, Zyrtec	Allergies	*Immune dysfunction is common on the spectrum, and your child may benefit from GI and immune support*
Antibiotics	Frequent ear or strep infections	*GI and immune support needed*
Adderall, Concerta, Daytrana, Focalin, Intuniv, methylphenidate, Ritalin, Strattera, and Vyvanse	Problems with attention and focus	*Child may benefit from GI and immune support, anti-inflammatory support, and food sensitivity testing*

Table 1-3

Don't settle for someone spending fifteen minutes in a room with your child and then telling you that he is on the spectrum. Why comprehensive testing? Because it may not be autism you're dealing with, or your child may have autism in addition to a mood disorder, attention-deficit/hyperactivity disorder (ADHD), obsessive–compulsive disorder, or an intellectual disability. Each child deserves a complete evaluation.

I often direct parents to the E2 Form on the Autism Research Institute (ARI) website. It was developed by Bernard Rimland, and research shows it is a reliable predictor of the likelihood that your child is on the autism spectrum. Go to Autism.com and fill it out. It is scored at no charge by ARI's wonderful volunteers. It is an easy and inexpensive way to see if your suspicions are on the right track.

Before you get started, take photos and videos of your child. You'll have something for comparison later, when you wonder if you're dreaming or not.

Let's go on a virtual "New Patient" visit to my office. Let's start at the beginning—with your pregnancy—and look for early indicators that your child may need specific health support. Watch your Action Plan components build as you work through each section. Write down any suggestions as you go, especially if a suggestion comes up repeatedly for different sections of the questionnaire. When you're finished, you'll have an idea of which protocols you will need (many can be found in Chapters 6, 7, and 9 and others in the Chapter 9 Online Action Plan), what other therapies and professionals to add to your team, and which testing might be of use. We'll arrange them in a logical order later. I'll teach as I go.

The Pregnancy

Any problems with the pregnancy?

☐ Bacterial Infections

☐ Antibiotics

Why I ask:

Antibiotic use may reduce the beneficial bacteria in your birth canal for when the baby comes through, setting him up for tummy troubles and other health issues.[7]

The Birth

☐ Vaginal

☐ C-section

   ○ If yes, did your doctor transfer birth canal bacteria to your baby with gauze?

Why I ask:

Babies delivered vaginally have the opportunity to pick up good bacteria from the birth canal. Colonization of the GI tract in C-section babies is more haphazard and suboptimal.[8]

☐ Did the baby receive any antibiotics at the hospital?

THE TAKE-HOME MESSAGE

For many of my young patients, their gut has turned into a ghetto, starting with events on their first day of birth.

How Does a "Gut Ghetto" Start?

Your child's beneficial bacteria—crucial for GI and immune health—may have gotten off to a poor start. A baby's gastrointestinal tract is thought to be sterile at birth (although that information may be changing[9]) and is initially colonized with good bacteria when he passes through the birth canal during a vaginal birth. Figure 4-2 on page 107 shows how stressors can cause mothers to not have enough beneficial bacteria for an optimal transfer to the baby during the birth. C-section babies skip the birth canal inoculation altogether.

Without a strong initial colonization of beneficial bacteria in the GI tract, babies are at higher risk for immune and metabolic differences, celiac disease, diarrhea, thrush, eczema, poor sleep patterns, obesity, allergies, asthma, and frequent ear infections and colds.[10]

Research is now examining the benefits of giving probiotics to pregnant mothers, and the preliminary findings look promising.[11] Cutting-edge delivery rooms are using gauze to wipe down newborns with bacteria from the mother's birth canal after a C-section to help the gut microflora get off to a better start. (Chapter 4 describes the benefits of these essential bacteria.)

ADD TO THE ACTION PLAN:

✓ Probiotics (see Chapter 4)

Infancy/Toddler Years

Research indicates that children on the spectrum may struggle with GI dysfunction including reflux, Candida, constipation and diarrhea, mitochondrial dysfunction, and alterations in their immune system.[12] Answer the following questions and see if your child may be affected, too:

☐ Breast-fed or bottle-fed

Why I ask:

Breastfeeding helps strengthen the immune system.[13] The AAP recommends breastfeeding for a full year.

- History of thrush (white overgrowth of yeast in mouth)
- Prone to diaper rash
- Prone to body rashes
- Red ring around the anus/cracking/bleeding
- History of strep infections
- Sinus infections
- Ear infections
- Caught a lot of colds as an infant

The gut is the "local neighborhood" for the immune system and 70 percent of the immune system lives there. How nice the neighborhood is determines how healthy the immune system is. GI support becomes important here.

- Asthma
- Allergies
- Age solid foods were introduced
- Sleep habits as an infant and as a toddler

Why I ask:

Children with ASD are more prone to Candida and microbial imbalance in the GI tract.[14]

Why I ask:

Children with ASD may have altered immune systems.[15] This section alerts me that your child may need immune support.

Why I ask:

A study by the Centers for Disease Control and Prevention (CDC) says introducing solid food before six months of age makes it more likely that your child will be obese or overweight and more prone to eczema, ear infections, and respiratory infections, which means more doctor visits and prescriptions and ending up in the hospital more often.[16]

Why I ask:

Why I ask: A telltale pattern of frequent night awakenings leads me to suspect acid reflux and tummy troubles. Such a child will likely need GI support, not sleep and reflux medications.

ADD TO THE ACTION PLAN:
✓ Basic GI Support Protocol (see Chapter 6)
✓ Basic Immune Support Protocol (see Chapter 7)

Milestones

☐ Did your baby hit milestones on time and then regress?

☐ Did your baby hit milestones on time and then hit a plateau?

☐ Was your baby just different from the beginning?

☐ Was head circumference larger than average?

Why I ask:

Researchers at the UC Davis MIND Institute are beginning to identify subtypes of ASD that may help in developing specific interventions for better health and improved function.[17]

Language and Communication

Research indicates that children on the spectrum may have inflammation,[18] including brain inflammation,[19] oxidative stress[20], and nutritional deficiencies,[21] that may affect their language, social skills, and communication. Answer the following questions and see if your child may be affected, too:

☐ Does your child understand what is being said to him?

☐ Does she use low-tech methods of communication like sign language or picture communication systems?

☐ Does he use high-tech communication such as an iPad app like Proloquo2Go?

☐ Can your child speak?

☐ Does he express needs and wants?

☐ Does he use "I want" statements?

Why I ask:

I'm getting a feel for your child's level of expressive and receptive language, which may show improvement after his GI and other medical symptoms are effectively managed. I want to make sure you are working with a good speech-language pathologist or using assistive communication devices. (See Weeks 19 and 33 in the Chapter 9 Online Action Plan.)

Why I ask:

Certain supplements support neurological health or have anti-inflammatory effects that may support an increase in language in certain subsets of ASD children.[22]

☐ Will she go get items that you ask for?

☐ Does he answer by repeating your question?

☐ Does she initiate conversations?

Describe his speech:

☐ 0 words, mumbles, makes some noises

☐ 1–2 words in a row

☐ 3–4 words in a row

☐ 1 sentence at a time

☐ 2–3 sentences in a row

☐ Many sentences in a row

☐ Language highly developed and appropriate

☐ A "wall" of one-way conversation

☐ Can sustain a back-and-forth conversation, not just reply to questions

☐ Repeats stories he/she has heard on TV (scripting)

☐ Echoes or repeats what you say

☐ Repeats some words or phrases over and over all day

Why I ask:

It is not unusual for my patients with GI dysfunction to gain new vocabulary words and begin speaking in longer sentences after starting the basic support protocols.

Why I ask:

Impairments in methylation chemistry are common in ASD.[23] The methylation cycle is a crucial biochemical pathway in the body involved in detoxification, immune function, switching genes on and off, protein synthesis, and controlling oxidative damage. Supporting this cycle may improve neurological health and support improved language and communication.

Why I ask:

The gluten-free, casein-free (GFCF) diet and enzymes with DPP-IV (pronounced "Dee Pee Pee 4") do not treat or cure autism, but may improve cognition and language in the subset of children with GI dysfunction and constipation. See Chapter 3 for more information on the gut-brain connection.

- □ Speaks in a mechanical voice

- □ Speaks in a singsong voice

- □ Shows concrete thinking (does not understand slang phrases, takes words literally)

- □ Has a sense of humor, but does not get jokes most of the time

- □ Cannot keep up with peer conversations that involve a lot of slang

Why I ask:

Learning verbal and nonverbal slang will help him be part of the conversation and learn to understand jokes. Unintentional Humor *by Gund Anderson and Brent Anderson, Volumes 1 and 2, are fun, helpful books for mastering slang.*

Learning

How is your child doing in school?

- □ Has learning difficulties

- □ Performs work at his/her grade level

- □ Has been held back a grade before

- □ Is being homeschooled due to difficult behaviors

- □ Is in an Autism or Special Education class

- □ Has poor handwriting

- □ Is hyperactive or has trouble sitting still

- □ Hits, kicks, or bites other students or teachers

Why I ask:

Your child may need a referral for a psychological educational evaluation (a "psych-ed eval") to understand his learning style, get more time on standardized testing, and get help at school and at college. I sometimes suggest Lindamood-Bell Learning Processes, a special center that can improve learning and comprehension.

Why I ask:

The Feingold diet has an 80 percent success rate with attention and hyperactivity issues. It even helps improve handwriting. As an autism clinician, I know that food sensitivities should be checked before a child with ASD is prescribed ADHD medication.

THE TAKE-HOME MESSAGE

Difficulties in communication, language, attention, and learning, as well as difficult behaviors, may improve when the silent health issues of the autism spectrum are appropriately addressed.[24]

ADD TO THE ACTION PLAN:

✓ Basic GI Support Protocol
✓ Psych-ed eval
✓ Assisted communication device or system
✓ Work on learning verbal and nonverbal slang
✓ Supplements known to support language development
   (see Week 20 in the Chapter 9 Online Action Plan)

ADD TO THE TEAM:

✓ Speech-language pathologist

ASSIGNED READING:

✓ *Ten Things Every Child with Autism Wishes You Knew* by Ellen Notbohm
✓ *Ten Things Your Student with Autism Wishes You Knew* by Ellen Notbohm with Veronica Zysk
✓ *Unintentional Humor: Celebrating the Literal Mind* by Linda Gund Anderson and Brent Anderson, Volumes 1 and 2

THINK ABOUT FOR LATER:

✓ Mild hyperbaric oxygen therapy
✓ IgG food sensitivity testing
✓ The Feingold diet

Sensory Screening

☐ Rocking, hand flapping, jumping, twirling

☐ Sensitive to noise/sounds

☐ Sensitive to the textures of fabrics

☐ Sensitive to the textures of food

☐ Sensitive to hot or cold foods

☐ Sensitive to smells

☐ Sensitive to light

☐ Bothered by seams and tags on clothing

☐ Does not like to have teeth brushed

☐ Likes to be hugged or touched

☐ Pressure is calming

☐ Sensory seeker

☐ Sensory avoider (avoids playground equipment, textures are a problem)

☐ Gets overwhelmed by crowds, the mall, or parties

☐ High pain tolerance (see Connor's story)

Why I ask:

Clinical observation: About 30 percent of my patients see improvement in their sensory issues after underlying medical issues are addressed. It's all about balance.

Why I ask:

If your child has trouble processing sensory information, he may be seeing the visual input from each eye separately—in other words, what he sees is different from what others see. In the next section, the Developmental Optometry Screening, you're in for a real eureka!

Connor's Story

Connor was four and half years old, and Marie, his single mother, was at her wit's end.

"I don't think he ever feels pain!" she exclaimed. After breaking his arm when he was three, he didn't cry or complain, and she didn't discover it for several days. In another incident, he fell while running and snapped off his two front teeth. He reached in his mouth, pulled out the loose pieces, and kept on playing.

Other children are *too* sensitive—to everything: noise, tastes, textures, smells, clothing, even socks. I don't "treat" sensory issues, but I do see these behaviors calm down in many children as their neurological and overall health improves and balance is achieved.

Developmental Optometry Screening

☐ Does a lot of sideways glancing

☐ Holds toys up very close to eyes

☐ Leans in to look very closely at things

☐ Head frequently tilted to one side

☐ History of a lazy eye

☐ Has been diagnosed with dyslexia

Why I ask:

Sometimes the different visual fields, including peripheral vision, are not smoothly integrated and the child experiments with the crazy jumble of images he is seeing. A developmental optometry evaluation may even reveal he's seeing double. One eye may become "lazy" and not track correctly as the brain ignores it to avoid this double vision.

☐ Avoids homework; has been called "lazy"

☐ Is very intelligent, but makes poor grades in school

☐ Skips over lines when reading

☐ Dislikes or avoids reading

☐ May dislike movies in 3-D

Why I ask:

I don't believe in lazy children. If vision is jumbled, this means your child is working much harder than everyone else in school and getting only half the credit.

☐ Is careful on the stairs: holds the rail, moves one foot at a time, sits down to do stairs

☐ Cannot catch a ball very well (ball avoidance)

☐ Sometimes trips or stumbles over nothing; tends to be clumsy

☐ Sometimes bumps into the door frame when going through a doorway

Why I ask:

Depth perception is poor when the visual input from both eyes is not coordinated. This may translate to difficulties walking stairs, catching a ball, driving, and reading.

THE TAKE-HOME MESSAGE

A developmental optometry evaluation is the miracle referral at my office—I have seen children go from making Ds and Fs in school to top of the honor roll. They cannot see correctly, they don't know it, and neither does anyone else. "He never told me!" many of you exclaim. Whatever he is seeing has always been his "normal," so he didn't know to tell you.

Most of you have no doubt already taken your child for an eye exam. And many of you will insist that your child's eyes are healthy and their vision is normal, *because the eye doctor said so.* And yet, here I am, wanting you to take your child to a different kind of eye doctor.

Think of this other eye exam as a *brain* exam. Specifically, developmental optometry looks at how the brain is handling all of the sensory information from the eyes. Remember, vision is one of the five senses, and man, do these kids have sensory integration issues! If the input from both eyes is all mixed up, your child may actually be seeing double.

As one of my eight-year-old patients said upon getting his new prism lenses, "Now I know which ball to kick!"

ADD TO THE ACTION PLAN:
✓ Developmental optometry evaluation
✓ Occupational therapy evaluation for sensory integration problems
✓ A "sensory diet"
✓ Chiropractic adjustments
✓ Music therapy
✓ Yoga for children
✓ Massage therapy

ADD TO THE TEAM:
✓ Developmental optometrist
✓ Occupational therapist who specializes in sensory techniques
✓ Chiropractor

ASSIGNED READING:
- ✓ *Seeing Through New Eyes* by Melvin Kaplan
- ✓ *The Out-of-Sync Child* and *The Out-of-Sync Child Has Fun* by Carol Kranowitz

GI and Immune System

☐ Very pale skin

☐ Dark under-eye circles

☐ Puffiness under lower lashes

☐ Frequent runny nose

☐ Asthma

☐ Allergies

☐ Frequent, brief grabbing at penis or vaginal area, as if itchy

☐ Food sensitivities

☐ Celiac disease

☐ Seasonal allergies

☐ Cheeks and ears sometimes flush bright red after eating for no reason

☐ Eats inedible things (pica)

Why I ask:
My patients with GI troubles are often very pale, with deep, dark circles under their eyes.

Why I ask:
Your child may be feeling a little itchy due to Candida or a bacterial imbalance.

Why I ask:
Observant clinicians report that red ears and cheeks may be a food sensitivity reaction as well as a soft clinical sign of increased intestinal permeability.

Why I ask:
Pica may be a sign that your child is not absorbing nutrients and minerals from a dysfunctional GI tract, and therefore craves them.

- ☐ Exposed to secondhand smoke (do any smokers live in the home?)

- ☐ Strep infections

- ☐ Sinus infections

- ☐ Ear infections

- ☐ Has ear tubes

- ☐ Catches every cold "coming and going"

- ☐ Had tonsils removed

- ☐ Has an autoimmune disease

- ☐ Seems less autistic when she has a fever

- ☐ Gets warts that are refractive to treatment

- ☐ Has molluscum contagiosum

- ☐ Cold sores

- ☐ Thrush

- ☐ Candida

- ☐ Clostridia difficile

Why I ask:

Children who live in homes with smokers are more susceptible to ear infections and upper respiratory infections[25], and miss more days of school.[26]

Why I ask:

Is your child a "frequent flyer" at the doctor's office? Missing a lot of school? A simple Immune Support Protocol will get him back in class in no time. See Chapter 7.

Why I ask:

Children whose autistic symptoms improve when they have a fever may respond favorably to an extract of broccoli sprouts rich in sulforaphanes.[27] Studies are ongoing.

Why I ask:

Unusual susceptibility to viral infections like the common cold, warts, molluscum, and fever blisters, or fungal infections like thrush or yeast may indicate a type of immune dysfunction seen in ASD called the "Th1 to Th2 shift."[28]

Why I ask:

Some children with ASD struggle with high levels of "C. diff."[29] These bacteria produce propionic acid, which may contribute to neuroinflammation, oxidative stress, glutathione depletion, and other factors that are suspected of exacerbating ASD symptoms. If you answer yes, add S. boulardii to your support protocols.[30] See Chapter 5.

> ### ADD TO THE ACTION PLAN:
> ✓ Comprehensive stool testing
> ✓ Basic Immune Support Protocol
> ✓ Chiropractic adjustments
> ✓ Broccoli sprout extract
> ✓ Saccharomyces boulardii, a beneficial yeast
> ✓ Don't smoke in the house or the car
> ✓ Test for Vitamin D level

Candida Screening

Research shows our children are prone to candidiasis. Read this list and see how many of these characteristics describe your child.

☐ Silly, "drunken" laughter that is inappropriate

☐ Cheeks have bumpy red patches

☐ Rashes around the crotch and buttocks

☐ Red ring around the anus (may also be due to perianal strep, parasites, sexual abuse)

☐ Rectal or vaginal itching

☐ Eczema

☐ Cracking or peeling hands or feet

☐ Ridged, discolored nails or toenails

☐ Jock itch or athlete's foot

☐ Wet hair that smells funny or like a wet dog

☐ Crusty or flaky scalp

☐ Dry flaky skin around the ears, eyebrows, or nose

☐ Persistent cradle cap

☐ Urinary tract infections

Why I ask:

You've probably tried creams, special shampoos, and nail treatments. What your child really needs is basic GI and immune support.

☐ Kidney infections

☐ How many rounds of antibiotics has your child had in her entire life?

Pediatricians are using creams, powders, even steroids to combat eczema, rashes, and the painful red ring that forms around the anus. However, the main culprits, microbial imbalance and Candida within the intestinal tract,[31] go untreated. Basic GI support is needed here.

You know how you usually get a yeast infection when you're on an antibiotic? Your new secret weapon is a powerful beneficial yeast you can take *during* a round of antibiotic. Saccharomyces boulardii (pronounced "Sac b" ☺) is the most researched probiotic on the planet. It hates other yeasts and helps keep them under control when taken with your antibiotic.

If every round of antibiotic was partnered with a month or two of high-potency probiotics and "Sac b," I doubt we would see so many GI, sleep, behavior, allergy, and immune problems in our children.

Here are more signs of a Candida imbalance:

☐ Cravings for desserts and sugary foods

☐ Depression or irritability

☐ Has needed to use Diflucan (fluconazole), nystatin, or other antifungals

☐ Spaced out, foggy, in a different world

> **Why I ask:**
>
> *Don't write these things off as autistic behavior. Scientific studies show our ASD children are more prone to candidiasis and dysbiosis. Bacteria and yeast make a lot of metabolic by-products, including toxins and alcohol. The brain is downstream from all this pollution, and the end result is brain fog, irritability, and a really mean sweet tooth.*

Do you have to say your child's name several times before you get a response? Does it seem like your child has to power through some serious brain fog to speak or respond to requests? Don't just assume this is "who he is." Try the Basic GI Support Protocol to see if his brain is simply downstream from some pollution in the gut.

ADD TO THE ACTION PLAN:
✓ Basic GI Support Protocol (which includes Sac b)
✓ Basic Immune Support Protocol

✓ Reduce sugar and refined carbohydrates in the diet
✓ Immune Support Protocol
✓ Antibiotic Support Protocol

Sleep Patterns

☐ Difficulty falling asleep occasionally

☐ Difficulty falling asleep most of the time

☐ Stays asleep all night but body is restless (e.g., tossing and turning, covers all torn up)

> **Why I ask:**
>
> *Autism parents have horror stories to tell of the frequent night awakenings and infamous poor sleep patterns on the spectrum— problems that are mostly due to acid reflux and GI discomfort. You will be glad to know your child's sleep pattern is often one of the first things to improve when the Basic GI Support Protocol is started. Hallelujah!*

☐ Awakens maybe once a night and goes right back to sleep

☐ Frequent night awakenings; does not go back to sleep easily

☐ Not unusual to "be up for the day" at an extremely early hour (e.g., 3 a.m.)

☐ Moans or cries in sleep

☐ Nightmares or night terrors

☐ Sleep walks

☐ Sleeps less than normal

☐ Sleeps more than normal

> **Why I ask:**
>
> *I've had several cases where overwhelming fatigue and excessive sleeping were found to be due to intestinal parasites.*

☐ Takes melatonin, clonidine, or other medications for sleep

☐ Antipsychotic or antidepressant medication is strategically taken at night to help with sleep

☐ How many caffeinated drinks are consumed each day?

Children with autism tend to get significantly less sleep than non-ASD children.[32] They go to sleep later, get up earlier, and may wake up several times a night. Poor quality of sleep significantly affects the daytime functioning of autistic children, and from personal experience, I can assure you that sleep-deprived children equals sleep-deprived parents. This leads to difficult behaviors and high levels of family stress. I spent years in a crabby stupor before I learned how easy the sleep patterns are to restore.

ADD TO THE ACTION PLAN:

✓ Follow the Basic GI Support Protocol (believe it or not, sleep will usually respond and improve)
✓ Try the sleep tips (see Week 4 in the Chapter 9 Online Action Plan)
✓ Reduce and eliminate caffeine in the diet
✓ Alpha-Stim 20 minutes a day (see www.alpha-stim.com)

THINK ABOUT FOR LATER:

✓ Lab testing of specific hormones and neurotransmitters (rarely needed, unless nothing else works for poor sleep patterns)

ASSIGNED READING:

✓ *Go the F**k to Sleep* by Adam Mansbach ☺
✓ *Healthy Sleep Habits, Happy Child* by Marc Weissbluth, MD

Dietary History

A healthy diet is the best medicine, and yet many of us can count on one hand the number of foods our children eat. What's up with those restricted eating patterns? Fill in the blanks below and see what pattern emerges for your child:

☐ Organic foods

☐ Nonorganic foods

☐ Partially organic diet

☐ Fruits

☐ Vegetables

☐ Meats

Why I ask:

Individuals with ASD may have impaired detoxification status.[33] A diet free from chemicals, dyes, preservatives, additives, hormones, and antibiotics can be an important foundation of health for them.

- [ ] Beans and lentils

- [ ] Grains

- [ ] Seeds, nuts, and nut butters

- [ ] Snack foods

- [ ] Dairy products

- [ ] Bread, pasta, pizza

- [ ] Difficulty chewing and swallowing

- [ ] Picky eater

- [ ] Consumes diet high in processed foods

- [ ] Consumes artificial sweeteners

- [ ] Attitude or mood changes after meals

- [ ] Demands or wants certain foods every day

- [ ] Drinks a lot of milk (white/chocolate/strawberry)

  - o Number of glasses per day:

  - o How much would your child drink if you let him have all he wanted?

- [ ] Ever been on a gluten-free/casein-free diet?

  - o Was it done strictly?

  - o What happened?

Why I ask:

I am looking for restricted and addictive eating patterns. If there is such an eating pattern, your child may benefit from enzymes with DPP-IV or one of several special diets.

Why I ask:

Picky eaters with low muscle tone or an extreme sensitivity to textures, smells, and tastes may benefit from a referral to a feeding specialist.

Why I ask:

I'm looking for addictive eating patterns. If a child drinks a gallon of milk a day, or eats chicken nuggets, macaroni and cheese, and pizza likes it's his job, I might jump ahead to the next section of the questionnaire to see if he's constipated. Chapter 3 also explains why gluten and casein can cause constipation, and why enzymes with DPP-IV can help.

Who'd have thought food—ordinary, everyday food—could have such dramatic effects on cognition, mood, learning, processing speed, ADHD, irritability, hyperactivity, and being "zoned out"?

Science and clinical observation are revealing that food is powerful for ASD children. And you can harness its power for evil or for good. We will explore why our children eat addictively and how it affects them in

Why I ask:

Your child will likely surprise you by trying new foods once he's on the enzymes with DPP-IV for about a month.[34]

Chapter 3. No matter what else I share with you in this book, remember that a good diet is the foundation of anything we do. And I'll show you how to overcome the picky and addictive eating habits in as painless a way as possible.

ADD TO THE ACTION PLAN:
- ✓ Enzymes with DPP-IV (part of the Basic GI Support Protocol)
- ✓ A good quality multivitamin
- ✓ Go as organic as you can afford, especially with meats, milk, and eggs

ADD TO THE TEAM:
- ✓ Feeding specialist

Bowel Habits

Next, I ask about the frequency, texture, and well, yes, the *smell* of your child's poop and gas. Some parents and even children look a bit taken aback by this line of questioning. (Some even laugh.) But many of you exclaim, "Finally, someone who's asking about all these weird things that we deal with every day!"

☐ How often does he have a bowel movement?

☐ Has he had to use laxatives or stool softeners?

Why I ask:

Children with ASD are significantly more likely to have constipation and diarrhea[35] and may need a GI support protocol or special diet. Keep reading!

☐ Has he been hospitalized for constipation?

☐ Bowel movements are very foul-smelling.

☐ Gas is very foul-smelling.

☐ He is excessively gassy.

Why I ask:

Gassiness may indicate poor digestion and insufficient digestive enzymes. The foul odor may indicate a microbial imbalance (unless, of course, you ate some spicy food last night!).

Look at the following chart, and mark all the stool types your child has:

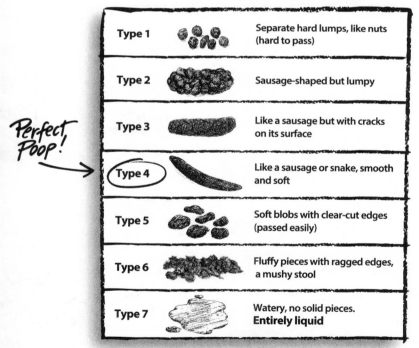

The Bristol Stool Chart

Perfect Poop! →

Type 1		Separate hard lumps, like nuts (hard to pass)
Type 2		Sausage-shaped but lumpy
Type 3		Like a sausage but with cracks on its surface
Type 4		Like a sausage or snake, smooth and soft
Type 5		Soft blobs with clear-cut edges (passed easily)
Type 6		Fluffy pieces with ragged edges, a mushy stool
Type 7		Watery, no solid pieces. **Entirely liquid**

Dr. Ken Heaton, at the University of Bristol, United Kingdom, developed the Bristol Stool Scale, or the Bristol Stool Chart. He first published it in 1997 in Lewis S. J., and K. W. Heaton, "Stool Form Scale as a Useful Guide to Intestinal Transit Time," *Scandinavian Journal of Gastroenterology* 32, no. 9 (1997): 920–24.

- How often does your child have a bowel movement? *The goal is daily type 4s.*

- Do you give any enemas, suppositories, or laxatives?

- Does your child have to crouch/perch on the toilet seat to have a bowel movement? *This can be a tip-off to constipation.*

- Enormous bowel movements: *Colon has become stretched out from impacted stools.*

- Diarrhea *and* constipation.

- Undigested food present in stools: *Many ASD children do not make sufficient digestive enzymes.*

- Mucus in the stools: *This is a marker for inflammation.*

- Sticky stools: *May indicate gluten or lactose sensitivity.*

- Foul-smelling bowel movements and gas: *May indicate a microbial imbalance.*

- Gassiness: *May indicate maldigestion or microbial imbalance.*

Why I ask:

Constipation may contribute to:
- *Reflux*
- *Candida*
- *Pain and discomfort*
- *Irritability*
- *Aggression*
- *Poor sleep*
- *Impaired detoxification*

Why I ask:

Let me explain about an alternating pattern of diarrhea and constipation: Our food begins the process of digestion as a rather liquid slurry. If a hard, impacted mass of poop is blocking the colon, the liquid poop will simply go around it, making you think your child has diarrhea.

Why I ask:

I am disturbed by doctors telling autism parents it's just "toddler constipation" or "toddler diarrhea." Giving it a name does not make it normal. How long do these children have to be miserable?

ADD TO THE ACTION PLAN:
✓ Basic GI Support Protocol

ASSIGNED READING:
✓ *Poophemisms: Over 1737 Fun Ways to Talk About Taking a Poop* by Douglas Fir
✓ *Digestive Wellness for Children* by Elizabeth Lipski, PhD

LAB TESTS TO CONSIDER:
✓ Comprehensive stool test
✓ Organic acids test
✓ Amino acids test

Stool and urine testing may reveal dysbiosis or nutritional needs.

TREATMENT TIP

Addressing GI dysfunction and eliminating constipation should be the centerpiece of any health plan. Taking MiraLAX forever is not acceptable.

Aaron's Story

The story of six-year-old Aaron's visit to a gastroenterologist baffled me. His mother, Katherine, listed MiraLAX, fiber, frequent enemas, and stool softeners on the list of interventions. She described attempts to pry the hardened stools from his rectum and said that untreated, he had bowel movements every twelve to fourteen days. With MiraLAX, he had them every five to seven days. Aaron's pediatrician referred him to a GI doctor for chronic severe constipation. The GI specialist was over an hour's drive away. After Katherine filled out papers, the nurse refused to put them in an exam room. "The doctor says he has to be constipation-free for six months before he can evaluate his GI tract." Katherine thought she must have misunderstood. "But we're here for the constipation!" she cried. The nurse would not budge. Six months.

Within three and a half weeks of starting digestive enzymes with DPP-IV, the first step of the Basic GI Support Protocol, Aaron was having glorious daily bowel movements, and his aggression began to smooth out.

TREATMENT TIP

By eliminating constipation, it is very likely your child will need far less, if any, medications for reflux, sleep, and behavior problems.

- □ Breath smells:
  - ○ Not bad
  - ○ Like freshly baked bread
  - ○ Stinky, bad
  - ○ Just like poop[36]
- □ Abdominal bloating
- □ Drapes his tummy or leans over tables, chairs, or arms of couches
- □ Presses his tummy up against the edges of tables
- □ Random self-injuring behavior and head-banging
- □ Random sadness or crying, or unexplained tantrums
- □ Spotting of feces in underwear
- □ Not toilet-trained
- □ Bed-wetting

Reflux Screening

- □ Has known reflux
- □ Swallows or clears throat frequently
- □ Tooth enamel is being eroded by gastric acid (here's your sign)

Why I ask:

Bad breath may come from a microbial imbalance, a Candida overgrowth, or poop and bile refluxing back up into the stomach. (Yes, really!)

Why I ask:

Bloating may be due to gas from maldigestion and Candida, stool impaction, or even severe malnutrition due to not being able to absorb nutrition.

Why I ask:

Don't miss this clue! These "random" incidents may be pain behaviors indicating belly discomfort.

Why I ask:

I never make promises, but I often see these last three issues disappear with a solid Basic GI Support Protocol.

Why I ask:

If your child puts off going to sleep or wakes up a lot during the night, he probably has reflux. Reach for the Basic GI Support Protocol in Chapter 6 first, not reflux medications.

> ### TREATMENT TIP
> Relieving constipation can reduce or eliminate reflux. The answer: enzymes with DPP-IV to the rescue!

☐ Facial grimacing

☐ Gritting teeth

☐ Wincing

☐ Sighing, groaning

☐ Burping

☐ Paces around the house, jumps up and down, is hyperactive

☐ Puts off going to sleep

☐ Frequent waking at night

☐ Falls asleep propped up in bed, sitting up on couch, in an armchair, or in the car seat

Why I ask:

Sleeping in a propped-up position is the "reflux position," a tip-off that your child likely has reflux.

Reflux is one of the most unsuspected conditions in children. Read that sentence again. Most parents say their child does not have reflux, but upon persistent questioning, a pattern emerges that is consistent with reflux. Reflux is a significant factor in poor sleep patterns and irritability on the autism spectrum.

> ### ADD TO THE ACTION PLAN:
> ✓ Basic GI Support Protocol
> ✓ Chiropractic adjustments
> ✓ Elevate the head of the bed with a mattress wedge

Behavior

- ☐ Easily frustrated
- ☐ Easily angered
- ☐ Tantrums or outbursts
- ☐ Irritability
- ☐ Aggression
- ☐ Self-injuring
- ☐ Destructive around the home

Why I ask:

"Symptoms associated with gastrointestinal disorders, especially pain, may function as setting events for problem behaviors."[37] These behaviors indicate pain and discomfort—missing this clue can lead to inappropriate use of antipsychotics and ineffective, time-consuming behavior programs. Go for the Basic GI Support Protocol first.

Few realize these behaviors can be an expression of pain and dysfunction in a child with poor communication and social skills.

Health professionals seem to assume that the high levels of constipation, irritability, aggression, rages, nighttime awakenings, hyperactivity, and self-injury that many of the children display are simply inexplicable "autistic behaviors." Hello?

These behaviors are due to real medical problems that children on the autism spectrum have. There are simple, natural protocols to correct these problems, calm your child, get rid of the GI issues, and let you and your child get well and get some real sleep. Now, that sounds like just what you need!

Let's peek at Isaac's story.

Isaac's Story

Every day, children with autism are asked to do their best while they feel their worst.

Two-and-a-half-year-old Isaac is on the autism spectrum and was having a bad day at the pediatrician's office. The doctor was annoyed and told the family that he wouldn't get any stickers: "This is not autistic behavior, this is bad behavior. We don't reward bad behavior with stickers." He told all of the nurses not to give Isaac any stickers and wrote it on the outside of his chart. When Isaac began head banging, the doctor instructed the angry family to admit him to the psychiatric floor of the local hospital via the emergency room.

I started Isaac on the Basic GI Support Protocol, and he is now a much mellower and happier ASD child.

Like many health professionals, Isaac's pediatrician doesn't understand that pain and dysfunction in the GI tract can affect mood and behavior for those on the autism spectrum. Isaac wasn't giving the doctor a hard time, he was having a hard time.

Toddlers like Isaac are routinely referred for psychiatric medications to control behaviors when a simple, natural GI support program would clear up most of the problems. We need to change the conventional approach to ASD so that every child can have a good day (and get his stickers!).

This book teaches parents and health professionals to recognize and address these unseen health challenges and support vibrant health on the autism spectrum. With improved health comes improved clarity, cognition, and clearing of the brain fog, as well as improved mood and behavior.

If you try the Basic GI Support Protocol, yet your child still has loose stools and behaviors such as hitting, screaming, biting, kicking, and head banging, it's time for a comprehensive stool test and more targeted treatment. Why? Studies indicate our children are more prone to Clostridia difficile and other bacterial infections in the GI tract that are associated with these behaviors.

Why I ask:

"Lactase deficiency not associated with intestinal inflammation or injury is common in autistic children and may contribute to abdominal discomfort, pain, and observed aberrant behavior. Most autistic children with lactose intolerance are not identified by clinical history."[38] Read Chapter 3 to get inspired about using digestive enzymes.

Your treatment plan is developing as we go. Are you beginning to feel like there might be some hope?

ADD TO THE ACTION PLAN:

- ✓ Comprehensive stool testing
- ✓ Basic GI Support Protocol
- ✓ Applied behavior analysis (see Week 23 in the Chapter 9 Online Action Plan)
- ✓ GABA and other calming support tips (see Week 3 in the Chapter 9 Online Action Plan)

Tics and Obsessive Tendencies

- ☐ Sudden, brief involuntary muscle movements or jerks (I am not talking about hand flapping or finger twirling)

- ☐ Repetitive blinking, snorting, or coughing; touching the nose, smelling objects

- ☐ Picking at skin until it is raw

- ☐ Sudden, brief involuntary vocalizations or sounds

- ☐ Tic disorder such as Tourette disorder

- ☐ Obsessive–compulsive disorder or tendencies

Why I ask:

Tics and obsessive tendencies seem to run with our crowd[39] and may be triggered by antibodies to strep species cross-reacting with certain structures in the brain. Antibiotics are sometimes used, and some patients successfully manage tics with the Xylitol Support Protocol. (See Week 48 in the Chapter 9 Online Action Plan.)

My Story

I'll share a story that illustrates how strep infections can contribute to an increase in tics. One of my sons has Tourette disorder. We brought the noises and twitches under good control with the Xylitol Support Protocol, which I provide in the Chapter 9 Online Action Plan. After a couple of quiet years, we became complacent and didn't always use the xylitol nasal and oral care products regularly.

We were on a family trip to a dude ranch out west, when he said, "Hey, Mom, watch this!" His entire arm shot up in the air and back, quick as a wink.

"Was that a tic?" I wondered. I was mystified. We hadn't seen one in months, and never one that dramatic. Two days later, he was transported by ambulance to the medical center in Jackson Hole, Wyoming, with strep pneumonia. His strep titers (antibodies) had been building while the infection was subclinical, and we had missed the clue of the newly reappeared tics.

ADD TO THE ACTION PLAN:
✓ Xylitol Support Protocol

ASSIGNED READING:
✓ *Saving Sammy: Curing the Boy Who Caught OCD* by Beth Maloney

Mitochondrial Screening

For this material I owe special thanks to Nancy O'Hara, MD, and Elizabeth Mumper, MD:

☐ As an infant:

- ○ Difficulty latching on

- ○ Difficulty swallowing

- ○ Excessive drooling

- ○ Poor head control ("floppy baby")

☐ Poor muscle tone

☐ Problems with fine motor skills (e.g., difficulty writing letters)

☐ Curved back, "C" shape when sitting

☐ Difficulty knowing self in space

Why I ask:

I am looking for signs of low muscle tone due to mitochondrial dysfunction, which may be due to chronic oxidative stress. We can provide "mito" support if appropriate. (See Week 23 in the Chapter 9 Online Action Plan.)

☐ Tires easily

☐ Poor eye-hand coordination

☐ Hyper-flexible joints

☐ Poor speech, expressive and receptive

☐ "Crashes" when he gets sick (i.e., gets dehydrated or even hospitalized)

It is estimated that up to 60 percent of ASD children may struggle with mitochondrial dysfunction,[40] which may be due in part to oxidative stress created by chronic inflammation. This translates to low muscle tone and being easily fatigued. Proper support includes antioxidants, anything that reduces inflammation, and supplements known to support mitochondrial function.

ADD TO THE ACTION PLAN:

✓ Mitochondrial support tips (see Week 23 in the Chapter 9 Online Action Plan)

✓ Antioxidant Support Tips (see Week 17 in the Chapter 9 Online Action Plan)

✓ Anti-inflammatory Support Tips (see Week 17 in the Chapter 9 Online Action Plan)

Seizures

☐ Staring spells

☐ Seizures

Why I ask:

Staring spells could be due to:
- *Seizure activity*
- *Opioid peptides from the gut*
- *Fatigue from sleepless nights*
- *Brain fog caused by Candida and dysbiosis*
- *Inflammation and oxidative stress*

Some autism clinicians have noted that some of their patients report a reduction in frequency of seizures when a healthy balance is achieved in the GI system, although we aren't sure why. I have noticed this in my own practice as well.

Why I ask:

Does your child chew his shirts to pieces? Studies show children with ASD tend to be low in zinc.[41] I always give zinc for the "chewies."

Signs of Zinc Deficiency:

☐ Has white dots or horizontal white lines on multiple fingernails

☐ Acne/sparse hair/psoriasis

☐ Canker sores

☐ Chews on toys, objects, clothing

Benefits of Zinc (one of my "Fab Five" favorite supplements):
- *Healing to the gut*
- *Improves appetite[42]*
- *Supports immune health*
- *Important for attention and focus*
- *Competes with copper and mercury for absorption, two things children with ASD may be high in[43]*

Signs of a Magnesium Deficiency:

☐ Muscle twitches/tingling

☐ Sighing

☐ Salt craving

☐ Chews on toys, objects, clothing

Why I ask:

If zinc doesn't get rid of the "chewies," I add magnesium to the Action Plan. Of course, chewing may be a sensory need as well.

Signs of an Essential Fatty Acid Deficiency:

☐ Keratosis pilaris (little bumps on the backs of the arms)

☐ Dry, coarse hair

Why I ask:

Essential fatty acids or EFAs are very beneficial for children with ASD.[44] They are another one of the "Fab Five" supplements I love.

ADD TO THE ACTION PLAN:

✓ Zinc
✓ Magnesium
✓ Essential fatty acids

Dental

☐ Does your child have regular dental visits?

☐ Does your child tolerate visits to the dentist?
If not, arrange a few "practice runs."

☐ Does your child have cavities, now or in the past? *Add xylitol to the plan.*

Why I ask:

Xylitol is great for oral health—it works against the mutans streptococci bacteria that cause cavities, reducing both plaque and cavities.

☐ Has the tooth enamel been eroded by gastric acid? *It's a sure sign of acid reflux.*

☐ Have steel caps been placed on the teeth? *Yep, acid reflux!*

☐ Is your child sedated for procedures? *If so, prevention becomes very important.*

☐ Tolerates brushing? *Occupational therapy may help.*

☐ Regular flossing? *Floss picks may make this chore easier.*

☐ Has had molars sealed? *Dental sealants smell so very toxic, yet they are worth the trade-off if they prevent cavities and sedation.*

☐ Uses a probiotic toothpaste or rinse.

☐ Uses xylitol toothpaste and mouthwash.

ADD TO THE ACTION PLAN:
✓ Basic GI Support Protocol for the acid reflux
✓ Xylitol Support Protocol
✓ Probiotic toothpaste and rinses
✓ Get molars sealed
✓ Dental hygiene tips (see Week 48 in the Chapter 9 Online Action Plan)

Focus, Attention, and Impulsivity

- ☐ Has been diagnosed with ADD or ADHD

- ☐ Poor self-control

- ☐ Impulsive (acts before thinking)

- ☐ Poor memory for directions and instructions

- ☐ Dreamy, distracted type

- ☐ Needs special seating in the classroom

- ☐ Trouble following directions

- ☐ Frequently interrupts

- ☐ Is the class clown

- ☐ Disorganized

- ☐ Poor planning

Why I ask:

Food sensitivities, including foods high in salicylates, may cause significant troubles with attention and hyperactivity. IgG food sensitivity testing and the Feingold diet may help your child avoid powerful stimulant medications.

Why I ask:

Neurofeedback can help with ADHD, executive thinking, and disorganization. It is worth the investment.

Exercise

What is your child's exercise level?

- ☐ Completely sedentary

- ☐ Not much exercise

- ☐ Moderate level of exercise

- ☐ High level of exercise

Why I ask:

Exercise is great for hyperactivity and ADHD. If your child avoids sports, consider a developmental optometry evaluation.

Activity

- ☐ Restless, roams around

- ☐ Fidgety

- ☐ Difficulty staying seated

- ☐ Hyperactive

- ☐ Headaches

- ☐ Talks excessively

- ☐ Touches everything

- ☐ Easily excited

- ☐ Lethargic/fatigued

Why I ask:

I often see hyperactivity and impulse control improve as families work through the basic protocols and balance health.

Compliance

- ☐ Has difficulty following the rules

- ☐ Argumentative

- ☐ Engages in negative behavior to get attention

- ☐ Destruction of household items, furniture, or walls

- ☐ Gets physically aggressive with family members

- ☐ Gets physically aggressive with classmates, teachers, or aides

Why I ask:

Too many children are being labeled and medicated for "oppositional defiant disorder" (ODD) instead of getting the help they need with their belly troubles. I expect many of these symptoms to improve or disappear as GI health is restored.

ADD TO THE ACTION PLAN:

- ✓ Exercise
- ✓ Feingold diet (see Week 41 in the Chapter 9 Online Action Plan)
- ✓ IgG food sensitivity testing (see Week 39)
- ✓ Neurofeedback (Week 40)
- ✓ Developmental optometry evaluation (Week 30)
- ✓ Tests for detoxification status (Week 24)

Peer Relationships and Behavioral Difficulties

☐ Would like to have friends

☐ Truly prefers to be alone

☐ Parallel play (plays *near* other children, not *with* them)

☐ Has trouble with group activities

☐ Blames others

☐ Is a "provocative victim"

☐ Bullies or bosses other children

☐ Teases excessively

☐ Unpredictable behavior scares other children away

☐ Is rejected or avoided by others

Why I ask:

There are many resources for teaching social skills: counseling, therapies, books, DVDs, supervised playdates, and even summer camps.

Emotional Difficulties

Research indicates that individuals on the spectrum are more likely to have mood disorders such as anxiety or depression.[46] Look at the following and see if your child may be affected too:

☐ Has been diagnosed with a mood disorder

☐ Frequent mood swings

☐ Irritable

☐ Often anxious

☐ Depressed or unhappy

Why I ask:

Supplementation with Lactobacillus rhamnosus early in life may reduce the risk of developing neuropsychiatric disorders later.[45]

Why I ask:

Your child may need a referral for psychiatric medications or counseling. Up to 84 percent of those on the spectrum may experience anxiety to some degree.[47] See Week 43 in the Chapter 9 Online Action Plan for tips for handling anxiety.

☐ Does your child wander or run away?

Why I ask:

Project Lifesaver is a GPS bracelet that finds a zippy little runaway in an average of twenty minutes instead of hours or days. (See Week 22 in the Chapter 9 Online Action Plan for more safety tips.)

Maturity

☐ Behavior resembles that of a younger child

☐ Prefers younger relationships

☐ Prefers the company of adults

Why I ask:

I find that many ASD children are less mature for their age than their peers. Just be patient and let them develop at their own pace.

Home Situation

☐ How many homes does the child live in, or divide time between?

☐ If more than one home, will both homes be cooperative with the health plans?

☐ Are there any difficult family situations that may hinder treatment?

Why I ask:

I keep the protocols very simple for complicated home and marital situations.

Who Lives in the Primary Home?

☐ Mother

☐ Father

☐ Stepmother

☐ Stepfather

☐ Girlfriend

☐ Boyfriend

☐ Brothers

Why I ask:

To be honest, the answer to this question gives me an idea of the "chaos status" of your home. It's usually more difficult to maintain the protocols when there is a revolving door for various relatives, friends of friends, and strays.

☐ Sisters

☐ Grandmother

☐ Grandfather

☐ Others

Why I ask:

On the other hand, I see great success when family members join together to support the health protocols.

ADD TO THE ACTION PLAN:
- ✓ Project Lifesaver or other ideas from Week 22 in the Chapter 9 Online Action Plan
- ✓ Social skills resources such as books, DVDs, counseling, and camps
- ✓ Referral to a psychiatrist

Okay, so far your child may be nonverbal, or only able to get out a few words at a time. You've discovered he may struggle with GI and immune dysfunction, a nightmare of sleep patterns, a very restricted diet, sensory integration dysfunction, anxiety, and ADHD, to name a few concerns. His world may make more sense after a visit to a developmental optometrist. You've discovered medications may help, but aren't the complete answer, and you're putting new tools into the toolbox.

I would love for your child's true personality to shine through and not be dulled by the fog of chronic inflammation and oxidative stress, opioid peptides, immune dysregulation, or depression and anxiety.

Want the Science?
For sources of information found in this chapter, turn to the Endnotes.

What's in Your Toolbox?

You'll get to choose from a suite of protocols to address and support these challenges in Chapters 3, 4, and 5. Then, in Chapters 6, 7, and 9, I will pull it all together for you. Don't settle for just MiraLAX, clonidine, and risperidone; there are lots of natural tools that work beautifully for these children and that address the problems on a deeper level.

The Action Plan isn't a buffet where you can eat dessert first if you feel like it; there is a logical order for each step. Let's continue to explore and learn what you can do to restore and enhance your child's health over the next few chapters. Chapter 6 will show you how to begin your Action Plan, and Chapters 7 and 9 will keep you going. And remember, these are just the basics for supporting vibrant health on the spectrum. Find a good MAPS—Medical Academy of Pediatric Special Needs—physician for complete medical management of your child's metabolic and genetic challenges. But first, let's get organized in Chapter 2.

2

Get Organized Before You Start

Living in continual chaos is exhausting, frightening.
The catch is that it's also very addictive.
Lorna Luft

Uh-oh, the little people were in charge.

I stood over the stove in our cramped, crowded laundry room, cooking a quick meal while trying to keep an ear out for the boys. Evan, seven years old, was playing under and around my feet, "helping" me get lunch on the table.

During our big remodel in 2002, the makeshift kitchen—with appliances squeezed into the eight-foot by eleven-foot laundry room—was a nightmare. To keep the fun going, what was supposed to be an eight-week project ended up taking eight months.

A pair of dirty underwear plopped down the clothes chute onto my head. I yanked it off and kept trying to cook three things at once.

Without warning, a five-pound sack of flour shot out of Evan's hands and exploded on the floor, blanketing the limited floor space. Plumes of flour hung in the air like smoke after a bomb goes off.

I sprinted into the hallway to get something to clean it up and ran into my two-year-old strolling out of the bathroom with a can from the recycling bin in his hand.

"I'm swiggin' a beer!" he crowed.

"Where'd you get the 'beer'?" I asked, pausing briefly. He pointed to the open toilet. It had pee in it that someone hadn't flushed.

"Yuck! Dump it out!" I yelled, dashing away to get the dustpan and

broom. When I returned to the five-pound sea of flour, Eli had poured the pee water all over it. Yes, a very funny story now, but not so much at the time. The chaos in our home was at a crazy-maker level. I spent entire days battling catastrophes.

One of the biggest obstacles to managing health and maintaining a multitude of therapies for the autistic child is the staggering amount of unpredictability in the autism household. That chaos creates a dysfunctional environment that can sabotage even the most Herculean efforts of the most extraordinarily dedicated parents. Missed appointments, clutter, messy piles of papers, exhaustion, and frustration become the hallmarks of what is truly a vicious cycle—until you banish the "chaos monkey," that is.

Autism parents eat, sleep, and breathe the daily details of the medical challenges and therapies for their child, often to the point of tunnel vision. This chapter brings you the structure and organization you long for but haven't had the time or wherewithal to figure out—a change that will also mean *other* parts of your family and adult life can come back into focus.

There is such a range of chaos in autism homes that I've included suggestions for all scenarios, from mild to wild. Do you have a naturally organized, calm, and neat son or daughter? Just move on to the next suggestion or chapter if this scenario doesn't apply to you. Do you have a child with no impulse control or with destructive tendencies? If your children are dedicated agents of chaos, many of these suggestions will be helpful. Keeping family life organized is *waaay* more difficult when the child lacks internal structure and impulse control. You will have to be the external frontal lobe until those skills can be learned. This chapter shows you how to free up your time to focus your amazing "Autism Parent Super Powers" on getting your child feeling better. Although our lives as autism parents are not easy, there is joy in the journey as we see our amazing children blossom and become able to use the tools that make for a happier, healthier life.

Some of these tips will save you time *and* money; some of them will save you time but *not* money. There were times I had to resort to spending a little more to have something delivered to my door because a short trip across town was out of the question—and many of you know what I mean!

Get the Medical/Therapy Plan Under Control

Are you tired of spending precious time madly searching through drawers and piles of miscellaneous papers looking for a form or document you desperately needed, like, yesterday? How many times have you showed up for an appointment with a doctor, therapist, or teacher and realized you were missing most of the paperwork? Can't remember why your child is taking a certain supplement? Ashamed because you used to be very organized before you had children and now you never know where any important papers are?

I've collected and refined tips and checklists over twenty years of living with autism—at home and in my clinic. I share my best hacks and help you create an organizer that suits your needs and personality. You need to manage the mess of records that have come swirling into your life, creating a mental "whiteout" and obliterating any sense of direction. Notes from doctors and teachers, business cards, appointment slips, prescription refill orders, supplement lists, protocol schedules—it's a must-do step to get it all under control so that you can concentrate on steps to improve your child's health and language and skills.

This binder can easily be carted along to any doctor appointments or Individualized Education Plan (IEP) meetings. I *love* it when a mom or dad pulls out a large, organized binder during a visit to my office! Your organizer will come in handy when going over a history with a new doctor or sharing information with another parent of a newly diagnosed child. Sometimes it's nice to flip back through the notes and realize just how much progress your child has made.

There is nothing complicated or fancy about this system. In fact, I've found that really elaborate systems end up abandoned by the side of the trail, so simpler is better. Ultimately, your binder is a powerful tool that allows you to manage your child's customized Action Plan. But it's more than that. I encourage you to fill it with photos and personal notes as well. It's okay to write in the margins and even to laugh at what it sometimes takes to get through the day with an autistic child. Instead of the usual loneliness and isolation autism parents face, I want you to start the journey to vibrant health on the spectrum with a friendly, experienced autism mom and clinician walking beside you. Someone who has made all the mistakes, figured out what works, and marked the trail with signposts.

Create an Organizer

Over the years, I've seen a number of different notebooks and organizing systems used by autism families. Most families didn't have any system at all.

Therapies, appointments, prescriptions, school schedules, IEPs, and the like usually form a crazy quilt of autism life that is not very cohesive, as each professional designs a therapy or prescribes a medication within the scope of their training and practice. Many treatments, whether medical or educational, work for *subsets* of children with autism, and it is up to skilled and intuitive parents and clinicians to figure out which ones are beneficial. If records are kept and observant parents and doctors continuously choose to "keep what works and ditch the rest," then a custom Action Plan develops for the child.

And that's nearly impossible when records and notes are hopelessly scattered and lost.

At the time of publication of this book, new apps for smartphones and tablets were either coming onto the market or in beta mode to help with this chore. You can try one of the new apps, like Birdhouse for Autism (see Week 18 in the Chapter 9 Online Action Plan), for example. Whether or not you use an app, I still recommend creating a binder for office visits. It will be much easier for your child's clinicians and therapists to review than scrolling through electronic screens.

You'll never get rid of all the chaos—that's not our goal—but you can throw a saddle on that monkey and ride like hell! Don't put off creating your organizer until you have time to go to the office supply store; it'll never happen. There were weeks at a time that I couldn't get away to do any shopping. Instead, go online and order what you need *today* and have it delivered to your door ASAP.

Here is a simple binder system that has everything you need and nothing that you don't. I can remember the "ahh" feeling after creating Evan's first journal. I felt like I had reclaimed some semblance of control over the chaos. Like everything else about this book, I've pared it down to the most basic necessities so that you can get back to doing what you do best—creating the best life possible for your child with autism. This binder system can be laid out in different ways, and you should keep it as simple and straightforward as possible, but here's what works for me and what you need to get started:

1) A heavy-duty three-ring binder. Get the kind with a D-ring that allows papers to lie flat. If you get a binder with a clear plastic cover, you can slip a photo of your child underneath so that he is the star of your journal.

2) Three-hole punch. Alternatively, you could use **plastic sheet protectors** that you can insert papers into.

3) Tabbed subject dividers with pockets. Quick tip: You can temporarily stash any loose papers gathered at an appointment in the *pocket* for that therapist or doctor. When you get home, hole punch everything and put the papers in the notebook if applicable.

4) Appointment cards. Place a specialized plastic sheet created to hold business cards at the *front* of the binder to hold all appointment cards. These are available at office supply stores.

5) Business cards. Use another business card sheet holder in the *back* of the binder. Keep business cards handy for every professional on your child's team.

6) Calendar option. Alternatively, some parents insert a three-hole-punched monthly calendar and mark appointments on it; then they can see all appointments for the month at a glance. Quick tip: No matter which style you choose—appointment cards or monthly calendar—create a calendar alert on your smartphone if you have one. Set an alert for a day or two in advance of each appointment, and a second alert for two hours before each appointment.

7) **Use the tabbed pocket dividers to create sections for:**

- ☐ *Physicians.* Have a section for each doctor your child sees. Keep records of any diagnosis, treatment plans, correspondence, and reports.

- ☐ *Therapists.* Again, have a section for each therapist your child sees. Keep records of any diagnosis, treatment plans, correspondence, and reports.

- ☐ *School.* Keep a record of only the latest school testing, IEP and goals, orders for special diets, and pertinent notes written by teachers. Note: If the school section is substantial, create a separate binder for educational records.

- ☐ *Legal Papers.* Proof of guardianship, foster care, adoption, court orders all go here. You will need these documents the first time you visit any professional.

- ☐ *Medical Releases.* Notes from parents are essential for giving permission to other family members or caregivers to take the child to appointments.

- ☐ *Insurance Information.* Include copies of Medicare or Medicaid coverage here, too.

- ☐ *Allergies.* List all allergies, sensitivities, and intolerances here, including foods, pets, grasses and trees, mold, medications, and supplements.

- ☐ *Lab Testing.* If you're a "lumper," just insert lab results as they come in and you will have them in rough chronological order. If you're a "splitter" and have more time, you can create sections for Blood tests, Stool, Urine, or Genetic testing, for example.

- ☐ *Psychiatric Testing.* Include reports from comprehensive psychological testing and any testing done by the school.

- ☐ *Vaccination Records.* Note any adverse reactions or allergies to vaccine ingredients here. Don't know what to do about the current vaccine controversy? Want to vaccinate your child but minimize risk? Some parents follow an alternate vaccine schedule that allows their child to be vaccinated, but on a more spaced-out schedule, one vaccine at a time, just in case their child is in a minority subset of children who seem to be sensitive to some vaccines. A great website to explore your vaccination schedule options is www.askdrsears.com.

☐ *Procedures.* List all surgeries here, such as tonsillectomies, tubes in the ears, etc.

☐ *Photos.* Photos of before, during, and after treatment. This is very important. You will be encouraged by how much healthier and advanced your child has become. Videos are invaluable, especially after your child improves so much that your doctor may try to claim "it really wasn't autism to begin with." Some doctors are only just learning that certain aspects of autism respond positively to appropriate health support, and your photos and videos will help back that up.

☐ *Journaling and Observations.* Here is one organized place to keep daily journal notes, a food diary, and observations, which are very important throughout the course of any treatment or intervention.

☐ *List of Emergency Contacts.*

8) Create a Medication and Supplement Section:

☐ *Prescription Medication Information.*

    ○ *Drug Inserts.* Who has time to create a detailed list of medications, their side effects, and other information? When you fill a prescription, save the drug insert that explains the drug's effects and side effects. Put the printed drug insert into a clear plastic sheet protector and put it into this section of your binder. It has all the information you need on a drug. Write the date started and why at the top of the page.

    ○ *Causes and Symptoms.* Think about it. Is this medication a temporary bandage? Does it suppress a symptom or address the root cause of a symptom? For example, reflux is a symptom of GI dysfunction, so your approach should address the GI dysfunction, not just the reflux itself.

    ○ *Dosage and Duration.* Ask yourself: How long should my child take this medication? Have a plan. If a medication is increased due to a specific episode (e.g., a temporary episode of anxiety), when should it be lowered again? Or is it a permanent increase in dose and why? Some doctors will increase the dose for a bout of anxiety but not have a plan to lower it after the temporary situational stress goes away.

☐ *Over-the-Counter Supplement Information.* Create a section for information on natural and over-the-counter (OTC) supplements. They don't come with drug inserts like prescriptions do, but you can go to WebMD.com and print out information on them. Some OTC products can interact with prescription medications or even other natural supplements and herbs. Always tell your pharmacist and doctor about all over-the-counter supplements. Better yet, bring the bottles to your office visit.

> **TIP: KNOW THE PLAN.** How long should your child be on this supplement or prescription, and is there a Maintenance Plan (see Chapters 5 and 6)? Just because your child was anemic or had Candida long ago doesn't mean he should still be on an iron supplement or an antifungal two years later.

☐ *Master Medication/Supplement Schedule.* Create a log of medications and supplements that your child takes daily, as in Figure 2-1. Create a new updated log any time there are changes.
☐ *The "Ditch."* I like to keep records of medications, supplements, and therapies that have been tried and discontinued, because knowing what *didn't* work provides insight into your child's health challenges. Jot down any negative or paradoxical reactions to medications and supplements here, as well as when you tried something and there was simply no benefit or improvement observed.
  ○ *Discontinued Medications.* If your child stops a medication for any reason, pull out the drug insert, write down the date and any notes explaining why it was dropped from your child's regimen, and put it here in the ditch.

> **Dosing Tip:** Always start low and go slow. If your child is one of the super-sensitive-to-everything kind or has paradoxical reactions to common medicines, never start with the full dose if you can help it. Start with a partial dose and increase very gradually until the desired results are achieved. What if you see great results at only half the dose? Discuss it with your child's doctor, but there is probably no reason to give a higher dose.

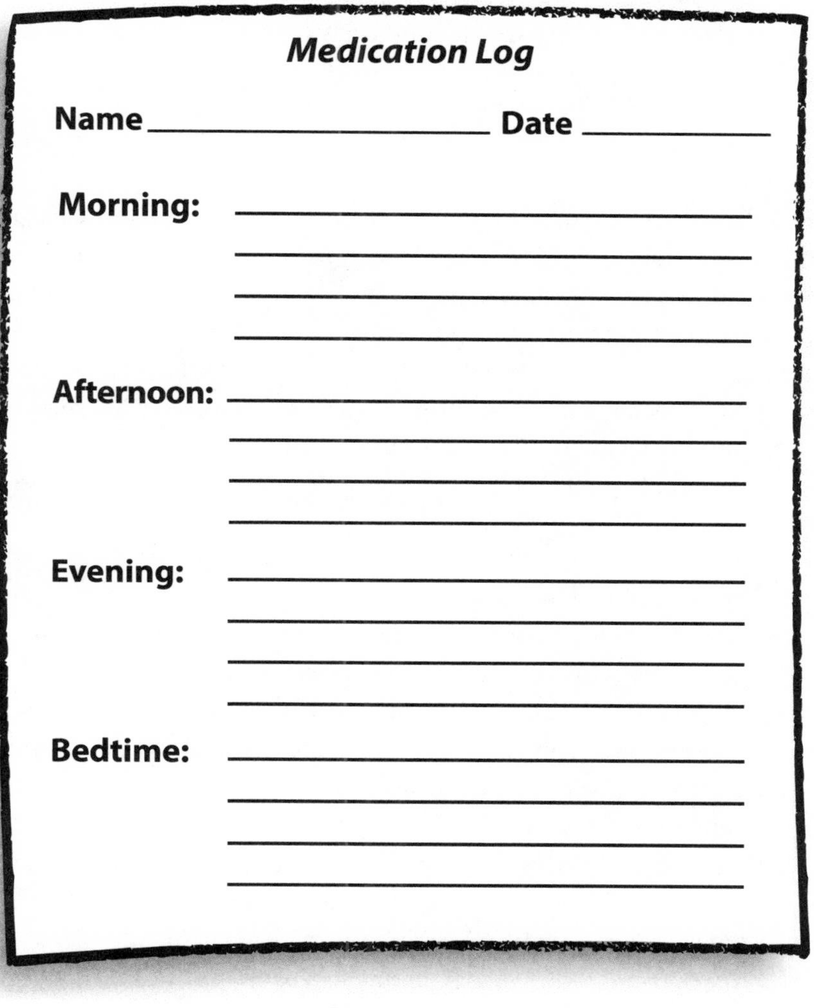

Medication Log

Name _____ **Date** _____

Morning: _____
_____
_____
_____

Afternoon: _____
_____
_____
_____

Evening: _____
_____
_____
_____

Bedtime: _____
_____
_____
_____

Figure 2-1

All righty, papers and records are organized and you should now be in better shape to track the total medical, therapeutic, and school plan for your son or daughter. Let's take it a bit further and free up some time, while restoring peace and order to your home.

Take Back Control

I think frankly when it comes to chaos
you ain't seen nothing yet.
Nigel Farage

First things first. If your child is a wanderer, or uncontrollably destructive around the house, and leaves no drawer, closet, or shelf unmolested, you will need to go into lockdown mode. Put locks on doors, use child gates, purchase a locking metal cabinet for papers and photos if you have to. Sometimes most of our day is spent two steps behind a very active child, making sure he doesn't get hurt or cleaning up some crazy mess he has made. Step one: Stop this madness and take control of your home. See if any of these ideas can help *your* situation:

- ☐ *Safety Fencing.* Install fencing about four to six feet high around your yard with gates that you can lock.
- ☐ *Put a Lid on It.* Install a locking key-coded cover on the swimming pool or hot tub. Water is the first place they go when they dash off.
- ☐ *Sound Alerts.* Install a system that will chime when a door or window in your home is opened. I don't mean an alarm that will sound like a burglar has invaded, just a clear signal that lets you know your child may be getting out.
- ☐ *Tracking Technology.* Quickly locate a child who has wandered. See Week 22 in the Chapter 9 Online Action Plan for ideas on GPS bracelets, clothing, and tracking apps.
- ☐ *Extra House Keys.* Avoid getting locked out of your own home. It's really scary when a young child is inside who can't or won't cooperate to unlock the door. Keep an extra key at your office and a neighbor's house, or use a key-code pad on one door. You might even use a key-code lockbox with a key inside—it works for realtors!
- ☐ *Open Sesame.* A new app called Open Sesame will allow you to unlock the door to your home using your smartphone.
- ☐ *Within Your Sight.* If your child is destructive to his room when put there for a time-out, install a peephole looking *into* the room so that you can monitor your child's safety. We did this with one of

our children, and when he gained self-control and matured a bit, he asked if we would switch doors with him. The inside of his bedroom door had been kicked to pieces, and it served as an embarrassing reminder of his former behavior. We complied and forgot about it. Months later we noticed our builder's crew whispering and giving us odd looks after working on a renovation in our master bedroom. We'd forgotten that our door looked like a wild animal had clawed away the bottom of it, plus it had a peephole looking *in*. No wonder they were talking!

☐ *Safety Glass.* Cover windows with clear packing tape if your child likes to hit them with his hands or tends to throw things at them. It won't keep the glass from breaking, but it will keep it from scattering and leaving dangerous shards.

☐ *High Access Locks.* Install slide bolts near the tops of doors if your child is an escape artist, or if you need to control access to certain rooms.

☐ *Dutch Style.* A split door where you can lock the bottom half, while leaving the top half open to keep an ear on everyone, works especially well with younger children.

☐ *Upper Limits.* If your child is especially destructive with your papers and records, install a high shelf along the top of the wall to keep these things out of the reach of a younger child.

☐ *Child Locks.* Install a childproof lock on the refrigerator and cabinets if your child eats inappropriate things (like uncooked meat), eats too much (resulting in medically concerning weight gain), or eats foods that are banned on his special diet, or if he just likes to paint your kitchen with all the condiments from time to time.

☐ *Wall Busters.* I have had parents tell me that they cannot keep anything out of the reach of their child because he could kick in a door, tear out door frames, and break through drywall. Now, those are extreme cases, but here are a few tips:

   ○ No hollow doors—use metal or solid wood doors.

   ○ Replace the access to at least one room with a metal frame and door, and use that room to store your papers and records.

   ○ *Brilliant* hack—when repairing large holes your child has made in the walls, fill the interior of the wall space with wooden two-by-fours turned on edge and nailed in place to form a solid fill before covering with drywall. This makes it extremely difficult (and painful) to kick in the next time.

Safety Tips I've Collected

- ☐ Get an anti-tip kit for the kitchen stove. Contact the manufacturer of your appliance and order one if your child pulls down the oven door and uses it to climb. Several hundred children a year die after tipping the stove over and getting crushed.
- ☐ Prevent drowning. Put a child lock on the toilet.
- ☐ Hide the knife block!
- ☐ To nail shut the window in his bedroom or not? Now that's an icky decision to make! If you've ever found your child out on the roof of your home, it makes that decision easier. Our son was quite adventurous. We'd put him in his room for a time-out and find him on the roof ("just wondered what it was like out here," he'd say). Once he even jumped off into the flower garden below and then rang the doorbell.
- ☐ Notify the 911 Call Center if your child is nonverbal or intellectually disabled and may not be able to respond during an emergency.
- ☐ Stick a decal on your child's bedroom window and your car window to alert emergency personnel that your child is nonverbal and may not respond in a typical manner. (Products are available at www. MagnetAmerica.com.)

Get Time Management Under Control

There are so many schedule/calendar tools available these days, it really makes me jealous. Let's review your many options.

Visual Thinkers

- ☐ Hang a huge calendar and bulletin board on the wall and keep the whole family's schedule and notes available at a glance.

Smartphones (Your Best Tool)

- ☐ Use your phone as your executive secretary, setting reminders for *everything.*
- ☐ Create prescription refill alerts. Set a phone alert for *two weeks ahead* to contact the doctor for a refill (some doctors take a long time to get hold of, even to get the refill).
- ☐ Set up your email and banking on your phone. I attend to these tasks in what would otherwise be wasted time in the doctor's waiting room or in line at the grocery store.
- ☐ Never get lost again! The newest models of smartphones can work as navigation systems, calling out turn-by-turn directions as you drive.
- ☐ Never forget where you parked again. Take a photo of your parking space at the mall or airport.
- ☐ Use your smartphone to take photos of your child's rashes or to video behaviors to show the therapist or doctor.

Now if they'd only invent an app to take down the Christmas tree!

Personal record for taking down the Christmas tree:
April 10!

Guard Your Time

- ☐ No guilt—use caller ID so that you can screen pointless calls or avoid long rambling ones.
- ☐ Respond via email instead of texting or phone calls. This way you can correspond when it's convenient for you, even if it's the middle of the night when you're up with a sleepless child.

Shop Online

- ☐ Online shopping is a great timesaver.
- ☐ For security purposes, use PayPal, or designate only one credit card for online ordering. It should not be connected to your bank account.
- ☐ No autoship—for anything. Although it seems like a good idea at

first, if you cannot regularly use up the item (e.g., coffee, skin care products, vitamins, or whatever) it will just pile up and ultimately cause you more stress and expense. Autoship was always a disaster for me.

Bill Paying

- ☐ Make online payments. I love paying online because I can do it day or night when it's convenient for me.
- ☐ Pay ahead. Pay utility bills quarterly or even a year at a time if the budget allows (e.g., trash pickup, water, sewer). This gets rid of a million annoying little bills every month and frees up your time.
- ☐ Set up ACH payments. Pay as many bills as you can via Automated Clearing House services, which are automatic withdrawals from your checking account. Set up an ACH payment for your credit cards that will pay the minimum monthly payment due every month and avoid those late fees. You can always go online later and either pay it off in full or at least make a bigger payment.

Junk Mail and Spam

Back in the early chaotic days, I was overwhelmed by the sheer amount of mail and email I was receiving, most of it unwanted.

- ☐ To reduce spam in your inbox, register for the Email Preference Service at www.dmachoice.org.
- ☐ Favorite email hack—have a junk email account for online ordering. Even reputable online companies always start sending junk emails right away, even if you uncheck the box before ordering. That is why I have one email address that I use solely for online ordering. Those junk emails never clog up my real email account, because I always protect that address from spam.
- ☐ Reduce junk mail, including:
  - ○ Eliminate catalog chaos. One drawback to using online shopping is that your name will end up on countless junk mail lists and will even get sold and rented out to other catalog companies. Cut off the back cover of the catalog and mail it back to the company with a note to remove your name from all mail and

marketing lists, and to not share, sell, or rent your name. It will take two or three months, but your junk mail load will decrease dramatically, making mail more manageable.

- ○ Register at www.dmachoice.org for the DirectMail.com National Do Not Mail List. It's free and lasts for six years.
- ☐ Reduce telemarketing calls (doesn't apply to charities):
  - ○ Get off their radar by calling 1-888-382-1222 from the phone number you want to register.
  - ○ Go online at www.donotcall.gov and sign up for the National Do Not Call list.
- ☐ Stop the prescreened credit card and insurance offers:
  - ○ To opt out for five years, call toll-free 1-888-5-OPT-OUT (1-888-567-8688) or visit www.optoutprescreen.com.
  - ○ To opt out permanently, go to www.optoutprescreen.com and make your request. You will be given a Permanent Opt-Out Election form to sign and return.

Get the House Under Control

Chaos was the law of nature;
Order was the dream of man.
Henry Adams

Organize the home—but first *simplify*. I always tried to organize and containerize all of our stuff, but true progress was made only after I learned to simplify and *get rid of stuff*. Here are my best tips and resources for giving your junk the heave-ho.

Simplifying

- ☐ *FlyLady.* If I had to pick only one system to get organized, it would be this one—and it's free. Go to Flylady.net and start your journey back to sanity today. FlyLady gets us. She starts you out with a Baby-Steps program and within two to three months you will be sane and organized.
- ☐ *How to Simplify Your Life* by Elaine St. James. This resource gave me that lightbulb moment when I realized less is more. . . .

- ☐ *Organizing from the Inside Out* by Julie Morgenstern. This book explores *why* we hang onto our clutter, and gives you permission to let it go.

Organizing

- ☐ *Pinterest.* It's porn for organizing, with lots of great ideas. Pin while you pee if you have to. Check out our organizing and other ideas on the Autism Health! boards.
- ☐ *Favorite Tip.* Set nothing on the floor. I was struck by this beacon of sanity after seeing a demonstration of a closet organizing system that kept the floor space empty and pristine. It looks great and makes cleaning a snap. Have you noticed that once you set something on the floor, it attracts other homeless objects like a magnet? Soon there is a growing blob of stuff next to it, and then you begin to set stuff *on top* of it. It grows like an alien egg sac!
- ☐ *Basket Case:*
  - ○ Containerize. Group things in bins and baskets; you don't have to organize each item, just group them together. (The look on my face when I'm at The Container Store says it all—a trip there is better than sex!)
  - ○ Put baskets by the front door (to hold shoes), on the stairs (to make carrying items up and down easier), in the garage, and in the closets of bathrooms and bedrooms.
- ☐ *Plan Ahead.* Use weekly pill cups and organizers and make up a week or two of supplements for your child at a time. There are all shapes and sizes available on the Internet or at your local pharmacy.
- ☐ *Label It.* Here's a story of when a labeler would have come in handy: One of our beloved guinea pigs passed away during a bitter winter, and it was impossible to have a burial ceremony. We wrapped him up and placed him in the freezer for a spring burial. Of course, we forgot about him, and months later I had a nasty surprise when I was rummaging through the freezer for last-minute dinner ideas. Label everything.
- ☐ *Have Only One Scary Room.* If you're doing your best, but your house is still cluttered, sacrifice one room and stick all the clutter

in there. I know that's not advice you're going to find anywhere else, but sometimes ya gotta do what ya gotta do!

☐ *Hoarder Patrol.* Obsessive–compulsive disorder (OCD) and anxiety are more common in those on the spectrum, and hoarding can show up in that category. Some children are "collectors" and end up acquiring lots of items that feed their area of intense interest: LEGO kits, stuffed animals, toothpaste, plants, vacuum cleaners, radios, toys, etc. I include pets in this category, too. Even though it is difficult, set boundaries on collecting and hoarding and curate the collection on a regular basis. Your child can learn self-control and discipline, and, who knows, these areas of interest may even become a profession someday.

Best School Hack Ever

☐ Beg, borrow, or buy an extra set of your child's textbooks each year. One set is kept at school and one set is kept at home. This eliminates that quagmire at the end of each day, when your child spreads out everything from his desk, locker, and book bag all over the floor and tries to decide which books to bring home. It eliminates those panicky days when you are phoning friends to get screenshots of assignments in books that were forgotten at school.

Wardrobe

☐ Wear a "uniform" if you're overwhelmed; choose a neutral such as black, brown, or taupe plus a complementary color, and buy all of your clothes in those two colors.

☐ Make getting dressed a snap. Find a flattering and comfortable pair of pants or a skirt in a basic color, and buy four or five of them. Ladies, don't fall into the trap of wearing mom jeans! Wear the same basic pants, boots, or shoes each day and just pair them with a different pretty top for a quick outfit that looks and feels great. Guys can put together a quick go-to outfit by pairing the basic khaki pant with different colors of the basic polo shirt. For a neater look, tuck in the shirt, add a belt and you are good to go!

☐ Really pinched for time? Make your whole wardrobe one color such as black or taupe, and wear a few different vests or cardigans. Ladies could add a variety of scarves tied in a variety of ways every day.

☐ Go for clothing that you can toss in the washer and dryer.

☐ Keep changes of clothing for your child in the car, at school, and at daycare. This will reduce unnecessary trips back to the house when accidents happen. I can remember being on a field trip to a children's museum. Every child on the trip got soaking wet playing with a delightful interactive water exhibit. I was the only mom who had an extra school uniform handy.

Laundry Room

☐ *Best Thing Ever*—vertical stacking laundry bins. Use a vertical stacking system such as Stack'n Sort by Rubbermaid to free up a ton of space in your laundry room. Label each one with the type of load it will be, such as Towels, Darks, or Lights. This is a great teaching tool for children, as they can bring down their dirty clothes and sort them into the baskets. When the basket is full, it goes right into the washer.

☐ *Sock Police.* Use plastic clips or safety pins to keep socks together.

☐ *Better Yet . . .* buy all socks alike so that no matching is needed.

☐ *Ditch the Iron.* Use a steamer to get rid of wrinkles. Buying tip: Only a commercial-quality steamer will get the job done.

☐ *Color-Coded Hangers and Baskets.* Children can learn life skills and help with the laundry chores if you use color-coded hangers and baskets for each family member. Keep the baskets on a shelf (remember, nothing on the floor).

Make a Stash

☐ *Party Stash.* Did you ever skip a party because you didn't have time to get a gift? No more surprise parties—stock a few age-appropriate gifts, gift bags, bows, and cards for when your child gets invited to a party.

☐ *Power Outage Stash.* What is important to your child that you must have, even during a power outage? For many of us, it's extra battery-charging packs for portable DVD players, iPads, and cell phones. Solar chargers may do in a pinch, but are a little iffier. Stash a few of your child's favorite snacks and drinks, too. Sometimes I bought a movie or game he hadn't seen before to catch his interest during trying times.

Supplements for Sleepovers

For those times when your child is staying at Grandma and Grandpa's or at the ex's house or is invited to a sleepover, here is a great tip for staying organized with the supplement schedule. I call them Travel Boards or Overnight Boards, and they make it easy for others to remember your child's supplements and medications. They are large rectangles or squares of sturdy cardboard, at least one foot by one foot in size. Enzymes and supplements are sorted into snack-size plastic bags for each anticipated meal or snack and stapled in vertical chronological order to the cardboard (see Figure 2-2).

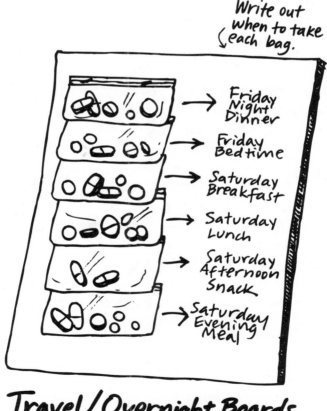

Figure 2-2

Let's use an example of your child staying at Grandma's house on Friday night and coming home Saturday evening after dinner:

1. Start at the bottom left-hand side of the board and staple the plastic bag with the supplements (for example, enzymes and a probiotic) for Saturday's evening meal.
2. Right above it and a little higher on the board, overlapping it slightly, staple the bag with the enzymes for the Saturday afternoon snack.
3. Next, a little higher above that one, staple the bag with enzymes for Saturday's lunch.
4. Next up, any enzymes or meds for Saturday's breakfast.
5. We continue to work backward time-wise and attach the bag with Friday's bedtime pills above the previous one.
6. The very top bag is the one with enzymes and a probiotic for Friday's evening meal.

As you can see, the very top bag is the one that will be grabbed first at dinner on Friday evening, leaving Friday's bedtime bag in plain sight as a reminder. You can send more than one board for longer stays.

Here are the benefits of using these Travel/Overnight Boards:

☐ They are hard to lose or overlook because of their size (obnoxious, really!).
☐ They are convenient to prop up on the kitchen counter.
☐ They are a gentle visual reminder for forgetful grandparents.
☐ They are a thoughtful visual reminder for your dear friend who is hosting your child for a sleepover.
☐ They are a lie detector for your lazy-ass ex who never bothers to give the meds and supplements. If the board returns home with bags still attached, you will know exactly which supplements were forgotten.

Nurture Yourself—No Guilt!

She is delightfully chaotic; a beautiful mess.
Loving her is a splendid adventure.
Steve Maraboli

- Schedule time for yourself once a week at least. Sleep, see a movie, take a walk, read a book.
- Make your bedroom a haven. Keep your bedroom neat and clutter-free, even it means you have to pile the garage sky high with stuff. Create a haven for the end of the day.
- Sleep once a month at a hotel if you are completely sleep-deprived; you can't take care of others if you are burnt out. Make sure the hotel alarm clock isn't set for 5 a.m.
- Nurture your brain. Music, audiobooks, and podcasts help keep your mind fed, especially when the routine of your day can be numbing.
- Recommended book: *The Happiness Project* by Gretchen Rubin.
- Watch only happy movies and comedies for a while. Laughter increases endorphins, strengthens the immune system, and decreases stress.
- Turn to prayer or meditation that matches your beliefs. It's very centering, relieves anxiety, and can be done anywhere, anytime. Serenity is very important when caring for a child who requires constant vigilance.
- Wear a Vitamin B12 patch. This is an amazing hack for better energy and memory. Add a margarita and it's a party!
- Yo GABA GABA. Gamma-aminobutyric acid, or GABA, is your new best friend. It is a calming neurotransmitter our own body makes. It's also sold over-the-counter and won't break the bank. I take it three times a day.
- Try Alpha-Stim. It's great for the anxiety and insomnia that autism parents experience. I was very skeptical at first, but had great results and now love it. Cranial electrical stimulation (CES) is an old yet effective therapy. Wear this device (www.Alpha-Stim.com) twenty minutes a day and soon you'll be more relaxed and sleeping better.

Nurture Your Children

- Let them be children and just play; it cannot be all therapy all the time.
- Get rid of yelling and dump the sarcasm. Many ASD children cannot interpret the meaning of a raised voice or sarcasm and it just agi-

tates them further. Their mood will mirror yours. Your house will be calmer if you modulate your voice.

Nurture Your Friendships

☐ Something has to give time-wise, but you can stay in touch. I never had time to be one of those "ladies who lunch," but my true friends were delighted to see me once every month or two (or three). Don't let your friendships die.

Nurture Your Love Life

Remember that beautiful, lazy Saturday morning move of lying half-asleep in bed and hooking your ankle over your spouse's ankle—and all that it says? I love you, I'm perfectly happy, I'd love some coffee, but I don't want to get up and leave you. . . . I don't think I ever got to do that again after my children were born.

☐ Try to have a date night every week or two, even if you don't think you have the time.

☐ Leave love notes for each other around the house and in the car. These create little bright spots in an otherwise sometimes thankless day.

☐ Attend seminars, read books, or listen to audio courses on strengthening your marriage.

☐ Recommended book: *The Five Love Languages* by Gary Chapman. I learned so much about my husband after we attended a weekend seminar on this book, hosted by our church.

☐ Kick pets out of the bedroom. You'll breathe better, sleep better, and avoid Sit-Com Sex (more on that in a moment).

☐ Did having a special needs child affect your love life? I know it did mine. I hope the "sex chart" in Table 2-1 gives you a much-needed laugh.

An Example of Sit-Com Sex

We were in the middle of silent Street Mime Sex one time, and our miniature dachshund Puddles took advantage of my silent "O" face to give me a *deep* French kiss. It was totally horrible, and we couldn't stop laughing for

Types of sex an autism parent might have

I'm Hot but Not for You	*One of you has a fever of at least 101.*
Chalk Outline	*One of you is completely exhausted and just lies there.*
Street Mime	*When there is a child with Vulcan hearing in the house, you resort to miming your passion with elaborate facial expressions. (We often dissolved into spasms of laughter—silent, of course— at the funny faces we made as part of this effort!)*
Drive-By	*Hurry-up-before-one-of-the-kids-wakes-up sex.*
Sit-Com	*When love making doesn't go as planned....*

Table 2-1

hours. Alan would just look at me and start laughing. Kicking pets out of the bedroom helps minimize such disasters. And lock the door.

All of these tips, hacks, and advice should get you in better shape to tackle the real-life challenge of getting your child healthy enough to get the most out of school, therapy, and social opportunities. Let's go on to Chapter 3 and start your child's journey back to vibrant health on the autism spectrum.

THOU SHALT NOT:
✓ Let the Little People be in charge.
✓ Neglect your mind, your health, your marriage.
✓ Store anything on the floor.
✓ Wear "mom" jeans! (ladies).
✓ Wear "baggy butt" pants (guys).

3

You Are What You Don't Poop:
Be Amazed by Enzymes

"**H**ave you *fa-a-awted*?" When my husband Alan, was in medical school, he had a roommate who nailed their attending physician's accent and signature line. On hospital rounds, checking on postsurgical patients, he'd sing it loudly from the doorway as he strode into a patient's room without so much as a hello, his flock of medical students trailing him, startling and often embarrassing the unsuspecting man or woman in the bed.

Anesthesia and opiate pain medications, such as morphine, are notorious for shutting down the bowels and causing opioid-induced constipation (OIC).[1] If you've ever had surgery, you may recall that you were not released to go home until you had a bowel movement or at least passed gas; the doctor or nurse checking on you had to be certain that your bowels had awakened from the opiate coma. Or, if you've ever been on pain meds like Lortab or Oxycontin, you probably remember how constipated you were.

My husband and his medical school classmates knew the potential problems drugs could cause in the bowels and weren't surprised by the doctor's daily query. But they were highly amused by his manner and distinctive accent, which is why "Have you *fa-a-awted*?" became fodder for late-night antics. In those sleep-deprived days, we thought the impersonation—and the question—was hilarious, and we were always ready for a laugh.

Up to 70 percent of autistic children suffer from chronic constipation,[2] which can lead to sleep disruptions[3] and aggressive behaviors.[4] Prescription medications that address sleep or aggression issues can be helpful, but most have an undesirable side effect—constipation![5] This creates a vicious cycle of more sleep disruption and aggression. Until the bowels are moving on a daily or near-daily basis, not much else can be accomplished.

TREATMENT TIP:
CONSTIPATION MUST BE TREATED FIRST

Job one on the path to your child's improved health is getting rid of his constipation. There are generally three approaches:

1. Give MiraLAX, stool softeners, and enemas for the rest of his life. (Ugh—for everybody!)
2. Begin the gluten-free, casein-free (GFCF) diet. (Yikes! What *can* we eat?)
3. Find an easy way to "fake" the GFCF diet. (I vote for this one!)

Before I explain how to fake this diet, let's explore what it is.

The GFCF Diet

Most of you will have heard of the gluten-free, casein-free diet—often referred to as the "autism diet" in the same breath—and you've either tried it and quit or shied away from it because it's so challenging. Don't worry. You don't have to start this diet, but it is a great tool for GI health if you're interested. When we first started the GFCF diet with our son Evan, we didn't understand *why* it worked. We just knew that it calmed Evan down, like magic. Friends and relatives kept asking us what new medication he had started! It didn't cure or treat his autism, but it did change his behavior.

GFCF Diet

GFCF stands for gluten-free, casein-free. Gluten is a protein found in wheat, barley, rye, and spelt. Casein is a protein found in milk and milk products. Following a GFCF diet means eliminating these foods from your child's diet. That's challenging when you stop and think about how many foods that includes. Bread, pasta, pancakes, cookies, crackers, to name a very few common (and beloved) foods, are on the "forbidden" list in the GFCF diet, along with milk, ice cream, butter, cheese, cream cheese, and a host of other foods kids (and their parents) love. To learn more about the GFCF diet, including websites, cookbooks, and general tips, see the Helpful Resources section at the end of this book.

As we continued to attend autism conferences, surf the Internet, and question our doctors, we learned that two major food proteins (gluten and casein) were only partially breaking down in our son's digestive tract *and* that these partially digested proteins, or peptides, are very similar in structure to *morphine*—in fact, they are called caso*morphins*[6] and gluteo-*morphin*.[7] Because these peptides can leak out of the GI tract and enter the brain[8] through the bloodstream, they are classified as neuropeptides. Once in the brain, the opioid neuropeptides can affect mood and cognitive function and affect an area of the brain in the temporal lobes that handles speech and auditory integration. Wow, your child's favorite foods might be affecting his brain![9]

The Opioid Effect

Talk about an *aha* moment! These morphine-like substances were coursing through our son, keeping him in the steady grip of opi-

> *Opioid peptides have been found in the urine of people with autism and schizophrenia.*[10]

oids that have the same effects as a powerful prescription painkiller—right down to the constipation and addictive habits. While Evan was eating the *same foods* the rest of the family consumed, because of his gastrointestinal inflammation and poor intestinal health some of the food was only partially digested. The physiological results were making him act bizarrely.[11] A case report published in July 2015 confirms a new clinical entity, "Gluten Psychosis," which can lead to neuro-psychiatric manifestations in adults and children. It is unrelated to celiac disease or wheat allergy.[12]

I began to understand why traditional methods of discipline were completely ineffective for Evan.

The GFCF diet is controversial, and research studies are mixed, with most failing to show any benefit for ASD. Dr. Susan Hyman at the University of Rochester has led two studies using a handful of autistic children that purport to show the GFCF diet doesn't have any benefit for ASD. The most recent study states, "we excluded children who had known gastrointestinal disorders, who might have been more likely to respond positively to dietary restriction."[13] She excluded those with GI issues from her previous study[14] as well. Apparently, Dr. Hyman is investigating if a GFCF diet affects autism itself, but didn't investigate if the GFCF diet helps the gastrointestinal issues that affect subsets of autistic children and adults. That's a fair angle. Dr. Hyman didn't study autistic children with GI problems, so please do not be misled by the media headlines announcing the GFCF diet has no benefit for those with ASD. Although I do not expect a GFCF diet to cure or treat autism, I do use it quite effectively to help with the gastrointestinal issues of autism.

The opioid effect explains why so many ASD children will eat only a few foods, and in an addictive manner: Macaroni and cheese, pizza, and chicken nuggets are common favorites. These foods are a rich source of opiate-like peptides, making them—to some children with autism—as addictive as narcotic drugs. I have two- and three-year-old patients who want to drink a gallon of milk or more a day or eat "bread sandwiches." Many of you autism moms and dads reading this know what I'm talking about.

When Alan and I first began following the GFCF diet for Evan, we were skeptical. We weren't initially aware of all the science behind it, but we couldn't argue with the astonishing results we saw when foods containing gluten and casein were removed from his diet. His wild rages began to lose their grip on him, he began sleeping more consistently, and his eye contact improved. Even his thought processes became more clear and rational. People who didn't know he had started a special diet thought he had started a new medication. I was grateful for the improvements, but I wished there were an easier way to get these results. (This chapter will show you how!)

There are some myths concerning gluten and casein and the GFCF diet that should be addressed here.

MYTH #1: A CHILD WILL ONLY BENEFIT FROM THE GFCF DIET IF HE IS *ALLERGIC* TO GLUTEN AND CASEIN.

Gluten and casein form opioids, not necessarily allergies. If the child has allergies, those must be addressed, but allergies do not have anything to do with the opioid effect.

MYTH #2: GLUTEN AND CASEIN *CAUSE* AUTISM.

Gluten and casein do not cause autism, although they can cause an increase in behaviors and symptoms, making a child's autism seem more profound than it really is.

DEALING WITH THE OPIOID EFFECT.

I have seen the opioid model bashed, and I have seen it applauded. That's not unusual in medicine. But I will say this: As a clinician working with ASD children, I haven't found a better explanation yet for the dramatic results of the diet or the digestive enzymes that break down these opioids[15] and "fake" the diet. So, until a better reason is developed, I use the opioid model to explain things to my patients.

Understanding that your child's gastrointestinal problems have essentially turned him or her into a drug addict will help you see why the opioid problem *must* be treated before anything else can be attempted. School, therapies, and social opportunities won't be as successful until your little addict is no longer high. Trust me—I see patients all the time whose parents have avoided the diet or the enzyme supplements, trying instead a multitude of other time-consuming therapies and interventions and remaining puzzled over why nothing seems to work well for their child. Think of it this way: Trying other therapies while he's high and fogged out is like washing the car instead of changing the oil. The car may look good but it isn't running too well. Once we put these children on enzymes, we usually see big leaps in their levels of function and ability. And when the child has been freed from the grip of opioids, other therapies finally have a chance of being successful.

Why I Stopped Recommending the GFCF Diet to *Start*

I no longer put my patients on the GFCF diet as a first line of GI support. For years, I did. I wore myself out telling families about the GFCF diet. I conducted workshops, met with parents privately, and gave away hundreds of dollars' worth of books about how to follow the diet. I cooked and baked delicious GFCF meals to serve at the workshops, eager to show families how good (and simple) the diet could be. I arranged to meet with parents at the grocery store, showing them where the GFCF products were located, giving tips on which ones tasted good and which ones were just plain nasty. I shared recipes and helped people convert their family favorites to GFCF. I printed and gave away instructions for following the diet on a tight budget, even food stamps. I talked until my voice gave out. Let's just say I gave it my best effort.

There were families who put the work in, implemented the GFCF diet, and were delighted with the improvements they saw in their child. I admire those families to this day. I finally had to admit, however, that of the dozens of families I worked with at any given time, *very* few children were being put on the GFCF diet. It was just too challenging for their already-overburdened parents.

"Dr. Jae," parents would say, "this diet makes sense and sounds wonderful, but my child only eats five foods. How am I ever going to do a diet that takes away the few things he's willing to eat?" Others said they were too stressed out or couldn't afford it.

Timing Is Everything

I noticed time and again that parents turned away from the *entire* vibrant health program because of the difficulty this first step, the GFCF diet, presented. Once they determined they couldn't master the diet, or even get started on it, they gave up and never came back to the clinic.

As the first step of a comprehensive health program, the GFCF diet was being attempted at a time when the child's behaviors were extremely difficult and parents were mentally worn out. I began to see that parents needed an *easier* way to calm their children. I needed to give them a simpler way to start the process. If I could get them past the challenge of the diet yet accomplish the same short-term goals of reduced aggression, improved sleep, and daily bowel movements, we could get down to the real work of those beautiful long-term goals: increased language, better social skills, and improved cognition.

The Role of DPP-IV

DPP-IV is an enzyme that's made in the lining of the small intestine and breaks down gluten and casein, which are highly resistant to breakdown by other enzymes. This enzyme is suspected to be deficient in some children with autism, either through intestinal damage or less genetic expression, and is sensitive to damage from environmental toxins.

Rumors were circulating on the Internet back then suggesting that autism families could chuck the GFCF diet and just slip their kids some enzyme supplements that contained DPP-IV, an enzyme that breaks down the dietary opioid peptides.[16] It sounded too good to be true. Nothing that easy happens with autism. *Ever.* I was skeptical. When Dr. Devin Houston, a renowned enzymologist, spoke about enzyme supplements at a local autism conference, I was initially unconvinced. (I hate to admit this now—sorry, Devin!) Were the enzyme companies trying to make money selling autism families a false hope? When I opened my clinic, I was so concerned that enzymes were, at best, a sloppy imitation of the GFCF diet, I suggested them only in extreme cases, when I knew the parents were too overwhelmed to pull off the diet.

Tired families, homes broken by divorce, and single parents with cranky, sleepless children wanted the results the GFCF diet offered, but the plan was just too difficult for most. So, more and more, I began using the enzymes to buy time. Now mom or dad could get started on the child's Un-Prescription Action Plan right away, rather than spending weeks or months planning and implementing a special diet.

Over time, I created a four-week "step-down" program in which the enzymes were introduced gradually, minimizing the significant withdrawal symptoms that occur when a child is coming off the opioid-producing foods. This approach made it easier on the child, the family, and the school system. The results were so good and the plan so simple, many parents chose to continue with enzyme supplements *instead* of a GFCF diet. My fears that the enzymes would be a lazy, sloppy imitation of the diet were unfounded. The results were great.

Physiology Is Destiny

As I continued tracking down research data and attending conferences, I learned that over half of children with autism may be deficient in certain digestive enzymes. Their bodies just don't produce enough of them, making it difficult to digest gluten, casein, lactose, and some carbohydrates and starches.[17] In fact, it's really *good* for these kids to take enzymes as a supplement. As time went on, so many families with whom I worked were having such great results with the enzymes alone, I bailed on the diet as a must-do first step. Nowadays, I wholeheartedly recommend the enzyme supplements alone for most of my patients. I feel like a bit of a traitor to the GFCF diet, but it is simply too high-maintenance for most of my stressed-out/in-crisis families. Once the child is out of pain and in a calmer, healthier state, any of the special autism diets are much more doable. The enzymes can be used as a transition to a healthier diet.

How do these enzymes work their magic? Remember, gluten and casein don't cause autism, but they can form opiate-like substances in your child's gastrointestinal tract. Opioids dull your child's cognition and increase difficult behaviors. And opioids cause chronic constipation, which can lead to reflux and night awakenings.

Before enzyme supplements came along, the only way to get the opioids out of a child's system was to take away the foods that formed them. Now we can break down the opioids using the magic of digestive enzymes. It's like having an Easy Button! Enzymes break down the partially digested opiate-like "trouble makers" from gluten and casein and, essentially, *fake* the GFCF diet.

Children with reflux tend to stay very busy, almost hyperactively busy, during the day, trying to keep their mind off of the burn and discomfort of acid reflux. They put off going to sleep for hours, because lying flat makes it worse. Many children will fall asleep sitting up on the couch, or propped up on pillows. This is a clue your child may have reflux.

How do enzymes eliminate constipation, sleeplessness, and aggression?

How is constipation connected to night awakenings? Chronic constipation can contribute to reflux. Think of it this way: If the flow of acid, bile, and food isn't moving through your gastrointestinal tract toward your hind end, it's moving in the other direction, up toward your throat! Gastroesophageal reflux disease (GERD) is common among ASD children and adults.[18] Experienced clinicians know that reflux and belly pain are most likely what keeps waking your autistic child throughout the night. During the day, when the child is walking, running, or sitting, gravity helps keep stomach acid where it belongs—in the stomach. There is a muscular sphincter at the top of the stomach that helps keep a lid on things, but it doesn't always do its job well since these children are prone to low muscle tone. At night, when the child lies down in the horizontal position, the stomach acid can flow up into the throat more freely. It's the reason children with reflux will put off going to sleep *for hours!* The burning pain not only delays sleep, but may cause restless sleep or frequent night awakenings.

Constipation contributes to overgrowth of undesirable bacteria and yeast in the gastrointestinal tract (or gut) as well. The longer it takes food to pass through the bowels, the longer it acts as a nutrient source for bacteria and yeast. The bowels are warm, dark, and moist, and they become an incubator for these unwelcome critters. When bacteria and yeast take over the playground, it creates inflammation and pain. Add the discomfort of constipation to reflux, inflammation, sleep deprivation, and chronic pain, and it is not surprising that these children are irritable or aggressive.

First Things First

Many autism doctors, including me, suggest probiotics and antifungals for ASD children to address bacterial and fungal imbalances and infections. But if you give these supplements to a *constipated* child, the toxic substances produced by dying yeast and bacteria cannot be easily flushed from your child's body if the bowels are not moving. Your child will *absorb* these "die-off" products and become quite irritable and edgy. Constipation must be addressed first. Stop and read that sentence again. Circle it, and then highlight it in yellow.

Many autism parents try detoxification or chelation products they find on the Internet. But if you are trying to detox your constipated child, he may be reabsorbing those toxins if he cannot eliminate them through the bowels. Trust me, detox comes much later in the overall plan, if at all.

Quite literally, you are what you don't poop. The bowels are a major route of excretion and detoxification. That is why you must focus on breaking the constipation before going on to other gastrointestinal interventions such as probiotics and antimicrobials. But I don't mean you should just rely on laxatives. Once your child is free of chronic constipation and the resulting symptoms, he will probably calm down a *lot*. In addition, his improved behavior will mean the doctor will be far less likely to suggest psychiatric medications such as risperidone.

This Is Your Child's Brain on Drugs

What kinds of problems do these opiate-like neuropeptides contribute to? Take a look, and see if you recognize any of your child's problems in this list:

□ Social withdrawal
□ Limited use of language, even if he can speak
□ Addictive eating patterns
□ Constipation, or diarrhea *and* constipation
□ Reflux
□ Fuzzy thinking, being "zoned out"
□ Poor concentration
□ Poor eye contact
□ Disrupted sleep patterns
□ Irritability and aggression
□ Anger-related issues (easily angered)
□ Lack of impulse control
□ Self-injuring behaviors
□ High pain tolerance

Sound familiar?

Obviously, these opioid peptides cause lots of symptoms that can make children seem autistic, or more autistic than they really are. Our son Evan had many of the problems on this list; they began to clear up dramatically when we removed the opioid peptides from his diet (which was our best course of action, because we didn't have the enzymes back then). If he accidently ate wheat or cheese, the bizarre behaviors and anger returned. If you're skeptical, let me assure you—*so was I.* But what do you have to lose at this point? Behavioral and educational interventions are great therapies, and your child will need them, but they can't treat underlying medical conditions in the gut.

Joey's Story

Joey was just shy of three years old when I met him. He had recently been diagnosed with autism. As I interviewed his mom, I learned that the pregnancy had been uncomplicated and his birth and infancy had been trouble-free. Her health was good and she did not smoke, use drugs, or drink. Little Joey had never been bothered by colic or thrush, had rarely been sick, and had "slept like a dream from day one." He did not have allergies, asthma, or sinus infections; he had not had diaper rashes or the telltale red ring around the anus; and he had normal bowel movements once or twice a day, with normal odor and texture. She had never needed to give him laxatives or enemas, although recently Joey began having bowel movements only every other day. Still, he was not displaying aggression, irritability, or pain behaviors like draping over furniture. But his cognition was foggy, and he was pale with dark under-eye circles and did not speak more than one to two words in a row. He had been receiving speech and occupational therapy, but with limited success. He did not seem like a candidate for enzyme supplements, except for his eating pattern. He did not eat any vegetables or fruits, but favored chicken nuggets, fish sticks, pudding, yogurt, crackers, cookies, waffles, and toast. Hmmm . . . Joey's mom agreed to try diet changes and the enzyme protocol and Joey responded strongly. The speech and other therapies began to show powerful results as his cognition cleared.

Frequently Asked Questions About the Enzyme Protocol

Q: *My child does not have any of the gastrointestinal problems; no reflux, constipation, or a high pain tolerance. He sleeps just fine and is good-natured. He will eat anything and isn't picky at all. Can't I just skip the enzymes?* (About one-fourth of my patients raise this question.)
A: *I still want you to try the enzymes anyway.*

Why? Because I have seen so many children like yours respond to the enzyme protocol. For the price of a bottle of enzymes, you can find out if this approach will help your son or daughter. I have been surprised many times to see improvements in children and adults who did not seem like ideal candidates for the enzyme protocol. Their GI problems might have been present but at such low levels that no one suspected them. If your child has a subclinical opioid effect, he or she could respond well to enzyme therapy. Go ahead and look under that rock! Little Joey's parents are glad they tried it!

One huge bonus to using enzymes in place of the GFCF diet is that you don't have to take anything away from your child's already-limited food choices. As an autism mom, I know how impossible it seems to take away the dairy, pasta, or breads these children demand every day.

Another bonus is that if you do not take away dairy foods and many grain products, you do not have to put *back* the calcium and other nutrients in the form of vitamin supplements. The vitamin supplement regimens for children using the GFCF diet can be expensive and time-consuming to dole out. Plus, many parents find it very difficult to get so many supplements into their picky eaters.

Here's another reason I no longer recommend the GFCF diet first: Researching and implementing the GFCF diet is a front-loaded project. Most of the work you'll put in finding GFCF recipes and foods that your child will agree to eat, stocking your kitchen, checking websites to see if products are GFCF, and so on, is done *before and during* the early stages of the diet. All of this is a lot of work. Once you get going, the diet is definitely much easier, but many stressed-out families just cannot manage to pull off all of the initial work that goes into starting the diet. Autism parents are some of the smartest, most tenacious people I know, but the chaotic early days make everything harder.

Q: *What if my child is already GFCF?*
A: *I strongly encourage you to consider the enzymes even when your child is already on a special autism diet.*

Why? Over half of these children do not make enough of their own digestive enzymes to properly break down foods.[19] A number of my GFCF diet patients have easily identifiable foods in their bowel movements, foods that have barely undergone any digestion or breakdown. Parents can sometimes tell what their children ate simply by looking at their stools. Even with an organic, gluten-free, casein-free diet, their digestion and absorption may still be impaired. Enzymes increase the efficiency of digestion. Ava, whose story we heard at the beginning of Chapter 1, was GFCF and hadn't had a bowel movement in *years*—only "little bits" that slipped out in her diaper at night. After four weeks on the enzymes she, too, was having daily Bristol Type 4 stools and was making progress with toilet-training.

Jon's Story

When Jon's mother, Jeannine, heard me speak at a state conference for the National Association of Social Workers, she felt like she had been "hit by a truck," as she later told me during her first appointment at my center. Listening to me describe case studies of my patients gave her a sense of hope that had been absent from her life for years.

Jon was five years old then, and already gluten- and casein-free. He was taking many of the appropriate supplements for a child with autism, thanks to his mom's research on the Internet. While he showed much improvement from the time of his original diagnosis, he could say only a few words in a row, still suffered from constipation and diarrhea, was not doing well in school, and was still sick all the time.

I convinced Jeannine to start with the enzymes and the Basic GI Support Protocol, and then go on to the entire Un-Prescription Action Plan. Jon astounded us all, making rapid leaps in health, language, and academic performance soon after starting.

Eating Out

Boy, did I miss eating out in the years before we knew about the enzymes. Years ago, when we were using a strict GFCF diet with Evan, we had to practically interview the chef about how foods were prepared in the restaurant's kitchen and what was on the grill before my child's food was cooked. At our local Outback restaurant, the owner himself would clean the grill and personally prepare Evan's meal each time we came. Once we learned about enzymes, however, we could relax and not be so vigilant. If a gluten-free, casein-free child grabs the bread that the waitress set on the table when you aren't looking, the enzymes are there to save the day. If breaded fish was cooked on the grill before your child's grilled chicken, enzymes are there to bat cleanup. It certainly makes eating out much less of a hassle!

MYTH #3: MY CHILD DOESN'T HAVE TO REMOVE
BOTH GLUTEN AND CASEIN.

We took out milk, but wheat doesn't seem to cause a problem (or vice versa).

I have heard this refrain from a number of families: Don't fall for this type of reasoning. You are deceiving yourself because gluten and casein form neuropeptides so similar in sequence to each other and to morphine that both should be removed. Get a free pass—you can leave the favorite foods in place and use enzymes! *Both* types of neuropeptides will be digested away when using enzymes with DPP-IV.

Some Great Reasons to Use Enzymes for Autism

- ☐ You can start immediately.
- ☐ They "fake" the GFCF diet by breaking down opioid-like peptides.
- ☐ They are far easier to administer than the diet.
- ☐ They give you time to research the GFCF diet and decide if it will work in your household.
- ☐ You don't have to remove foods from your child's diet.
- ☐ They eliminate both gluten- *and* casein-derived peptides.

- ☐ You don't have to give as many vitamin supplements as with the GFCF diet.
- ☐ Enzymes make it easier to eat out in restaurants.
- ☐ Enzymes are safe, relatively inexpensive, and readily available.
- ☐ They help decrease GI inflammation.
- ☐ They provide digestive support.
- ☐ They minimize the domino effect of poorly digested food and its subsequent sensitivities and allergies.
- ☐ They improve your child's nutrition since insufficient enzymes cause poor digestion and absorption.

We can encourage a nice weight gain in undernourished children by using digestive enzymes.

- ☐ If foods are not broken down, the nutrients remain locked inside. A small number of my patients had such severe gastrointestinal problems they were actually malnourished and had that third-world look of starvation, with a bloated belly and stick-thin arms and legs. Digestive enzymes help "unlock" your child's food and help him get the nutrition he needs.
- ☐ Partially digested foods become a source for bacterial overgrowth in our colons. We are constantly fighting dysbiosis (microbial imbalance) in these kids; enzymes ensure there is less undigested food hanging around for bacteria to grow on.

Ready to Start Your Action Plan?

There are four big improvements you should see within the first four to five weeks of using enzymes. You won't be nearly finished, but you should definitely see significant improvements. Look for the following *short-term goals*:

1. Reduced aggression and irritability
2. Falls asleep easier
3. Fewer or no night awakenings
4. Daily bowel movements

Love that! ♡

Some of our long-term goals may begin to show up as well. An increase in language, clarity, and affection as well as eye contact are frequently noted during this early period.

What's the Catch?

Your child may go through a period of *withdrawal* from the opioid peptides, and it can get pretty ugly. When I tell parents this, their eyes widen in concern, even alarm, and they immediately want to know how long this spike in behavior is going to last and how bad it's going to get. The honest answer is: It depends on the child.

Note taped to my fridge: "I'd like a mocha vodka marijuana latte, please!" Humor helps you through the tough times!

A few children may experience no side effects, some may have minor irritability that lasts a few days, a few others may become dramatically more aggressive for several weeks, and the majority are somewhere in between.

Symptoms of withdrawal are *temporary* and can range from irritability, whining, and some really mean, bad behavior to screaming, hyperactivity, and full-blown violence. Progressing slowly and taking four weeks or longer to implement the digestive enzymes (as described in Chapter 6) will greatly lessen these symptoms.

Here is a general rule of thumb, based on what I see in my practice: *The milder your child's behavior is now, the milder a withdrawal he will likely have.*

After the initial spike in difficult behavior has passed, this is truly a thrilling time for families. Finally, some positive results! Teachers and bus drivers are amazed, friends and relatives are all talking about the positive changes, and you are not imagining it. If a child who previously had a vocabulary of a few single words (and who would scream if you touched him) begins to speak in sentences and gives parents hugs and kisses, you are overjoyed. Not every child regains or improves in language, but many do.

Grandparents often tell me with tears in their eyes that they are getting affection from a grandchild for the first time in years. I hear remarks like,

"He looks *at* me now, not *through* me!" Parents report a strong move in the right direction for sleep and bowel habits as well. Four county school systems have contacted me to learn how we calmed down such aggressive children. These are real improvements in behavior and cognition.

> *Bonus! After the opioid effect is broken, children often branch out and begin to eat new foods, to the absolute amazement of their parents.* [20]

Three Speeds for Your Action Plan

- "Go!" The basic Un-Prescription Action Plan as we do it in my center (see Chapter 6). This pace is usually neither too fast nor too slow. It takes four weeks to implement the enzymes completely.

> *HOW LONG WILL IT TAKE? If your child responds positively, expect to use the enzymes for anywhere from one to five years or longer. See Chapter 6 for when to stop.*

- "Slow!" This is a baby-steps plan for families in crisis. It takes twice as long to do each step, minimizing the opioid withdrawal even more.
- "Whoa!" How not to do the plan! A recipe for disaster, usually.

If your child is already gluten- and casein-free, you can introduce the enzymes at a much faster rate (see Chapter 6 for the week-by-week, step-by-step suggestions and variations).

Are Lab Tests Helpful?

The following lab tests are all useful in a number of situations, but none can accurately answer the question of whether your child may respond positively to the enzymes.

Urinary Peptide Test

- ☐ Not a fan! Some children may test positive for opioid neuropeptides from either casein or gluten, but not both. These families are led astray as they remove only one of the proteins, but not both, from the diet. Remember, this is not about an allergy or sensitivity, but about how similar the two proteins are. With the enzymes, we don't have to argue this point—the child may have both gluten and casein, and the enzymes will break down both.

Urinary Peptide Test

"Measurement of urinary peptides has not been proven to be clinically useful as a marker for ASDs or as a tool to determine if dietary restriction is warranted or would be effective."[21] *Children with a negative urinary peptide test may respond very well to a GFCF diet and/or enzymes. Why allocate time and money for this test? It makes more sense to start the diet and/or enzymes right away, and let that be the test.*

Allergy Testing

☐ Doesn't matter. An allergy doesn't cause an opioid effect. Testing for allergies is a good idea, but it won't answer the enzyme question for you at this point. (The exception would be if you notice that eating wheat or dairy causes tremendous GI distress or difficult behaviors in your child—but then, do you really need a test to tell you to avoid those foods?)

Celiac Disease Testing

☐ See answer above.

Food Sensitivity Testing

☐ See answer above.

Applied Kinesiology Muscle Testing

☐ See answer above.

NAET (Nambudripad's Allergy Elimination Technique)

☐ See answer above.

Okay, are you getting the picture? In my opinion, these are all valuable tests in other situations, but all but one are based on some premise of intolerance, allergy, or sensitivity. None of these lab tests can answer the question, *Will my child respond to the enzymes?*

For those of you who choose to do only the enzymes, you are on your wellness journey. For those of you still interested in one of the special autism diets, the four-week step-down plan of enzymes bought you some time to read about the diet and to see if your child will accept any of the alternate foods and products, so you'll know if doing a diet is even an option for you.

Guidelines for Using the Enzymes

Which enzyme or blend should I use for my action plan?

When I first opened my practice, we were using pure DPP-IV (dipeptidyl peptidase-4) as our enzyme supplement. Since DPP-IV is the enzyme that digests the opioid peptides from gluten and casein, I knew this enzyme was the key to faking the GFCF diet. But as we have seen, many children with autism are deficient in more than one type of digestive enzyme, including those necessary to digest sugars, starches, and proteins. For

> How much does it cost? For a good-quality, broad-spectrum digestive enzyme blend containing DPP-IV, using about eight capsules a day, expect to pay from $60 to $70 per month.

this reason, a broad-spectrum blend of digestive enzymes is going to benefit your child the most.

When I switched to a broad-spectrum *blend* of enzymes, one that would help children digest not only gluten and casein but also fats, sugars, and starches as well, I saw dramatically better results. Parents began calling the office to report amazing changes in their children that we did not see when supplementing with DPP-IV alone. I've had new patients tell me they are already using the enzyme approach, yet their child still seemed foggy and constipated to me. A little detective work revealed they were using a formulation that did not contain DPP-IV. So here's the deal: Your enzyme product needs to be a broad-spectrum formulation *and* include

DPP-IV for the best results. These products are available as capsules, powder, or chewables.

A Note on Time-Release Medications

Most digestive enzyme blends contain an enzyme called *cellulase*, which will digest cellulose. Cellulose is sometimes employed as the protective time-release coating on prescription medications. For the few medications using pure cellulose as an extended-release coating, cellulase may prematurely release the medicine into your child's system. In that case, just get a cellulase-free formulation, such as TriEnza by Houston Enzymes. There is no research indicating that cellulase will release the contents prematurely, but I am being conservative here.

If you're not sure if your child's prescription is extended-release or if the coating is pure cellulose, ask your pharmacist to check.

TREATMENT TIP:
ONLY START OR STOP ONE THING AT A TIME
When you try any of the protocols or ideas in this book, or anywhere else for that matter, start or stop only one new thing at a time. This advice includes even things that your pediatrician or your DAN! or MAPS (see Helpful Resources to learn more) doctor puts you on. If you start two or more new supplements or therapies at the same time and see improvements or negative reactions, you will never know which one was responsible for the changes.

   I understand you're in a hurry to get your child better, but this is a rule that should be set in stone: Start only one new thing at time, give it several days or a week to observe the effect it is having on your child, and then decide to keep it or pitch it. Some supplements only take a few days to assess, such as zinc and Vitamin C. Some supplements take more than a week to assess, such as the digestive enzymes, probiotics, and antifungals. And some of them, like the enzymes, may produce initial negative side effects that must be worked through. By starting one new thing at a time, you will have a chance to watch your child progress through any side effects and benefits, as well as to look for allergic reactions or sensitivities. You will be able to make a more educated decision when you and your doctor decide what to keep in your child's custom health program.

This rule also applies when your child is sick, or has just started a new school, got a new teacher, moved to a new house or town, or is adjusting to your divorce or another life upheaval. If your child has, say, been fighting strep, thrush, and ear infections and has been on antibiotics for several weeks, this is not a great time to put him through the opioid withdrawal process. Wait a few more weeks until he feels better and is better able to handle the side effects. You may end up quitting everything and missing an opportunity to find something that really works for your child. We autism parents are often hampered by our desire to help our child *right now*, but we need to learn a little patience for this wellness journey.

We have some great long-term goals we are aiming for. Let's review them one more time, just for motivation:

These goals are the ones that are nearest and dearest to an autism parent's heart!

Long-Term Goals

- Increased language
- Improved social skills, like joining the family at the dinner table or joining circle time at school
- Better learning
- More affectionate
- Better cognition
- More imagination
- Less fogginess
- Improved eye contact

- Eating a wider variety of foods
- Decreased sensory issues
- Decreased stimming
- Decreased seizure activity
- Improved immune function
- Fewer colds and runny noses
- Reduced chronic inflammation
- Improved behavior
- Toilet training
- More independent life skills like dressing and bathing
- Able to tolerate things like going to the mall, parties, a fireworks display

Table 3-1 shows you the benefits of enzymes when used alone, and when combined with dietary changes.

Frequently Asked Questions about Enzymes

Here are some common questions and answers on enzymes. Dr. Devin Houston, an enzyme biochemist with thirty years of research experience, has graciously answered some of them. His answers are indicated by his initials, DH.

Q: *Are enzymes safe? Is it possible to give too much of the enzymes?*
A: *Enzyme supplements are most likely the safest products in the dietary supplement arena: You cannot overdose on enzymes, and studies have demonstrated no toxicity, even at extremely high doses. (DH)*
Q: *Are the enzymes destroyed by stomach acid?*
A: *These enzymes are acid-stable, which means that they can survive in and actually work in the stomach. (DH)*
Q: *What if my child is allergic to gluten and/or casein?*
A: *You should follow the GFCF diet if it is a true allergy, or go gluten-free for celiac disease. You should still give the enzymes with the GF or GFCF diet to aid with digestion.*
Q: *Can't I just take these papaya enzymes I have?*
A: *Papaya enzymes do not contain DPP-IV and will not remove the opioid peptides.*

Enzymes from a good, better, best perspective

	Pros	Cons
GOOD **1.** Do the protocols as presented, tailoring the timing and dosing to your own child	• Least expensive (great for really broke people) • Least time-consuming (great for really tired people) • It's a good way to get started • Skeptics won't need to invest much time or money. • Many, many people see great results with just the basics	• Your child still has a crappy diet
BETTER **1.** Do the protocols as presented, tailoring... **2.** Go GFCF	• Those sensitive to gluten and casein will show more improvement in GI health • Allergies may improve when dairy is removed	• You have to supplement calcium and possibly protein • Your child still has a diet high in carbs and processed foods
BEST **1.** Do the protocols as presented, tailoring... **2.** Go GFCF **3.** Clean up your child's diet: ✓ Reduce sugary foods ✓ Reduce sugary drinks including soda, sweet tea, and sports drinks ✓ Reduce processed foods ✓ Go organic ✓ Include lots of colorful, fresh fruits and vegetables ✓ Reduce meat ✓ Experiment with naturally fermented foods	• Your child will have a healthier GI system • Your child will get more nourishment for optimal growth and development • Your child will have better neurological health • Your child will have more vibrant overall health	• Very time intensive • Much more expensive

Table 3-1

Q: *We use raw milk from our own animals. Can I just depend on the enzymes it naturally contains to do the job, instead of supplementing digestive enzymes?*

A: *No.*

Q: *He eats a lot of raw, organic food. Doesn't that contain enough enzymes to fake the GFCF diet?*

A: *No.*

Q: *Can I take the enzymes with medications?*

A: *Yes, medications are developed to withstand our own digestive enzymes. (DH)*

Q: *Will my child "get used to" the enzymes, and will his body stop making its own digestive enzymes?*

A: *No worries!*

Q: *Can I put them into what I'm cooking on the stove or in the oven? How about the microwave?*

A: *Enzymes can take temperatures up to about 120° to 130° Fahrenheit but cannot be put into food that is being cooked, baked, or microwaved, as that will destroy them. (DH)*

Q: *What if I forget to give the enzymes at the beginning of the meal?*

A: *Go ahead and give them as soon as you remember. Food can stay in the stomach up to an hour and a half or more, so there is still time and opportunity for them to work.*

Q: *My child says his stomach hurts since we started the enzymes. What's going on?*

A: *The enzymes can help clear away any dead layers of cells on the lining of the stomach or intestines, which may expose new, more tender tissue underneath. It is actually beneficial in the healing process for a GI tract that has been inflamed or ulcered. (DH) You may have to go to the kinder, gentler Slow! speed of the enzyme protocol if your child is experiencing this type of stomachache. (JL)*

Q: *Can the enzymes give him diarrhea or constipation?*

A: *Different enzyme formulations can either loosen or firm the stools. The enzyme manufacturer will be able to guide you on which formulation to choose. For example, Dr. Houston has a chart that illustrates the effects of his different formulations. Just call the number on your bottle.*

Q: *We tried the enzymes for a week or two, but it made him worse. I guess the enzymes didn't work for us.*

A: *I suspect you were seeing the start of an opioid withdrawal. This is the very time to push forward with the protocol, not quit.*

Q: *We tried the enzymes for a week or two, but didn't see any results, so we quit.*

A: *It is very common not to see any results the first week or two. Some children don't show any negative side effects. It may be four to six weeks later that you begin to notice your child seems more clear-headed or is looking you in the eye. Perhaps he's starting to join the family at the dinner table, instead of staying in his room. We don't always see brimstone and fire with the enzymes; there is that occasional child who simply looks up and quietly begins the journey back to balanced health. If you do the enzymes consistently with every meal and snack for three to four months and see absolutely nothing, then you can drop them in good conscience and continue with the rest of the Basic GI Support Protocol in Chapter 6.*

Q: *My child is a "grazer" and snacks many times throughout the day. Do I have to give a full dose of the enzymes each time he eats?*

A: *For grazers, mix the enzymes into a drink, then keep it in the fridge. Shake it up and give him a few sips each time he nibbles a few bites. If kept icy cold, the enzymes will stay active for up to, but no longer than, four hours.*

Q: *We put the enzymes in a drink, and he says it makes the back of his throat tingle.*

A: *With certain formulations, such as AFP Peptizyde by Houston Enzymes, it's normal to feel a tingling or burning at the back of the throat. Use a straw to consume the drink and chase with water.*

Q: *I gave my child the enzymes, and then he didn't eat anything. Will this hurt him?*

A: *No, he will be fine.*

Q: *How should I store the enzymes?*

A: *Enzymes can take cold temperatures better than heat. Even freezing them won't hurt them. Just store them at room temperature. When you bring them on a trip, keep them in your purse or your pocket. A hot car won't bother them unless temperatures get above 120° to 130° Fahrenheit.*

Q: *How young is too young to take enzymes?*

A: *Once a child starts on solid foods, enzymes can be used. Enzymes should definitely not be used when breast-feeding, as there are antibodies and proteins in milk that could be inactivated by enzymes. If the infant is on formulas, enzymes may be used if the infant is having problems tolerating the formula, especially if the formula is soy-based. (DH)*

Want the Science?

For sources of information found in this chapter, turn to the Endnotes.

4

Dirty Jobs:
The Power of Probiotics

I don't want to be stinky poo poo girl,
I want to be happy flower child.
Drew Barrymore

Welcome to the dirty job of getting a handle on your autistic child's gastrointestinal problems. Inflammatory bowel disease, immune and autoimmune problems, ADHD, mood, and difficult behaviors can all be linked to gut health—and all can and do show up in a child with autism.

Don't shy away from the task. You are about to greatly change his life for the better, and yours too.

Beneficial bacteria are the unsung heroes of our gastrointestinal system. Our friendly bacteria function like an organ[1] (an *acquired* organ), are more metabolically active than our liver, and weigh more than our brain. Fully half of the contents of our colon are these important bacteria.

The foods we choose, the stress we feel, the life we live—all of these factors in turn affect this important organ. Our health and well-being are vibrantly intertwined with this microscopic world. When we talk about our friendly bacteria, however, most people picture the gut only. Take a look at Figure 4-1 and see where our microbiome *really* lives:

The human microbiome

Figure 4-1

The GI Tract: A Nice Neighborhood

Ideally, our microbiome should be a large diverse population of beneficial and benign species, with few yeast or pathogens. Think of the GI tract as a neighborhood. That neighborhood "opens for business" the day you are born. Research has revealed that the first few days and weeks of life are when we acquire our most important permanent strains of beneficial bacteria—our citizen strains. Yet our modern style of birth and infant care leaves our babies to haphazardly colonize their GI tract, instead of the way Mother Nature intended.[2] We have a high rate of C-sections these days (close to one in three births); babies don't pick up the good bacteria from Mom's birth canal when delivered via C-section and are then whisked away from Mom in the delivery room rather than enjoying immediate skin-to-skin contact; and in some hospitals babies spend a lot of time in the hospital nursery rather than in Mom's room. All of this means the baby is left to collect initial strains of bacteria in a haphazard fashion, and research shows we don't end up with the best bacteria this way.[3]

If your neighborhood is rather empty or thinly populated, then there is room for undesirable squatters to move in, set up shop, and create a "gut ghetto." You want to create a neighborhood thriving with hardworking citizens where there isn't an opportunity for undesirables. This is where probiotics come in.

I'm not going to wear you out with an exhaustive primer on the topic of probiotics—those books have been written. This chapter is about creating an Action Plan on how to use probiotics to help your child feel better and get better. We're picking up where Chapter 3 left off, and delving further into the relationship between probiotics, gut health, the immune system, and the effects on a child with autism.

Why do so many children and adults have tummy troubles, and children with autism in particular?[4] In Figure 4-2, we see how our modern world takes a big toll on our beneficial friends in the microbiome.

If our ASD children are more genetically vulnerable to the microbiome stressors shown in Figure 4-2, they may be at the center of a perfect storm for gastrointestinal problems. While research hasn't settled this question yet, the good news is that this chapter includes a step-by-step protocol for properly adding probiotics to the Action Plan and restoring many of the benefits we have lost to modern stressors.

Probiotics:
A Missing Piece in Helping Your Child

Probiotics are one of the missing pieces in most doctors' approach to helping children on the spectrum. Sadly, many pediatricians seem at a loss to help an ASD child's constipation, diarrhea, gassiness, foul odors, and poor digestion. Many repeat the standard advice of more fiber, water, and exercise, or they recommend a daily laxative and leave it at that (as if we haven't tried it already!). Parents are left to search the Internet for ideas, and many

Modern stressors on the microbiome

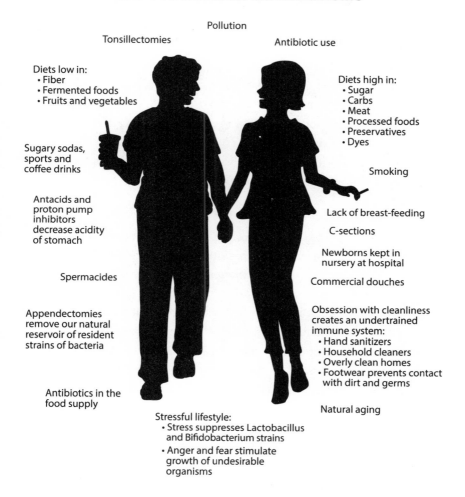

Pollution

Tonsillectomies

Antibiotic use

Diets low in:
 • Fiber
 • Fermented foods
 • Fruits and vegetables

Diets high in:
 • Sugar
 • Carbs
 • Meat
 • Processed foods
 • Preservatives
 • Dyes

Sugary sodas, sports and coffee drinks

Smoking

Antacids and proton pump inhibitors decrease acidity of stomach

Lack of breast-feeding

C-sections

Newborns kept in nursery at hospital

Spermacides

Commercial douches

Appendectomies remove our natural reservoir of resident strains of bacteria

Obsession with cleanliness creates an undertrained immune system:
 • Hand sanitizers
 • Household cleaners
 • Overly clean homes
 • Footwear prevents contact with dirt and germs

Antibiotics in the food supply

Natural aging

Stressful lifestyle:
 • Stress suppresses Lactobacillus and Bifidobacterium strains
 • Anger and fear stimulate growth of undesirable organisms

Figure 4-2

are ready and willing to try anything and everything for relief from the daily agitation of GI troubles on the spectrum.

When I am consulted by colleagues on stubborn GI cases in infants and children, I find that the mere mention of a high-potency probiotic brings on a knee-jerk response. A dismissive wave of the hand and a "yeah-yeah-yeah, but how would you *really* handle it," is the standard attitude. The answer for ASD children is often so simple no one *hears* it, not even health professionals. And that's why probiotics remain a missing piece for vibrant health on the autism spectrum.

Certain myths contribute to our underuse and poor understanding of probiotics.

PROBIOTIC MYTH #1: MY CHILD'S YOGURT HAS PROBIOTICS IN IT, SO I FIGURE WE'RE GOOD.

A lot of parents think giving their child yogurt should do the trick. (How's that working for you?) I'll share a few guidelines that will help your child get the most out of probiotics.

PROBIOTIC MYTH #2:
ALL PROBIOTIC SUPPLEMENTS ARE THE SAME.

The amount of research into probiotics is gratifying and growing. Now the hunt is on to discover each individual strain's health benefits and limitations.

A conservative approach is to use a brand from a company that is fanatical about quality and viability. I am a fan of multispecies probiotic formulations. My favorite is Ther-Biotic Complete by Klaire Labs. (Just because a certain strain is "the most studied" doesn't mean it is automatically the most effective.) I usually see better results when more than one strain of probiotics is supplemented.

PROBIOTIC MYTH #3:
ONCE THE PROBIOTICS ARE INGESTED, THEY WILL LIVE IN THE GI TRACT PERMANENTLY.

I used to think that once I took a probiotic it would permanently replenish my beneficial bacteria: Turns out, ingested probiotics are more like visiting angels,[5] only lingering a couple of weeks. This is another missing piece in your child's probiotic protocols. I'll provide you with a Maintenance Proto-

col to keep the great benefits of probiotics going—without breaking the bank.

PROBIOTIC MYTH #4: PROBIOTICS MAKE IT THROUGH THE STOMACH ACID.

There are some acid-resistant species and strains, such as lactobacillus and S. boulardii, that naturally survive the stomach acid. But beyond those, some reports claim that over 90 percent of the probiotic supplements we take may be destroyed in the acidic environment of the stomach. Great care must be taken to select a brand that has some type of specialized delivery system to protect the probiotics until they land safely in the small intestine. There are brands with enteric coatings and really cool space-age coverings to resist the stomach acid, and there is even one with a delivery system that contains prebiotics to nourish the bacteria once they arrive in the intestines.

PROBIOTIC MYTH #5: I HAVE TO STOP TAKING MY PROBIOTIC WHILE I'M ON AN ANTIBIOTIC.

That's right, it's a myth. Don't put away that bottle of probiotics just because your child started an antibiotic. Many strains survive antibiotics, and we can help out even more by taking the probiotic two to three hours *after* taking the antibiotic. It will actually help the GI and immune system if you continue to take probiotics during and after the antibiotic.

When autism parents get together, the conversation often shifts to how to help with the daily struggle of bowel problems on the autism spectrum. If your autism life centers on your child's painful, messy, or unpredictable bowel movements, you'll want to add some high-powered probiotics to your child's treatment approach.

You might be an autism parent if you can't go a whole day without talking about poop!

Oftentimes in my practice I'll meet a parent and child who obviously have a caring, thoughtful doctor helping with the child's health. Yet, while the child is on many good supplements, there is no probiotic in sight. You need to hear this message: A broad-spectrum, high-potency probiotic that will survive the stomach acid has incredible benefits for most children on the spectrum. If you haven't tried one yet, or if you're just using a weak, low-potency probiotic with only a few million colony-forming units (CFUs), a brand with only one or two strains, or one without safe delivery through the acidic pH of the stomach, prepare to be wowed by the improvement your child may see.

Great News on Probiotics

Research on probiotics has exploded in the last two decades. Studies indicate that activities in our gut can modulate systemic inflammation and autoimmune conditions as well as mood, behavior, and emotions.[6] As a matter of fact, in 2005, probiotics were suggested as a beneficial addition to therapy for major depression.[7] Probiotics such as Bifidobacterium infantis and L. acidophilus have a confirmed positive effect on emotions and mood and are called "psychobiotics."[8] Although research is still ongoing, let's look at what we know already about these powerfully beneficial bacteria:

Neurological Health[9]:

- ☐ May ease "autism-like" symptoms[10]
- ☐ Enhance mood, behavior, and brain function[11]
- ☐ Promote central nervous system maturation[12]
- ☐ Produce neuroactive compounds[13]
- ☐ Activate neural pathways[14]
- ☐ Activate brain signaling systems[15]
- ☐ Reduce inflammation[16]
- ☐ Impact brain development and subsequent adult behavior[17]
- ☐ Affect neuronal circuits that control motor function[18]
- ☐ Influence anxiety and depression[19]

Gastrointestinal Health:

- ☐ Reduce inflammation[20]

- ☐ Relieves constipation[21]
- ☐ Reduce abdominal pain[22]
- ☐ Relieve bloating[23]
- ☐ Attenuate stress-induced GI disorders[24]
- ☐ Defend against opportunistic fungi[25]
- ☐ Decrease pH of the gut[26]
- ☐ Keep harmful bacteria from attaching to the intestinal wall[27]
- ☐ Reduce undesirable bacteria in the gut[28]
- ☐ May protect against parasites[29]
- ☐ Reduce intestinal permeability[30]
- ☐ Make beneficial short-chain fatty acids to nourish the cells lining the colon[31]

Immune Health:

- ☐ Support the immune system[32]
- ☐ Produce natural antibiotics[33]
- ☐ Train our immune system to only attack pathogens
- ☐ Strengthen the mucus barrier[34]
- ☐ Influence the Th1-Th2 balance[35]

> *Th1 and Th2 represent different arms of our immune system. The Th1 to Th2 balance may be altered in ASD, leaving the immune system less efficient at recognizing and fending off viruses and fungi, as well as having a heightened allergy response.*

Probiotics Protect Against:

- ☐ Colds[36]
- ☐ Viruses[37]
- ☐ Infection[38]
- ☐ Food poisoning[39]
- ☐ Urinary tract infections[40]
- ☐ H. pylori[41]
- ☐ Clostridia difficile[42]
- ☐ Cancer[43]

Probiotics Help Fight and Prevent Diarrhea Caused By:

- ☐ Antibiotics[44]
- ☐ Clostridia difficile[45]

- ☐ Traveler's diarrhea[46]
- ☐ Other infections[47]

Probiotics Battle Toxins:

- ☐ Neutralize toxic substances[48]
- ☐ Chelate heavy metals[49]
- ☐ Target bacterial toxins[50]

Probiotics Generally Help Around the "House":

- ☐ Enhance digestion[51]
- ☐ Protect against environmental allergens[52]
- ☐ Manage dietary toxins[53]
- ☐ Down-regulate allergies,[54] hives,[55] hay fever[56]
- ☐ Reduce eczema[57]
- ☐ Improve oral health[58]
- ☐ Potentially help prevent cavities[59]
- ☐ Reduce symptoms of irritable bowel syndrome[60] and arthritis[61]
- ☐ Metabolize dietary carcinogens[62]
- ☐ Make vitamins[63]
- ☐ Enhance nutritional support[64]

That's a lot of benefits! And for a child on the spectrum who struggles with GI problems, probiotics are a must for the health plan. With all this in mind, let's take another look at our health goals for your child.

Short-Term Goals

- ☐ Normal bowel movements
- ☐ Better toilet training
- ☐ Less gas
- ☐ Improved odor of bowel movements and gas
- ☐ Clearing of eczema and diaper rash
- ☐ No more itchy bottom
- ☐ Better sleep

Are you getting happy just reading this list? ♡

- □ Few or no night awakenings
- □ Improved immune system
- □ Catch fewer colds
- □ Better digestion
- □ Fewer tummy aches
- □ Improved eating patterns
- □ Improved mood and behavior
- □ Reduced aggression and irritability
- □ Less fogginess, more clarity
- □ Return a healthy glow and the missing "sparkle" to your child's eyes

Long-Term Goals

- □ Optimal maturation of the brain and immune system
- □ Improved communication and language
- □ Enhanced eye contact and socialization
- □ Fewer allergies and less congestion

Eczema and Probiotics

Did you see that clearing of eczema is one of our short-term goals? Does your child keep a case of eczema or a rash around the privates going most of the time? Comes and goes, doesn't it, but you can never really kick it? Did you know it may be related to imbalance in the microbiome?[65] Listen to this mother's story.

Jax's Story

Paul and Mona brought Jax, their six-year-old son with ASD, to my office for a health support plan. He had a history of "lots and lots" of ear infections and subsequent rounds of antibiotics since two years of age. Although he wasn't constipated, his bowel movements were very foul smelling and his gas was "very, very stinky."

Mona sighed in exasperation about the constant rashes around his crotch, groin, and upper buttocks. Although a dermatologist told her they were due to "yeast," his treatment plan did not include getting rid of the yeast. Mona claimed to have a drawer full of creams and powders, including prescription steroid cream, but the rashes always came back. We've all done this, haven't we—rubbed in creams and lotions, soaked our kid in oatmeal baths, tried pre-scriptions—and yet seem surprised when the rashes come back? If rashes are the symptom of a yeast problem, why is no one treating the yeast?

My advice to start a high-potency probiotic was met with an uncomfort-able silence and furtive looks darting between the parents. They clearly were not expecting this advice. A few short weeks later Mona was practically singing with joy: "Three weeks and I can't believe all that clear skin I'm seeing!"

Jax did go through two predictable side effects of starting an effective probi-otic: The foul odor of his gas got even more disgusting for a week or two, and he had a spike in defiance before his mood smoothed out for the better.

Jax had been riding the antibiotic merry-go-round for years, and probi-otics helped him get out of that vicious cycle. In Chapter 7 (Why Is My Child Always Sick?), you'll learn more about this cycle and how to break it—or avoid it altogether.

What Are the Drawbacks?

I have learned the hard way that many children and adults with autism may experience a *big* increase in the amount of gas they produce when first start-ing a high-potency probiotic, as well as changes in the odor of the gas and a temporary change in their mood. In other words, it's likely they are going to fart their head off, it will stink like Pete, and they'll be grump muffins for a few days to a few weeks. In the spirit of transparency, Table 4-1 shows some of the early, and let me stress *temporary*, side effects reported by parents at my center.

Liam's Story

This story is about my own son Liam. His teacher got a good laugh and observed firsthand the power of starting a probiotic. She was seated behind him in the auditorium and knew he was off-gassing like road kill when she saw the boys on either side of him dive sideways for fresh air, while he remained upright in the middle. Luckily, she had been notified ahead of time that he was starting a probiotic and might experience some stinky gas. It paid off over the long run when Liam caught fewer colds and missed less school that year.

Temporary Side Effects You May See When Your Child First Begins the Probiotic Regimen	Parent Observations
GASSINESS: • Increase in volume • More foul in odor • Bloating, gas pain	"He couldn't possibly have more gas!" "It about drove us out of the house!" "Behavior improved after he passed gas."
MOOD: • Spike in irritability • Angers more easily • Increase in aggression	"She was meaner than a snake." "He was hard on his siblings for a while." "He got in trouble at school."
SKIN: • Rashes and itching • Eczema flares	"We had to trim his fingernails and keep him in long sleeves and pants." "Her skin got worse before it got better."
RARELY: • Increase in stimming • Increase in hyperactivity • Sleep disruption • Throwing up	(**Dr. Janet's note:** Parents should stop or cut way back if any of these rarer problems occur.)

Table 4-1

Over the years, each of my children has proudly confided he was voted the Best Farter in the class! #MustBeABoyThing

Getting Started with Probiotics

Here is what to look for in a probiotic:

- ☐ Look for the "B" word—*billions*. I use a minimum of 25 billion CFUs.
- ☐ Look for a brand that tests and guarantees the viability of its products. Just because a capsule contains probiotics does not mean they are alive.
- ☐ Arrive alive! Look for a brand that features an excellent delivery system *and* guarantees its probiotic will arrive alive in the small intestine.
- ☐ Until more research is done, include a multispecies product with a mix of at least four different species, preferably more, in your probiotic selections.

SUCCESS TIP 1: DO NOT GIVE A HIGH-POTENCY PROBIOTIC TO A CONSTIPATED CHILD OR ADULT. GET THE BOWELS MOVING *FIRST.*

Starting the enzyme protocol outlined in Chapter 3, or the GFCF diet plus enzymes, should be done first to relieve constipation, and then you can start a probiotic. Do not start the enzymes *and* the probiotics at the same time or else your child will be miserable, act out, and drive you crazy to the point where you will probably be tempted to quit.

SUCCESS TIP 2: NEVER START A PROBIOTIC:
- ☐ At the beginning of the school week (better idea: start on a Friday)
- ☐ Right before a field trip with the class
- ☐ Right before an important party, celebration, or dinner
- ☐ Right as you leave for vacation

☐ Anytime crabbiness and unexpected farting is a no-no (you get the idea!)

SUCCESS TIP 3: ALWAYS GIVE PROBIOTICS WITH A MEAL. You'll find a collection of suggested probiotic protocols in Chapter 6, and you may choose one as a guideline for your own child. Keep your child's pediatrician in the loop with anything you choose. Here, briefly, are some of the protocols I will discuss in Chapter 6.

Probiotic Support for Infants and Toddlers

It's not uncommon for a newborn to receive an antibiotic at the hospital for various reasons. Give your baby the gift of a great start and use an infant probiotic starting on day 1. Again, a high-tech delivery system that gets the probiotic powder safely through the stomach acid so it is delivered alive is crucial, especially since infants cannot swallow a capsule. Bonus: Infants given probiotics experience less eczema, allergies, and asthma.

Probiotic Support for Ages 2 and Up

☐ *The "Go" Plan.* Full speed ahead with probiotic support! I do break it in over two weeks to minimize side effects.
☐ *The "Slow" Plan.* If your ASD child is *this close* to getting kicked out of school or daycare for difficult behavior, or is still struggling with constipation, we don't want to rock that boat. Here's a kinder, gentler, slower plan to minimize the initial irritability side effect of starting a powerful probiotic.
☐ *The "Whoa" Plan.* Or how *not* to give probiotics.
☐ *Modified School-Year Approach.* This approach is also known as the weekend method. Depending on the age and level of social function of your child and his school situation, you must consider how the initial temporary increase in gas and irritability may affect the school day. Use a modified weekend schedule during the school year if the die-off turns out to be a stinky or cranky one.
☐ *The "Detective" Schedule.*
☐ *The "Already on a Probiotic" Plan.*
☐ *The Maintenance Plan.* What to do after gut balance is achieved.
☐ *How to take probiotics during a course of an antibiotic.*

Whatever maintenance schedule you choose, I do *not* recommend just stopping probiotics altogether for a child with ASD. Early research seems to indicate a predisposition to dysbiosis, and probiotics are one piece of the health plan I would never give up.

Good-Better-Best

Let's approach adding the probiotic piece to your child's Action Plan from a good, better, best angle (see Table 4-2).

Probiotics from a good, better, best perspective

	Pros	Cons
GOOD **1.** Do the protocols as presented, tailoring the timing and dosing to your own child	• Least expensive (great for really broke people) • Least time-consuming (great for really tired people) • It's a good way to get started • Skeptics won't have to invest much time or money • Many, many people see great results with just the basics	• Your child may not consume enough prebiotic fiber (think whole fruits and vegetables) to nourish colonies of good bacteria • You may miss something that comprehensive stool testing would reveal
BETTER **1.** Do the protocols as presented, tailoring... **2.** Add prebiotic fiber to feed and nurture beneficial bacteria	• Your child will have a healthier GI system • You will encourage stronger colonies of beneficial bacteria without encouraging "bad" bacteria	• Not too bad—just one extra supplement to give twice a day • You may miss something that comprehensive stool testing would reveal
BEST **1.** Do the protocols as presented, tailoring... **2.** Add prebiotic fiber to feed and nurture beneficial bacteria **3.** Add comprehensive stool testing	• You will have a better grasp of exactly what is going on in your child's gastrointestinal tract and can tailor your Action Plan to the results • You can specifically target any parasites or dysbiosis revealed by lab testing	• Bit of an "ick" factor • Comprehensive stool testing can be very expensive, from several hundred dollars to over $2,000 • Not always covered by insurance plans • Testing should be repeated on a regular basis for best results

Table 4-2

Who Shouldn't Take a Probiotic

□ Immunocompromised and immunodeficient, severely ill children and adults, including those with AIDS

□ Patients with short bowel syndrome (avoid Lactobacillus species, especially)

□ Those with pancreatitis

□ People who are hypersensitive to lactose and milk (avoid probiotic supplements that aren't certified free of traces of dairy products)

□ Anyone undergoing surgery (stop taking probiotics a week before surgery, and until any open surgical wounds are healed)

Frequently Asked Questions About Probiotics

Q: *Can I take the probiotic at the same time as the digestive enzymes?*

A: *Yes.*

Q: *Are probiotics safe for infants?*

A: *They are not only safe, they are beneficial, as research indicates they may reduce the risk of eczema, allergies, and asthma in infants receiving them.*

Q: *How long do I have to take probiotics?*

A: *There are no hard-and-fast rules, but I believe that everyone should take probiotics for life.*

Q: *I left my probiotic out on the counter overnight. Is it still good, or do I have to throw it away?*

A: *It's still good. A good probiotic brand should be able to withstand a night or two on the counter, just don't leave it in a hot car.*

Q: *The probiotic gave him diarrhea: What should we do?*

A: *Cut way down on the dose and only give the probiotic every two to three days until it is well tolerated. If the diarrhea doesn't stop, discontinue it for a while and try again using mere specks as a starting dose.*

Q: *His eczema flared up after he started the probiotic. Should I stop?*

A: *Only if it's severe. Just cut back on the dose and use it every two to three days until the rash settles down. Then gradually increase to the full dose as it is tolerated. It may be helpful to keep him in long pants and sleeves, and keep his nails trimmed until then.*

Q: *Can I open up the capsule and put the probiotic in his drink?*

A: *As long as it's not a hot drink.*

Q: *How long is the drink good for after I put the probiotic in?*

A: *Although there are no studies on this, my expert sources seem to think the friendly bacteria will live for an hour or two. The liquid does "wake up" the flora, so it's best to use right away if possible.*

Q: *Can I put the probiotic in his food?*

A: *Yes, as long as it's not hot food, or food that will be cooked.*

Q: *We forgot to give him the probiotic during dinner. What should we do?*

A: *Go ahead and give it as soon as you remember. Food stays in the stomach for an hour and a half, or even longer.*

Q: *Are there any chewable probiotics?*

A: *Yes. Probiotics come in powder, capsule, gummy, and chewable forms. There is even a liquid form, although it is less common.*

Q: *My other children aren't autistic, but have many of these signs and symptoms. Can they do these protocols?*

A: *Of course.*

Q: *My child is on an antibiotic. Should I wait until it is finished to start the probiotic?*

A: *No. It's very important that you DO give the probiotic during a round of antibiotics. Just give the probiotic three hours after he takes the antibiotic. See Week 6 in the Chapter 9 Online Action Plan for antibiotic support suggestions.*

Q: *Can I take probiotics with my other medications?*

A: *Yes, there are no known interactions with medications.*

Q: *My pediatrician says I shouldn't give children probiotics because not enough research has been done to say which strain should be taken for which problem. He says to wait until more research comes out.*

A: *Have your pediatrician babysit the poor wailing, gassy, rashy, shitty, sleepless thing for a week or two, and then ask him again.*

Q: *Should I take probiotics on an empty stomach?*

A: *Again, there are no hard-and-fast rules; however, the thinking is that taking a probiotic with food will help protect it from the stomach acid. If it has a strong delivery system that guarantees it will arrive alive in the small intestine, then it may not matter if it's taken with or without food.*

Q: *My child's lab results say she is high in lactic acid. Should I avoid probiotics?*

A: *No. According to Klaire Labs, "When elevated urine D(-)-lactate levels are encountered, the most effective approach is to resolve gut dysbiosis with pre- and probiotics, optimize digestion with enzymes, restrict excessive carbohydrate intake, provide nutritional mitochondrial support, and reduce elevated oxalate levels."*

Q: *My child has PANDAS (pediatric autoimmune neuropsychiatric disorders associated with streptococcal infections). Do I need to avoid probiotic products that contain streptococcus species?*

A: *According to Klaire Labs, "Group A beta-hemolytic streptococcus (GABHS) infection is believed to elicit production of antibodies that cross-react with neural tissues and thereby provoke the neurobehavioral symptoms associated with PANDAS. A review of the literature reveals no evidence that S. thermophilus promotes production of cross-reactive antistreptococcal antibodies and no indication that any streptococcal organism other than GABHS is associated with PANDAS or ASD."*

Q: *Are soil-based probiotics safe?*

A: *Yes, if the proper strains are used. Choose products from a company like Klaire Labs that tests and guarantees the genetic purity of soil-based strains.*

Want the Science?

For sources of information found in this chapter, turn to the Endnotes.

You are deep into your child's wellness journey now. Probiotics will be a great piece to add to your child's plan, but they're only part of what you need to restore vibrant health on the spectrum. Let's go on to Chapter 5 for one of the most overlooked and poorly understood areas of GI health.

5

Sh!ts and Giggles:
The Antimicrobial Rotation

I'm like a fungus; you can't get rid of me.
Adam Baldwin

Evan walked out of the bathroom at Sam's Club with an odd look on his face.
"There's poop on the ceiling."

My husband came out, an odd look on his face as well. "Get a manager.
And buy some clothes for Liam."

Apparently my middle child had become a diarrhea piñata, the grand
finale of diarrhea fireworks, giving the bathroom of our spanking-new Sam's
Club its inaugural christening, but without the traditional champagne. I had
no idea poop could exit the human body in a spectacular 360-degree detona-
tion. He had started his first dose of Diflucan that morning.

THE TAKE-HOME MESSAGE
Don't take antifungals or antimicrobials until you understand how
and why. This chapter will lead you through the swamp of confusion
that exists on this topic so you can avoid the land mines that lurk
there.

For far too long, autism families and some health professionals have focused solely on yeast as Public Enemy No. 1 for children with autism, yet there's more to the story than Candida. Bacterial overgrowth and parasitic infections are ignored in the stampede to treat yeast. My approach addresses all three.

Antimicrobial agents (AMs) are natural supplements and prescription medications that discourage or kill a variety of fungi, bacteria, or parasites. They are part of, or should be part of, the toolbox for individuals with ASD. But misunderstanding, underuse, and even overuse of these agents have created some vicious cycles for our children.

Outdated Approaches to Dysbiosis on the Autism Spectrum

Treatment-wise, it seems a lot of conventional pediatric practices are not yet acting on the emerging scientific support for dysbiosis (a microbial imbalance in the digestive tract) on the spectrum. As we see in Table 5-1, children

Common oversights at the pediatrician's office

- Unaware of tendency for dysbiosis
- Does not ask about it during the history
- Does not order laboratory testing for it
- Does not treat it
- Is waiting for more research
- Thinks parents have been on the Internet too much
- May do one round of nystatin if the parents beg
- Does not assess for GI pain and dysfunction, but may:
    o Suggest daily laxatives for constipation
    o Prescribe sleep medication for disturbed sleep patterns
    o Prescribe antipsychotics for irritability and aggression (see Bindee's story)
    o Prescribe medication for acid reflux
    o Prescribe ADHD medication for the ensuing brain fog and attention issues

Table 5-1

and adults with ASD aren't being regularly assessed, treated, or provided support for dysbiosis (pronounced "dis bye OH sis") in most of the cases I see at my office.

The Danger of Ignoring GI Problems on the Spectrum

Bindee's Story

Three-year-old Bindee's pediatrician wanted to put her on risperidone for her constant irritability and crying and on clonidine for her very disrupted sleep patterns. Clonidine is an older blood pressure medicine that is used for its sedating properties to help children with autism go to sleep. Risperidone is a powerful antipsychotic medication that is approved for treating irritability associated with autistic disorder, and Bindee was certainly irritable.

Her parents didn't want to use an antipsychotic in a three-year-old and said this seemed to annoy the pediatrician.

Since research indicates irritability and poor sleep might be a sign of GI problems on the spectrum, I ordered comprehensive stool testing, among other tests. We discovered Helicobacter pylori (a bacterium that may cause peptic ulcers), and a significant overgrowth of Candida and Blastocystis hominis, a parasite known for causing GI symptoms.

Along with a prescription from the reluctant pediatrician, Bindee started the Basic GI Support Protocol to restore and maintain good GI health.

Her crying, irritability, and poor sleep patterns resolved, and she felt and behaved much better for a number of months. The school she attended reported a huge leap in learning, unlike anything the teachers had seen before from Bindee.

Six months later, Bindee experienced a significant return of symptoms, complete with a bloated belly, and screaming and crying, and everything was worse than the first time. I ran another stool test and discovered a fearsome parasite called Ascaris lumbricoides, or giant human roundworms, typically a third-world parasite found in unsanitary conditions. The parents realized they had noticed "little white things" in her diaper, and it turned out she had picked it up at her school, where there was a cluster of these infections going on. Inexplicably, the pediatrician asked Bindee's parents to find another practice.

I contacted the health department for advice on appropriate treatment and connected Bindee's parents with a new pediatrician, and Bindee was once again returned to good health.

THE TAKE-HOME MESSAGE

Bindee's story is a call to action for parents and pediatricians everywhere to realize that irritability is a *symptom*, not a core deficit of autism. Just because risperidone is "indicated" for irritability on the autism spectrum does not mean it should be the first thing you reach for. Each child deserves a complete assessment to discover the source of the irritability.[1]

The GI Two-Step

Are you tired of taking three steps forward and then a giant step backward? Do you finally get control of diarrhea, constipation, tummy aches, and a bloated belly, only to see them return worse than before? I'll share five reasons for the dreaded relapse that often get overlooked and tell you how to get past it and get on with more important things for these children.

This chapter gives you the final piece in the Basic GI Support Protocol, and if you think probiotics are the missing piece, then antimicrobials are the Rosetta Stone.

Relapse Reason 1: Yeast isn't always the culprit.

Don't get stuck on treating yeast—it seems that is all some autism parents talk about. There are other possibilities to consider. Time and research are bearing out that individuals on the spectrum may be vulnerable to imbalances in the microbiome,[2] not just because of yeast, but bacteria and parasites as well. Individuals on the spectrum are candidates for dysbiosis, or microbial imbalance, thanks to:

- ☐ Genetic differences
- ☐ Overuse of antibiotics

- ☐ Extended use of antifungals
- ☐ Poor hygiene (poor hand washing and hand-to-mouth behavior)
- ☐ Clostridia difficile, which is a special problem for some on the spectrum[3]

What are some of the signs and symptoms of a microbial imbalance?

- ☐ Gas and bloating
- ☐ Foul breath
- ☐ Breath that smells like freshly baked bread
- ☐ Breath that has a "fruity" alcohol smell
- ☐ Fecal smears in the underwear
- ☐ Silly giddy behavior
- ☐ Headache
- ☐ Fatigue, apathy
- ☐ Irritability
- ☐ Brain fog, poor memory
- ☐ Reflux
- ☐ Abdominal pain or cramping
- ☐ Night awakenings
- ☐ Poor appetite
- ☐ Weight loss
- ☐ Nutritional deficiencies
- ☐ B12 deficiency
- ☐ Iron deficiency
- ☐ Sugar and carbohydrate cravings
- ☐ Carbohydrate intolerance
- ☐ Fat malabsorption
- ☐ Diarrhea
- ☐ Cyclic diarrhea
- ☐ Eczema
- ☐ Rashes and hives
- ☐ Vaginal or urinary tract infections

> *I've had to consult with the health department and even veterinarians on some of the bacteria and parasites discovered through stool testing. It's not always yeast!*

- ☐ Fungal infections of skin or nails
- ☐ Rectal itching
- ☐ Vaginal itching
- ☐ Achy muscles and joints

Obviously, most of these symptoms are vague and could be attributed to many things, including allergies, colds, inflammation, or anxiety. I know autism parents who want to "treat yeast" at the first sign of dark under-eye circles in their child, when this could just be a sign of fatigue or even allergies. That's why it is important to get proper stool testing and not try to treat "yeast" on your own.

How are these infections and imbalances treated? There are natural supplements and prescription medications to control most of these microbes. So why is there a problem? What's with all the relapse? As usual, the devil is in the details. Using these same tools in the *right* way can help your child get on with his childhood and leave GI relapse in the rearview mirror.

Relapse Reason 2:
Lack of rotation creates havens for bad bugs.

Dr. Sydney Baker brilliantly came up with the prescription "Antifungal Parade" for his autism patients who were struggling with stubborn dysbiosis. It was a breakthrough for restoring GI health at a time when the health challenges of autism were poorly understood. Some doctors implement this strategy but get stuck on using only a couple of antifungals instead of a wide-ranging rotation as originally designed by Dr. Baker.

MYTH #1:
DIFLUCAN AND NYSTATIN KILL ALL THE YEAST.

It's appropriate to use these two antifungals as part of your doctor's treatment approach to dysbiosis, but it's incorrect to think that one or two antifungals are all you'll ever need. If you've gotten in the habit of using only a couple of antifungals or antimicrobials ("He just seems to tolerate this one best of all," or "His doctor keeps him on just those two"), you are creating a haven for any microbe or strain of yeast not sensitive to the products you are using. By only using one or two antimicrobials on a long-term or even occasional basis, you are working against relatively few microbes and reducing competition for all the others that are not killed by it.

Simply put, it doesn't matter if it's a natural agent or a prescription; either can create a haven for unwanted microbes in a gut ghetto.

These drugs are being used outside of the recommended lengths of time of use, too, with some doctors renewing the prescriptions for months or even years. Some of our ASD children are given way too many rounds of antibiotics, and the same thing can happen with antifungals. I have some autism patients who have been on one prescription antifungal for four to five years, and these drugs were not intended for extended use.

And yet, thanks to the predisposition to dysbiosis on the spectrum,[4] Candida and all of its symptoms come back as soon as the antifungal is discontinued. Both parents and doctors would like to get off that merry-go-round.

> According to Drugs.com, "Long-term or repeated use of fluconazole (Diflucan) may cause a second infection."

MYTH #2: HE GOT USED TO THE NYSTATIN AFTER A COUPLE OF ROUNDS AND IT DOESN'T WORK ANYMORE.

Nope—although microbes can develop resistance, it's likely the nystatin is doing its job. It's just that other strains of yeast that aren't bothered by nystatin have moved in or flourished. In fact, they are thanking you for eliminating the competition! That is why using a variety of antimicrobials is an important strategy.

Sometimes a new patient hands me results from an old stool test that identifies one or more strains of microbes in their child's colon. I'll discover they've been using the antimicrobial agents specified in the report for a year or more. They'll say it initially helped their child feel better, but then tummy troubles returned. I believe they cleared the original infection and then created a haven for other microbes to move in.

Here's how to avoid that pitfall: Start with a rotation of the antimicrobial agents specified in the lab test, then transition to a wide-ranging antimicrobial rotation (use all the crayons in the box!) to keep any other bad guys from moving into the neighborhood. Then taper off to a light Maintenance Plan to prevent relapse—which leads me to the third reason relapse occurs.

Relapse Reason 3: You lack a Maintenance Plan.

Countless autism parents express surprise and disappointment when Candida and bacterial overgrowth recur, even though their doctor treated it. Treating a microbial imbalance in the gut microbiome is not like a slow cooker—"fix it and forget it." *Maintenance plans* are essential if you want to avoid relapse.

Keeping children on a daily rotation of antimicrobials forever—prescription or over-the-counter—isn't medically sound, but what to do about the inevitable relapse? I discovered that tapering the antimicrobial agents over time to every other day, then once a week, and eventually transitioning to using them one or two weekends a month was ideal for many children. Some children have to use them every weekend, but the beautiful improvements in health and lack of relapse are worth it. Progressing to a rotating maintenance program helps rest the liver and prevents resistance from developing. When children aren't struggling with GI relapse, they can enjoy more success at school and in social situations and get more out of therapies. (See Chapter 6 for details.)

Relapse Reason 4: SIBO or small intestine bacterial overgrowth may occur.

Here's another reason not to assume that everything your child does is due to yeast. Normally, very few bacteria hang out in the small intestine, but our modern lifestyle may set us up for bacterial overgrowth there because:

☐ Chronic use of antacids and proton pump inhibitors for acid reflux reduces protective stomach acid.[5]

☐ A lack of digestive enzymes may leave more undigested food available for bacteria.

Could these lead to a fermentation scenario in the small bowel?

SIBO is when an unusually large number of bacteria grow in the small intestine, whether they are beneficial, opportunistic, or pathogenic.[6] A comprehensive stool test is more indicative of what's going on in the large intestine, which makes what's growing in the small intestine pretty much of a mystery. (There is no *direct* method of testing for a small bowel overgrowth except perhaps to take a sample from an ileostomy bag.)

As the bacteria feed, they produce hydrogen and methane gases and create all the familiar signs and symptoms of a yeast overgrowth: reflux, bloating and belly pain, gas, belching, fuzzy thinking, and fatigue. Many autism parents and health professionals then double down on their yeast-fighting efforts, all to no avail.

So how can we tell the difference? Ask your autism doctor about the hydrogen (H2) breath test. It's an *indirect* method of assessing bacterial overgrowth in the small intestine and may offer some promise.

Your pediatrician should be involved in treating SIBO, as it will require a prescription antibiotic. For those who choose to avoid antibiotics, some experts suggest a selection of natural supplements that support small bowel motility such as Undecylex (a commercial over-the-counter blend), glutamine, and probiotics[7] may be helpful.

SIBO is an emerging area of research and clinical experience, so stay tuned. See www.siboinfo.com for more information. The take-home message: Not everything is due to yeast.

Relapse Reason 5: There are hidden colonies of microbes.

So far we've noted four reasons why GI health relapse happens:

☐ The assumption that it's always yeast
☐ Creating havens for bad bugs through lack of rotation of antimicrobial agents

- ☐ Allowing relapse due to lack of a Maintenance Plan
- ☐ The possibility of SIBO due to overuse of reflux medications and an insufficiency of digestive enzymes

So what's left?

Biofilm.

If you haven't heard of it, you will. Biofilm has been an active area of research for a number of years now and is emerging as of possible importance to autism spectrum disorder. Biofilm is a protective polysaccharide matrix manufactured by microbes, both beneficial and pathogenic, in the GI tract and elsewhere in the body.

Taking shelter in a biofilm is like taking cover in a nuclear bunker. Dental plaque is a biofilm and is a great example of just how tough and persistent this stuff is. Biofilms are made in nature and create problems in industrial and hospital settings as well.

Biofilm provides shelter to microbes from the following threats:

- ☐ Dislodgement
- ☐ Attack by other microbes
- ☐ The host immune system, both humoral and cell-mediated
- ☐ Prescription antibiotic, antifungal, and antiparasitic agents
- ☐ Botanical or "natural" antibiotic, antifungal, and antiparasitic agents

Microbes protected by biofilm are up to 1,000 times more resistant to antimicrobials than the free-floating planktonic form. This means powerful agents like fluconazole, nystatin, amoxicillin, or olive leaf extract go right over the biofilm, while bacteria and yeast shelter safely within the matrix, untouched and very much alive. And when our immune system tries to attack the biofilm, it can end up damaging our surrounding body tissues with no damage to the pathogens.

Free-floating or planktonic bacteria travel alone, are unprotected, and aren't known to communicate or cooperate with other microbes. The gene expression in bacteria and fungi associated with biofilm is different from that of planktonic microbes. Through chemical signals and quorum sensing, certain suites of genes are up-regulated or down-regulated. For example, for microbes residing within the biofilm, the genes for antibiotic resistance and making the components used in the matrix are up-regulated. Genes for motility are down-regulated. What's fascinating (creepy, really!) is that microbes in a biofilm actually communicate and are assigned specific metabolic jobs. It's like an entire city within the biofilm, complete with communication and public works departments.

Gastrointestinal relapses are about as welcome as thunder and lightning at a picnic, and biofilm may be responsible. Your efforts at reducing and eliminating yeast and other pathogens may be effective, but only for the free-floating microbes. The ones in the biofilm simply wait for you to stop using antimicrobials; the colonies then mature, rupture, and reseed the gut with a new wave of bad guys.

There are relatively new products and protocols on the market designed to break open and degrade biofilms. (InterFase Plus by Klaire Labs and Serralase by ProThera are two; Biofilm Defense by Kirkman Labs is another.) This leaves the microbes open to attack, and we often see new leaps in health, cognition, and clarity when a biofilm protocol is used.

Does everyone need to treat biofilm? *In my clinical experience—no.* I only use biofilm strategies when relapse is persistent and severe. I can almost always achieve vibrant health and good gut control using just the Basic GI Support Protocol and a wide-ranging antimicrobial rotation. So why do I even mention biofilm? So you'll understand why microbial imbalance can return again and again, and understand the importance of a light maintenance rotation to check the growth of any new seeding of the gut from down in the biofilm. I'm not sure it is healthy to completely eradicate biofilm—after all, even beneficial bacteria produce it—so don't set that as a goal unless clinically indicated. *Maintenance* is the message here.

Should You Use Natural or Prescription Antimicrobials, or Both?

Systemic antifungals like fluconazole and ketoconazole circulate in the whole body and can adversely affect the liver, the blood chemistry, the heart, and other body systems, and you may need to run blood tests to monitor for adverse effects (see Table 5-2). These helpful prescription agents weren't meant to be used for months and years on end. The prescription is hard on the liver, the blood draw is hard on the child, and the expense of it all is hard on the wallet. Yet the children seem unable to come off the prescriptions without the Candida coming back. Even worse, some patients on these drugs aren't being monitored with blood tests at all. I keep wondering, "What's the plan here?"

Drawbacks of prolonged treatment with prescription antifungals

- Stress and damage to the liver

- Abnormal blood tests

- Neutropenia (a low count of neutrophils, a type of white blood cell)

- Development of drug-resistant strains of fungus

- Failure to rehabilitate the microbiome

Table 5-2

Other antifungal and antimicrobial agents such as nystatin, oral ampho-tericin B, and a wide array of botanicals stay in the GI tract, don't enter the general circulation, and therefore don't affect the liver. Also, no blood draws are needed. These products are fine to use in rotation.

Depending on the style and preference of your doctor, good results can be obtained using both prescription and natural agents. With care, both can form the foundation of a safe and effective maintenance program to put an end to the dreaded GI relapse. Just be sure to use systemic prescriptions on a short-term basis *only*.

A Special Tool for Autism— The High Priest of Yeast

I always tell patients that the beneficial yeast Saccharomyces boulardii, or "Sac b" as we call it, is my favorite supplement for many reasons. It is widely available, inexpensive, helps heal the gut,[8] stimulates the immune system in a positive way,[9] has antifungal properties,[10] and curbs H. pylori[11] and Clostridia difficile.[12] Sac b has been shown to be helpful in children with autism, and it can be a real gem in your quest for vibrant GI health in your son or daughter with autism.[13]

It completes the trilogy of supplements that make up my Basic GI Support Protocol, and I usually get a lot of bang for the buck with this wonderful tool. It doesn't permanently colonize the gut in healthy individuals —another visiting angel—but it's useful for its many actions. Let's look at the amazing benefits of this powerful nonpathogenic yeast in Table 5-3.

How long to use S. boulardii? I advise my patients to use it for about

Benefits of Saccharomyces boulardii

- Inhibits yeast, clostridia, and some harmful bacteria[14]
- Anti-toxin activity[15]
- Healing effect on the lining of the gut[16]
- Reduces intestinal permeability [17]
- Powerful support in the treatment of diarrhea:
  - ✓ Antibiotic-associated diarrhea[18]
  - ✓ Traveler's diarrhea[19]— put some in your purse for that cruise to Mexico!
  - ✓ Clostridia difficile–associated diarrhea[20]
  - ✓ Acute diarrhea[21]
  - ✓ Also diarrhea in those who are tube-fed, and those with AIDS[22]
- Anti-inflammatory actions[23]
- Increases beneficial short-chain fatty acids in the stool — great for colon health![24]
- Acts as an immune stimulant and increases fecal sIgA[25]
- Beneficial effects in ulcerative colitis and Crohn's disease[26]
- Reduces side effects of H. pylori treatment[27]
- Beneficial support for children with autism[28]
- Helpful in maintaining and restoring healthy GI function[29]

Figure 5-3

one month, and then go on to an antimicrobial rotation. Don't throw away what's left in the bottle; just put the S. boulardii into the lineup for the weekly rotation. (See Chapter 6 for details on the Antimicrobial Rotation.)

S. boulardii has not been shown to cause a blood-borne infection in healthy individuals; however, it should *not* be used in immunocompromised patients, critically ill individuals, or those who have a central vascular catheter. It is a yeast, so I don't use it in patients who have a prominent yeast allergy or sensitivity.

How the Un-Prescription for Autism Approaches Dysbiosis

The Un-Prescription Action Plan for autism brings rotation, rotation, rotation and a *long-term* maintenance plan to the table. Using natural, over-the-counter supplements, the plan addresses yeast, bacteria, and parasites; it restores and supports GI health; and it avoids the dreaded relapse. It's how I achieve and maintain GI health for my patients.

A lot of the children I see have used countless rounds of antibiotics in the fight against recurring ear infections. In Chapter 4, we saw that antibiotics often ransack the neighborhoods and "real estate" of the gastrointestinal system and create gut ghettos. And we learned the wisdom of making sure the neighborhoods were rehabilitated by supplying them with good, hard-working citizens in the form of probiotics.

Now we've learned that even in the best of neighborhoods, security guards are often necessary to keep order and clear out any bad guys. I like to think of a gentle rotation of antimicrobials as the friendly neighborhood police officers walking their beat. Once you have balanced your neighborhood, you don't need a SWAT team, just a light security detail to keep things in order. Think of it as the "Yeast Police"!

If your child has had "too many antibiotics to count," or even just a few, plan on starting a Basic GI Support Protocol now. Antibiotics are often necessary for various childhood ailments, but probiotics and antifungals should be used *each and every time* to restore balance to the GI tract.

Even doctors who understand that autism patients are prone to dysbiosis get stuck on the prescription pad, keeping young children on prescription antifungals for years. Remember, the goal is not to eradicate yeast, but to rehabilitate the microbiome. I have discovered that balance can be restored without the use of prescription antifungals or antibiotics at all. Save those big guns for special cases (like Bindee's story).

What's in Your Toolbox?

What are these antimicrobials (AMs), and are they in your toolbox? There are prescription ones such as nystatin, fluconazole, ketoconazole, and oral amphotericin B. There are natural herbs and extracts that have antifungal, antibacterial, and anti-parasitic properties. In Chapter 6, you'll find a long list of some of the

HOW LONG WILL IT TAKE? This is a hard one, because it varies widely among individuals. Expect to use the Antimicrobial Rotation Schedule 1 daily for three to eight months, and hopefully transition after that to every other day, then to weekends, and then twice a month thereafter.

widely available ones that I use at the office to support GI health. I use many of the same ones that laboratories use when testing stool samples.

None of the antimicrobials I've listed in Chapter 6 are appropriate for infants or toddlers with the exception of S. boulardii. If, despite working

with your child's pediatrician, your infant is still prone to diaper rash or oral thrush, rely on high-potency infant probiotics designed to make it through the stomach acid to support microbial balance. Clean the diet of excess sugar and carbohydrates. The

HOW MUCH DOES IT COST? Natural supplements are relatively inexpensive. Your initial average monthly cost will vary from about $30 to $60 and will cost far less once you are on a Maintenance Plan.

Specific Carbohydrate Diet (see Helpful Resources) is an excellent choice.

You'll find out how to do an Antimicrobial Rotation and set up a Maintenance Schedule in Chapter 6. Your organizer is crucial here—enter all antimicrobials with dates and dosages used. It's really helpful if you also track the signs, symptoms, and behaviors at the same time. Tables 5-4 and 5-5 will remind you of our short-term and long-term goals.

Short-term goals for antimicrobial support

- ☐ Clear up eczema and diaper rash
- ☐ Reduce irritability
- ☐ Minimize yeast in the GI tract
- ☐ Minimize pathogenic bacteria
- ☐ Balance opportunistic bacteria
- ☐ Eliminate parasitic infections
- ☐ Minimize the toxins produced by fungi and pathogens
- ☐ Reduce GI inflammation
- ☐ Restore gut barrier function

Table 5-4

Long-term goals for antimicrobial support

- ☐ Restore balance to the microbiome of the GI tract
- ☐ Support and maintain gut barrier function
- ☐ Eliminate GI inflammation
- ☐ Restore vibrant health
- ☐ Support the immune system by supporting GI health and balance
- ☐ Prevent and reduce infections, including ear and urinary tract infections
- ☐ Fewer illnesses and missed days of school
- ☐ Support improved cognition, clarity, language, attention, focus, and sleep
- ☐ Give your child the best chance for success at school and with therapies

Table 5-5

Side Effects and Discussion of Microbial Die-Off Reactions

Autism is part of my family life. So I understand the fragile family dynamic that must be taken into account when designing health support protocols. I get better compliance and results when I design conservative protocols that put the entire family through less stress and frustration. It takes a little longer, but compliance and lasting results are worth it. Many families would have stopped antimicrobials altogether after the Sam's Club experience. What good is a protocol if the family quits the entire health journey?

You often have to walk through the fire to get to the other side when using antimicrobials. When yeast, bacteria, and parasites die, their toxin load gets dumped into the GI tract. This microbial death is called the die-off. Even though you've gotten your child's bowels moving daily, these toxins will still be absorbed into the bloodstream. It's like an oil tanker sinking in the ocean and the payload of oil gushing out to pollute the water. You will definitely see some side effects when you start antimicrobials.

Interpreting the side effects of microbial die-off might feel like taking a test you haven't studied for. Table 5-6 shows us what to look for.

As with the enzymes and probiotic protocols, you can use a regular antimicrobial protocol, go slow, modify it for the school or daycare calendar, and of course, there is always a way to go about it completely WRONG! (See Chapter 6 for specific protocols.)

COMMON-SENSE TIP: Never give children adult doses of over-the-counter supplements. I use only tiny doses of the mildest natural agents for children ages 5 to 12. I have seen parents and other health professionals give natural supplements to children in alarming doses. Just because it is natural doesn't mean it's not powerful or doesn't have side effects. Consult your doctor and use ⅛ to ¼ of the adult dose at most, depending on the age and weight of the child.

Tips for Minimizing and Handling a Microbial Die-Off

□ Work with your doctor.
□ Do not use antimicrobial agents in a constipated child. Big boom!

Possible temporary side effects of treating dysbiosis

- ☐ Increased volume of gas and bloating (a polite way to say your child will fart his brains out!)
- ☐ Really foul odor to gas and bowel movements
- ☐ Increase in irritability
- ☐ Easy to anger or have a meltdown
- ☐ Spike in aggression
- ☐ Diarrhea
- ☐ Increase in eczema, rashes, and breakouts
- ☐ Malaise with achy muscles and joints, headache, and fatigue
- ☐ Fever and chills
- ☐ An increase in rocking, flapping, spinning
- ☐ Hyperactivity
- ☐ Nausea
- ☐ Vomiting (very rarely)
- ☐ Scratching that worsens a rash and causes it to become infected (very rare, but keep your child's nails trimmed as a precaution)

Table 5-6

- ☐ Don't start while on vacation or right before an important event (antimicrobial support can be a messy business).
- ☐ Start on a Friday to avoid fireworks during the week.
- ☐ Start low and go slow with the dosing.
- ☐ Give with food if you have to, but on an empty stomach is best.
- ☐ Drink plenty of fluids.
- ☐ Take milk thistle to help support the liver during treatment. The liver processes the metabolic by-products of microbial death.
- ☐ In the case of a severe die-off, you should work with your doctor and

use your "mom or dad intuition." Back down on the frequency or the dose. Just give ¼ to ⅓ of a child's dose every other day, or even every third day. During the school year, I encourage parents to treat more actively on weekends and over school breaks such as Thanksgiving or Christmas.

☐ Wait at least two hours after you give the AMs, and then give acacia fiber or activated charcoal to absorb the by-products of microbial death.

☐ No spanking for die-off behaviors. You must draw the line and have consequences, but they should be short and nonphysical. These are predictable side effects, not a spoiled child having a tantrum.

☐ Nausea/vomiting is not common, but it can happen when there is a toxin dump into the child's system. Just cut back on the dose and/or frequency and keep going if you can. Or take a short break and try again at a much reduced dose. You may have to do heavy probiotics for a while before retrying.

☐ Brace yourself: Can you say C-R-A-N-K-Y? If your child is mild-mannered and dreamy, you will likely only see things like irritability and whining, easy frustration, or a little extra hitting with siblings. But, if your child is aggressive and destructive to begin with, brace yourself. You may see holes in the wall and have some furniture flipped over. You may have to have younger siblings stay with grand-parents or they will bear the brunt of the physical aggression. Hair pulling, screaming, anger, you name it, we see it. If the reaction is this strong, check with your doctor and reduce the dose and frequency until your child can tolerate the full dose. It may last a day or two, it may last for weeks—there is no way to predict.

☐ Try brushing and other calming sensory techniques. (Ask your occupational therapist.)
  ○ Swinging.
  ○ Water play in a warm bath.
  ○ Exercise.

☐ Keep busy! Go on lots of walks to the park.

☐ Try GABA and magnesium supplements (see Week 3 in the Chapter 9 Online Action Plan for calming strategies).

☐ Know when *not* to give up. Even if the die-off reaction is too nasty, he gets too mean, and you just can't take it, *don't quit*. Just use your "parent radar," cut way back on the dose, and give it every other day or even every third day. I had one parent tell me that her son got so mean and irritable on Week 2 that she just threw everything away. She was so rattled that she forgot that she could adjust the dose and control the microbial die-off side effects. She tried it again, taking twice as long to introduce it, and was able to get through the die-off process and achieve good results.

☐ Make it yours. It's okay to spread out the support protocol over two to three months. I remind parents that your child didn't get that way overnight, and he isn't going to dig his way out of it overnight. Yes, we are all anxious for results, but sometimes it is easier on the child as well as the family to restore balance in a slower, more controlled fashion.

COMMON-SENSE TIP: Reduce and eventually eliminate sugar and highly processed carbs in the diet.

Stool Testing

It's always a good idea to start with a stool test. (Because guessing isn't smart and the Internet isn't always right.) When should you do a stool test?

☐ When a child eats a sufficient amount of food, but appears malnourished

Be sure to call your insurance company first and make sure you know exactly what it is going to cost.

☐ In cases of failure to thrive
☐ If your child suffers from chronic diarrhea, or the bouquet of his bowel movements brings tears to your eyes
☐ In cases of cyclical diarrhea and GI symptoms, which may indicate a parasitic infection

If your child is in reasonably good health, it's reasonable to start by giving the Basic GI Support Protocol a trial for a few months. If his GI issues straighten out, you're fine. If not, it's time to test.

What Kind of Stool Test Should You Have Done?

There are stool tests and then there are stool tests. Some tests just give you the basic facts about bacterial, fungal, or parasitic infections. Others give digestion and absorption markers, inflammation markers, and information on commensal bacteria, opportunistic and pathogenic bacteria, fungi, parasites, and beneficial short-chain fatty acids. Comprehensive stool testing generally reflects what is going on in the large bowel or colon. See Week 31 in the Chapter 9 Online Action Plan for more information, as well as the Helpful Resources section for suggestions on laboratories.

At the same time, get an Organic Acids Test (OAT). This is thought by some to be an indirect indicator of what is going on in the small intestine, as well as a reflection of metabolic and nutritional status. I like to combine stool testing with the OAT and the amino acids test (both are urine tests) for nutritional factors to help me design a thorough support plan for my patients. See Week 32 in the Chapter 9 Online Action Plan for more information.

Occasionally, I'll have a patient whose stool test is nearly pristine (colon), but whose OAT test shows strong markers for bacterial overgrowth (small bowel). Since our children with autism are often on long-term medications that reduce stomach acid and the natural protection against infection it provides, I suspect they may have a small intestine bacterial overgrowth. Although there is a breath test available to confirm SIBO, it doesn't provide clues to the types of bacteria involved. Discuss the possibility of SIBO with your child's doctor.

"I Read It on the Internet"

The Internet is brimming with helpful information, but there is some dangerous misinformation out there as well. I cringe sometimes when I eavesdrop in an autism chat room, as the discussions there seem to think that treating yeast is the answer for everything.

I have had patients ask me about the "saltwater flush" or the "lemonade fast" they read about on the Internet as a way to treat yeast or break down biofilm. No. Hell no! I don't even put the word "fast" and "child" in the same sentence, unless I'm chasing him. These are dangerous ideas. You should ask about the science, research, and clinical observations on any treatment, even ones your doctor suggests. Yeast does pose significant problems for those on the spectrum, but as you saw in Chapter 1, there are many other health challenges that explain signs, symptoms, and behaviors on the autism spectrum. So don't overtreat for yeast and miss other important areas of health support.

Some protocols don't play well with others. This is true of treating a known fungal overgrowth and also trying to detox or "chelate" at the same time. Any form of detox enhances the growth of yeast and must wait until ironclad gut control is achieved. One of the most common mistakes that I see autism parents (and many autism doctors) make is to start chelation or detox protocols while still trying to get control of dysbiosis in the GI tract. The child ends up in a yeasty, rashy, irritable mess, and the family often quits everything in confusion and anxiety.

Patience, patience! Go about restoring health on the autism spectrum one careful, conservative step at a time. I used to test for metals and toxins on the first visit. Now, with clinical maturity, I know if I wait a year or two to test the body's detox status and focus instead on restoring health and balance, the vast majority of my patients will naturally begin to flush toxins from their system so that no detox support is needed. Read that sentence again.

Rule of thumb: If you save detox for last, you probably won't even need it. Your child's body will naturally begin to flush itself of toxins and metals as health and balance are restored.

The signs and symptoms of parasitic infections can be vague, and many people become convinced they have "parasites" and begin treating with ideas they got off the Internet. Long strips of intestinal mucosa can slough off from these "treatments" and appear as "parasitic worms." The individual takes this as proof that he has parasites and redoubles his efforts at treating parasites, usually with no medical oversight. I had one patient who had treated himself for "parasites" for years. I sent off the "parasites" to a lab, only to discover they were actually long strips of intestinal wall tissue that his harsh home parasite treatments were sloughing off his intestines.

Another gentleman in his thirties severely damaged his health after years of chelating himself for metals and toxins. He would lie on the couch for several days after each chelation, exhausted and ill. He felt the health problems caused by his "metal poisoning" cost him his marriage. He never felt well, and his gut could only tolerate a few foods. Only after I ran tests that did not indicate a high level of metals in his body or impaired detox status did he begin to change his thinking. He has enjoyed *much* better health since he stopped trying to detox himself without medical oversight and focused instead on restoring and balancing health.

Frequently Asked Questions About Antimicrobials

Q: *Does the Saccharomyces boulardii have to be refrigerated?*

A: *It does not have to be refrigerated, but it will last longer if kept in a cool place or refrigerated.*

Q: *Do the herbal AMs have to be refrigerated?*

A: *No.*

Q: *Can I take the antifungals and antimicrobials with the probiotics?*

A: *This is an area where there isn't much research to guide us, so to be conservative, I suggest taking antimicrobials in the mornings when the stomach is empty from its overnight fast. This gives the AMs direct access to microbes and fungi without food getting in the way. I give the probiotics with the last meal of the day.*

Q: *My child is too young to take these AMs (or refuses these bitter AMs). Is there anything else I can do?*

A: *Yes, double up on probiotics, rotate among different probiotic blends, and use a diet low in carbs and sugars. The Specific Carbohydrate Diet or the Body Ecology Diet work beautifully. (See this book's Helpful Resources section.)*

The take-away message: Always start low, go slow, and use your parent radar to decide if it's okay to go on to the next step in any protocol.

> ## Want the Science?
> For sources of information found in this chapter, turn to the Endnotes.

Ready to put some voodoo on that doo-doo? I know you can't wait to get started with specific strategies for supporting vibrant health for your son or daughter on the autism spectrum.

On to Chapter 6!

PART TWO

How—Taking Action

6

The Un-Prescription Action Plan for Basic GI Support

The road to health is paved with good intestines!
Sherry A. Rogers, MD

Like a good story, a good Action Plan has a beginning, a middle, and an end. The Basic GI Support Protocol is the foundation, *the beginning*, of your Action Plan. This chapter shows you how to get started with enzymes, probiotics, and antimicrobials, how to progress, and most important of all, how to transition to a Maintenance Schedule. More support: I have created a calendar app called "The Un-Prescription for Autism" to help you schedule these protocols with ease. You will also find a fun online game called "Fact or Fart?" at www.LoveAutismHealth.com that will help with FAQs and troubleshooting.

If you do nothing more than the Basic GI Support Protocol you would probably relieve 80 percent of the day-to-day discomfort and misery that a child on the spectrum may experience. By misery, I mean constipation, diarrhea, sleep deprivation, rashes, itching, nausea, stomachaches, irritability, and aggression. It isn't all your child will ever need, but it can be a huge step forward in improving his quality of life. Chapter 7 will add Basic Immune Support, and Chapter 9's Online Action Plan will lead you on a year of ideas to build out your child's team and health plan. My goal is for our beloved children to find that "sweet spot" of vibrant health on the autism spectrum.

The Basic GI Support Protocol

The New Patient Questionnaire (NPQ) that we explored in Chapter 1 has, no doubt, revealed areas of health to support and, at the same time, generated the building blocks of your child's custom Un-Prescription Action Plan. Now we learn when and how to put it all together, and it starts with the Basic GI Support Protocol. Don't skip any of the steps you are about to learn—through years of experience, I have developed these protocols in a sequence that maximizes results and minimizes undesirable side effects. Give each step a good effort, and do them in the order presented.

These protocols can be integrated with conventional or alternative methods. They can be used while on prescription medications or with natural supplements. These protocols do *not* treat or cure autism spectrum disorder. They are intended to support optimal health and function of children and adults *with* ASD so that your amazing child can have his or her best chance of success and happiness.

The Basic GI Support Protocol is the foundation of your child's health plan. Start with this protocol and then branch out and expand the plan from there. Let me show you an example of a Basic GI Support Protocol in Figure 6-1 on page 151, and then you can spend the rest of the chapter learning how to customize it for your own child. You can vary the speed and dosing to minimize side effects.

Then you can go on to add some basic supplements such as zinc or essential fatty acids indicated by the NPQ, or you can add the Basic Immune Support Protocol from Chapter 7 to help support vibrant health for your son or daughter. The Chapter 9 Online Action Plan gives you a year's worth of ideas with tips and suggested protocols.

Remember to keep detailed records in your Un-Prescription Organizer as you go, work with your doctor for oversight and lab tests, and transition to a Maintenance Schedule when the time is right.

Let's get started and customize the plan for your own child.

Step One: Enzymes

First, let's review the basics:

- ☐ Choose a broad-spectrum digestive enzyme blend that contains DPP-IV.
- ☐ Choose a delivery method: capsules, powder, or chewables (you can also open capsules).
- ☐ If your child is on one of the less common time-release medications with a pure cellulose coating, consider a cellulase-free formulation.
- ☐ Choose an appropriate dose, which is based on the size of the meal, not your child's age or weight.
- ☐ Check the ingredients for anything your child is allergic to, such as pineapple or egg white.
- ☐ Look for and read any cautions or contraindications with the brand you choose.
- ☐ Choose your Enzyme Schedule (options to choose from are explained later in this chapter).
- ☐ Work with the school and daycare so your child can have enzymes with meals and snacks.
- ☐ Take occasional "enzyme holidays" (discussed later in this chapter, plus an example is provided in Chapter 9).
- ☐ Transition to a Maintenance Schedule at some point.
- ☐ For the best chance of success and to avoid wasted time, go over the common mistakes that are made with the enzymes (see Chapter 10) before you start.

> WHAT TO EXPECT: A spike in irritability as opioid peptides leave your child's system (most often in Week 3), more bowel movements, better sleep, and improved eye contact. Some children may respond with more language.

Shortcut to Starting Tonight

If you're lucky enough to live in an area where you can purchase the enzymes today, you can get started with the evening meal. And if you aren't able to buy them today, just serve a meal that is gluten-free and casein-free for dinner all week, and you will already be starting the journey to free your child's system of opioid neuropeptides. Meanwhile, go online and order your enzymes *today.*

If your son or daughter cannot swallow capsules, you'll have to mix the supplements with food or drinks. For very resistant eaters, parents may have to take charge and simply mix the enzyme or supplement with a teaspoon or so of juice, draw it up into a needleless plastic syringe (available at pharmacies), and squirt it toward the back and side of the child's throat. Don't aim *directly* at the back of the throat, as that would trigger a gag response, but rather to the back and over to one side.

Once you have progressed to using enzymes with every meal and snack, the time has come to address the meals that your son or daughter is getting at school. Most state school systems will allow you to sign a medication order and will then administer the enzymes with the meals and snacks served to your child during the school day. Private schools and daycares will usually make the same accommodation.

You may have to provide a letter from your doctor stating that your child must have the enzymes with every meal and snack, along with the dosage requirement. It is very important that the letter specifies the enzymes must be given with *every* meal, snack, and carton of milk, and that they be given at the *beginning* of the meal, not an hour before lunch in the nurse's office.

If your school cannot give over-the-counter supplements, see www.Houston-enzymes.com for ideas on getting the enzymes to school mixed into food or drink. If it is impossible to have your child take the enzymes at school, you can pack a GFCF lunch and snack, or ask your doctor to order GFCF school meals and snacks, which can be eaten without the enzymes.

And since I know you're going to ask . . . if your child's diet is strictly GFCF, he does not *have* to take the enzymes with every single meal and snack. When it was first suggested to me that my GFCF child take the enzymes, I cynically thought that the doctor just wanted to make additional money and it really wasn't necessary. Science has shown that children with ASD may not make enough digestive enzymes and the digestive support may be very welcome, even if GFCF.

WHAT TO EXPECT: Your child may branch out and begin to eat new foods after the opioids have left his system. (Yes, really!) If not, consider a consultation with a feeding specialist (see Week 19 in the Chapter 9 Online Action Plan).

Overview of the Basic GI Support Protocol

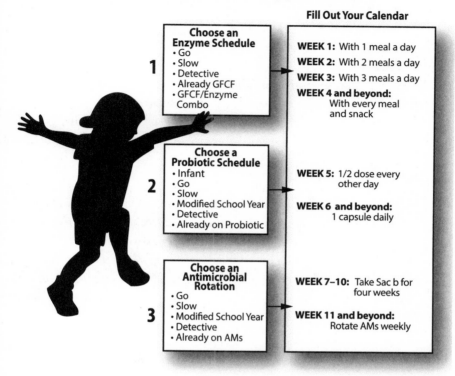

Figure 6-1

Dosing Suggestions

☐ Enzymes may be used in children as young as infants who are no longer breast-feeding and are eating solid food.

☐ In general, follow the manufacturer's dosing instructions.

☐ Dosing is based on the size of the meal, not the age or weight of the child. I've had to use conservative judgment and clinical observations to come up with suggestions for younger patients. Our goal is to support digestion, especially of gluten and casein, and ease constipation. Children one to two years of age do not eat large volumes of food, so I usually suggest using just a trace amount of the enzymes with meals and cups of milk. If constipation persists after a few weeks, gradually increase the dose until it clears.

- ☐ For children three to four years of age, I suggest starting with one-quarter to one-half the recommended dose on the bottle. If that clears up constipation by the last week of the plan, stick with that dose, otherwise increase to no more than the manufacturer's suggested dose.
- ☐ For children age 5 and up, follow the manufacturer's suggested dose.
- ☐ You'll know you're at the right dose when your child is no longer constipated. If stools are still large, hard, or in little balls, gradually increase the dose (up to the manufacturer's limits) until they normalize.

I've had a number of children who suddenly began to eat a lot more food at meals after starting the enzymes, much to the surprise of their parents. I suspect they are unconsciously attempting to overwhelm the enzyme dose (eating more food than the enzyme dose can handle), in a desperate attempt to get more opioids. If your child begins to suddenly eat more at meals, increase the dose of enzymes accordingly.

TIP: Choose one of the following enzyme schedules for your child.

The Basic "Go" Schedule for Enzymes

Here is the basic enzyme schedule that I suggest in my center. This pace is usually neither too fast nor too slow. You will likely see no changes in the first week, maybe some edginess in Week 2, but Week 3 is usually a doozy—loaded with irritability, possibly even anger and aggression as your child weans off of the alleged opioid neuropeptides.

Week 1: *Give the enzymes with one meal a day.*
Week 2: *Give the enzymes with two meals a day.*
Week 3: *Give the enzymes with three meals a day.*
Week 4 and thereafter: *Give the enzymes with every meal and snack.*

The "Slow" Schedule for Enzymes

This is a baby-steps plan. It's an extended plan for children who experience a really difficult withdrawal. Use this protocol if your child is considered aggressive and violent and at risk for getting kicked out of daycare or school. For those parents who are hanging on by their fingernails and cannot tolerate their child getting one bit more aggressive as they go through the predicted spikes in behavior and irritability, here's *your* plan!

It will take twice as long to do each step. Stay on each step for two weeks or even longer before progressing to the next step.

Weeks 1 and 2: *Give the enzymes with one meal a day.*
Weeks 3 and 4: *Give the enzymes with two meals a day.*
Weeks 5 and 6: *Give the enzymes with three meals a day.*
Week 7 and thereafter: *Give the enzymes with every meal and snack.*

The "Whoa" Schedule for Enzymes

I call this one "how *not* to give the enzymes." Some parents are overeager to get results and start giving their child the digestive enzymes with every meal and snack from day one. This strategy may throw him into an abrupt opioid withdrawal and is a bit harsh in my opinion. Choose a kinder, gentler schedule.

The "Detective" Schedule for Enzymes

When a child is an extremely sensitive food detective and can sense even minute amounts of supplements added to his food or drink, some parents get "extreme" too. They start the enzymes using only five to ten specks instead of a full dose in the food. Sometimes the full dose cannot be put into one item, such as a drink, without being detected. We then suggest putting a small amount in the drink, a few grains on the fruit sauce, a few specks in the mashed potatoes, and so on. Over the course of several weeks or months, the amounts are very gradually increased until the child accepts it. Of course, it takes much longer to get there this way, but hang in there—you can be the tortoise and still win the race.

> It does not matter how slowly you go,
> as long as you do not stop.
> *Confucius*

Month 1: *Give the enzymes with one meal a day.*
Month 2: *Give the enzymes with two meals a day.*
Month 3: *Give the enzymes with three meals a day.*
Month 4 and thereafter: *Give the enzymes with every meal and snack.*

The "Already GFCF" Schedule for Enzymes

I'm not worried about an opiate-type withdrawal if a child is already gluten- and casein-free, and I introduce enzymes faster in this case.

Week 1: *Give the enzymes with two meals a day.*
Week 2 and thereafter: *Give the enzymes with every meal and snack.*

The "GFCF/Enzyme Combo" Schedule

Use this plan if you are super gung-ho and want to start the GFCF diet *and* implement the enzymes. It's really simple: You are gradually introducing GFCF meals and giving them with enzymes. An easy-to-make mistake is to give enzymes with lunch and make dinner GFCF—but then you are taking away the opioid-forming foods too fast and will trigger a nasty withdrawal. Let me be clear: The GFCF meal is the one that gets the enzymes.

Week 1: *Give one GFCF meal a day with enzymes.*
Week 2: *Give two GFCF meals a day with enzymes.*
Week 3: *Give three GFCF meals a day with enzymes.*
Week 4 and thereafter: *All meals and snacks are GFCF and are taken with enzymes.*

The Maintenance Schedule for Enzymes

What do you do after gut health and balance are achieved?

Ideally, I would love for your child to be able to digest food and absorb nutrients without relying on digestive enzymes. However, I know you don't want to risk a return to the wild behaviors your child may have experienced before using the enzymes. So how do you know when to reduce or eliminate their use?

This is where art meets science, as it is completely individualized for each child or adult. A few children may be able to minimize or eliminate the enzymes after a year or less, many may be successful eliminating them after several years, and some individuals will always need enzymes for digestive support.

Indicators Your Child May Still Need Digestive Enzymes

☐ If there are behavior or mood changes after eating meals without the enzymes

☐ If constipation returns after eating meals without enzymes.

☐ If you can see undigested food in your child's bowel movements with the naked eye

☐ If comprehensive stool testing indicates low digestive enzymes or poor digestion and absorption

☐ If your child has gall bladder problems (anyone without a gall bladder would benefit from ongoing use of digestive enzymes)

I don't consider wheat and dairy to be good choices for those on the spectrum, but for parents who would like to include these foods in their child's diet, here's a way to evaluate if the child can tolerate them without enzymes.

☐ Try a simple test with a food that contains casein, *not gluten*. (Casein exits the body quickly in two to three days, whereas the effects of gluten may hang around for weeks.) On a Friday afternoon, try sampling a mouthful or two of a dairy product (ideally from an organic, grass-fed source) such as milk, cheese, or ice cream and don't give the enzymes with it. Then observe for the rest of the weekend. If you see a regression of mood, irritability, hyperactivity, sleep disruption, brain fog, or constipation, you have your answer—not ready yet!— and the ill effects should be gone in time for school on Monday. Wait a few more months and try again.

☐ If nothing bad happened after trying this simple test, you may continue to gradually reintroduce dairy products without the enzymes.

Most people find they can consume a daily serving or two of dairy without enzymes but cannot just feast on it all day long. Some are able to reintroduce it into their diet without problems.

☐ Once dairy is successfully introduced, try a bite or two of *organic* wheat without enzymes. (I strongly suggest consuming only organic wheat because glyphosates, which are herbicides, are sprayed on virtually all nonorganic wheat right before harvest in this country.) Again, I suggest a Friday afternoon so that any disappointing reactions happen at home and not at school. Better yet, try it when school is out for the summer.

My son can now eat small amounts of gluten without any negative behavioral effects, but he seems to have an *intolerance* to it on the GI level, because it causes gas, diarrhea, and a deep fatigue. He has made the decision to simply avoid wheat and gluten altogether. It's a sensible choice for many on the autism spectrum.

Who Gets a "Pass" on the Enzymes?

Some children won't need enzymes at all. If you tried the enzymes and/ or the GFCF diet *strictly* for 100 percent of meals, snacks, and glasses of milk for several months and saw absolutely no changes whatsoever, it's a good bet your child doesn't need to keep taking them. And if you let your child abruptly start eating gluten- and casein-containing foods without the enzymes and saw no negative behaviors or symptoms, it's also a good bet he doesn't need them. But if you did the diet or enzymes *some* of the time, or only for wheat but not milk (or vice versa) and other variations of that nature, you should still give them a good try. Many of you will be surprised.

Enzyme "Holidays"

Our children can become sensitive to anything that is consumed repetitively, and that includes the enzymes. It is a good idea to periodically forgo the enzymes completely for a few weeks or a month, and use the GFCF diet during that time instead.

> **TIPS FOR STAYING AT THE EX'S HOUSE**
> ☐ A cooperative "ex" can do the same protocols you do at home. Just keep a set of supplements at each house or use a Travel Board (see Chapter 2 for this great idea).
> ☐ If your ex is an uncooperative asshat, then just do the enzymes at his or her house and leave the other supplements at your home.
> ☐ If your ex refuses to do *any* of the supplements, don't give up on the protocols at your house. You can still see positive results.

Step Two: Probiotics

First, the basics:

☐ Only begin the probiotic schedule after your child is taking the digestive enzymes with DPP-IV with every meal

> *WHAT TO EXPECT: A spike in irritability, gas and odor; some children may experience rashes.*

and snack and is mostly constipation-free. He will continue to take the enzymes daily as you begin this step.

☐ Choose a multispecies or a single-species formulation.

☐ Choose a formulation (i.e., infant, children, or adult). Use an infant formulation for birth to two years of age. The formulation I use is a powder (Ther-Biotic Infant Formula from Klaire Labs), but it still has a delivery system to get through the gastric acid and deliver a full load of viable beneficial bacteria to the small intestine. Check with the manufacturer, but most infant formulas can be used from the day of birth.

☐ Choose capsules, powder, gummies, or chewables.

☐ Choose a strength. I suggest a minimum of 25 billion colony-forming units (CFUs) for ages two and up.

☐ Choose a Probiotic Schedule (described in the next sections).

☐ Eventually transition to a Maintenance Schedule (optional).

☐ Mix it up! Once your child is fully on the probiotic schedule, you can use different blends and formulations of probiotics.

Note: "Week 1" of the probiotic schedules is not the same as Week 1 of the enzyme schedules. The Probiotic Schedules are designed to be started after your child is able to take the digestive enzymes with every meal and snack.

> TIP: Choose one of the following probiotic schedules for your child.

The Infant Probiotic Schedule (Up to Two Years of Age)

Powdered infant formula probiotics are easier to digest than adult formulas; they can be dabbed around the nipple for breast-feeding or added to a bottle of breast milk or already-warmed formula for bottle feedings.

Healthy babies and toddlers up to twenty-four months of age can go with the manufacturer's dosing guidelines. If your baby is struggling with colic, diarrhea, painful gas, eczema, or diaper rash, here's a slower, gentler way that will minimize gas and crankiness to start:

Week 1: *Give ½ of the recommended dose, every other day.*
Week 2: *Give ½ of the recommended dose, daily.*
Week 3 and thereafter: *Give the full daily dose recommended by the manufacturer.*

Probiotic Support for Two Years of Age and Up

The Basic "Go" Probiotic Schedule
Week 1: *Take ½ dose of probiotic with the evening meal every day.*
Week 2 and thereafter: *Take the regular dose with the evening meal daily.*

> *HOW MUCH DOES IT COST? A quality probiotic with good viability and an effective delivery system doesn't have to be pricey. Your initial average monthly cost will vary from about $20 to $30 and will cost far less once you are on a Maintenance Schedule.*

The "Slow" Probiotic Schedule
Here's a kinder, gentler, slower schedule to minimize the initial irritability side effect of starting a powerful probiotic.

Weeks 1 and 2: *Give ¼ to ½ of the manufacturer's suggested dose every other day.*

Weeks 3 and 4: *Give ½ of the suggested dose every day.*

Week 5 and thereafter: *Try moving up to the full suggested dose once daily with a meal.*

The "Whoa" Probiotic Schedule

How *not* to give probiotics!

- □ Avoid giving full-dose, high-potency probiotics to a constipated child
- □ Avoid starting the probiotics at the same time you're starting the GFCF diet and/or digestive enzymes with DPP-IV
- □ Avoid giving a full dose if your child has painful gas

None of this will likely cause any physical harm to your child, and perhaps your child will just sail through the protocol with no problems. For some children, it's just no big deal. But siblings and classmates may bear the brunt of the irritability, so I urge you to start slow until you see how your child will be affected.

Here's why I introduce probiotics slowly: The way the gut feels pain is different from the way your arm or leg feels pain. You could probably slice through the intestine with a scalpel and not feel all that much pain. But if the intestine is s-t-r-e-t-c-h-e-d, it's exquisitely painful. Starting a high-potency probiotic can produce tons of gas, which inflates and stretches the GI tract and causes tummy aches and sharp gas pains, which can lead to explosive meltdowns and tantrums. It's not very nice to do this to a child. So I always start low and go slow with these powerful supplements.

The "Modified School Year" Probiotic Schedule

This schedule reduces embarrassing gas at school while your child's GI system gets used to the probiotic.

Month 1: *Take ½ dose on Fridays and Saturdays with the evening meal.*

Month 2: *Take the full dose on Fridays and Saturdays with the evening meal.*

Month 3 and thereafter: *Gradually increase the number of days per week you are giving a probiotic until your child can tolerate a full dose seven days a week with the evening meal.*

The "Detective" Probiotic Schedule

Use your judgment, but a very slow guideline would be:

Month 1: *Gradually introduce a few specks of probiotic daily with the evening meal.*
Month 2: *Try giving ⅛ dose or capsule each evening with a meal.*
Months 3, 4, and 5 and thereafter: *Gradually work up to one full capsule. If the most you can get up to is half a capsule, that is better than nothing.*

If you reach a certain volume (e.g., one-quarter of a capsule), after which your child can tell that you have put probiotic powder in his food or drink and refuses it, switch your strategy and try using a smaller amount with *every* meal so that you can get the full dose in by the end of the day.

The "Already on a Probiotic" Schedule

If my new patients are already on a daily probiotic, they are good to go and should just continue taking it daily, even when just starting the enzymes. If the probiotic they are already on is not a high-potency probiotic with a good delivery system, I have them switch to a better product and break it in over two weeks to minimize gas.

Week 1: *Take one dose every other day with the evening meal.*
Week 2 and thereafter: *Take one dose daily with the evening meal.*

Optional: The Maintenance Probiotic Schedule

So, how long should you keep giving a daily probiotic? If I had my way, *everyone* would take a daily probiotic for as long as they live. However, some families tell me that they don't

HOW LONG WILL IT TAKE? Expect to take probiotics for a lifetime. Some people will need them daily, some weekly, and some a couple of weekends a month. Health-wise, probiotics are pure gold.

like taking supplements every day, and some tell me it's a bit expensive for them.

So here is my advice: Once gut balance and control are achieved, I continue to give probiotics on a regular basis. For some children this may be a daily probiotic for the rest of their life, but others may do fine with every other day or even just on weekends.

How do you know when to cut back? When your child no longer has eczema or other rashes. When his breath is sweet and fresh, or she no longer struggles with tummy pain, diarrhea, and constipation. In other words, when your child is not sick all the time. You know your child better than anyone else, so just pay attention to your "parent radar" to find the perfect Maintenance Schedule for your child.

MORE TIPS ON HOW TO CUT BACK

□ Try giving the probiotics every other day for a few months, and watch for a regression of bowel symptoms, rashes, or tummy aches, or how often your child gets sick.

□ If everything goes well with the above step, try giving the probiotics just on weekends for a few months, and again, watch for regression of symptoms.

Early research seems to indicate ASD individuals may have a predisposition to dysbiosis, so probiotics are one piece of the health plan I would never give up.

Step Three: The Antimicrobial Rotation

This piece of the Action Plan is hands-down either the most abused or the most neglected area in supporting health on the autism spectrum. It's also a little trickier than the enzymes and probiotics. The heart of this piece of the health plan is *rotation* among different antifungal and antimicrobial agents. It may seem confusing at first, until you realize that basically it's just an antimicrobial (AM) in the mornings. The AM may be different every week, but your daily routine is just one AM in the mornings.

Figure 6-2 is a basic overview of how the rotation works.

Overview of the Antimicrobial Rotation

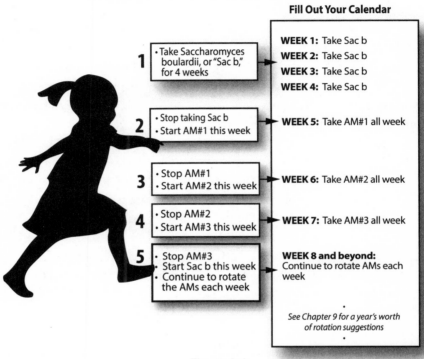

Figure 6-2

Just like with the enzymes and probiotics, the Antimicrobial Rotation can be started slowly, on weekends as a Modified School Year Schedule, in minute amounts for detectives, and so on.

Please note: I do not suggest an antimicrobial rotation for children less than five years of age without a doctor's supervision, and never for infants and toddlers.

- ☐ Continue to take the enzymes with meals and snacks, and the probiotic with the evening meal.
- ☐ Always work with your child's doctor.
- ☐ Use supplements formulated for children.

- □ Take the antimicrobial on an empty stomach in the morning (suggested), although it may be given with food or drink.
- □ Choose an Antimicrobial Rotation Schedule (see next sections).
- □ If your child has a prescription antifungal, you are welcome to put it into the rotation list *with your doctor's approval.*
- □ Eventually, transition to a Maintenance Schedule. (The Maintenance Schedule is discussed later in this chapter, and an example is provided in Chapter 9.)

Dosing Suggestions

- □ I suggest only minimal short-term use of S. boulardii for children ages 2 to 5, at a dosing range of 1.5 billion to 3 billion CFUs.
- □ With caution, I suggest using only ¼ to ½ dose of AMs for children ages 6 to 14.
- □ With caution, I follow the manufacturer's suggested dosing for those ages 15 and older, unless they are severely underweight.

I am very conservative in the dosing suggestions for children because we are not treating an infection but, instead, supporting GI balance and health. I find that even using a fraction of the children's dose can often improve balance in the GI tract. Never give your child adult doses. For children ages 3 and up, some parents have successfully used a tiny fraction of the dose of liquid herbal extracts (such as those suggested by Herb Pharm or KidsWellness). I recommend that you do this only under a doctor's supervision.

If you have results from a recent comprehensive stool test that indicate a fungal or bacterial overgrowth, look at the Sensitivity and Resistance information. This is where the lab grew out the invader and tested it against various prescription and natural agents to see what killed it and what did not. Rotate among the choices that the overgrowth is sensitive to for a month or two, then return to a wide-ranging general rotation. Just because a stool test from two years ago indicated you should use Caprylic acid and fluconazole doesn't mean you should only use those two agents and, worse yet, still be on them a year later. Treat appropriately, and then get back to a wide-ranging rotation. Otherwise, you are creating a haven for any microbe not sensitive to Caprylic acid and fluconazole.

I usually suggest beginning with S. boulardii for one month, followed by a weekly antimicrobial rotation, as shown in Figure 6-2.

> TIP: Choose one of the following Antimicrobial Rotation Schedules for your child.

The Basic "Go" Antimicrobial Schedule
To lay the groundwork for an AM rotation, I start my patients out with an initial four weeks of S. boulardii (Sac b) before beginning to rotate through various antimicrobial agents. It's a one-time only thing, is an inexpensive way to get started, and has a lot of bang for the buck. After the first four weeks, Sac b will join the list of antimicrobials to rotate through a week at a time. Sac b will usually cause a lot of really smelly gas (chil-

> HOW LONG WILL IT TAKE? This is a hard one, as it varies widely among individuals. Expect to use the Antimicrobial Rotation Daily for three to eight months, and hopefully transition after that to every other day, then to weekends, and finally twice a month thereafter.

dren in my practice have nicknamed it "the stinky pill") as well as irritability or even rashes; these side effects may last a few days or a few weeks.

After four weeks of Sac b, your child will then begin to use a different AM each week. It's not feasible (or necessary) for parents to purchase ten or twelve different AMs, so I have them just get three or four different varieties and rotate through those bottles on a weekly basis until they begin to run out. The parents then purchase different AMs to replace those bottles and continue the rotation.

Each week when you start a new antimicrobial, your child may go through another round of die-off symptoms. Usually these are smaller than when you first started. Some supplements may have no noticeable effect, but that's okay; they are still policing the "neighborhood" of the GI tract and doing their job. Once in a while, a new antimicrobial will set off some really spectacular gas and irritability. It's probably working to curb some yeast or bacteria that nothing else had killed yet and was living in there rent-free. You may need to cut back on the dose or the frequency of that particular AM, but don't discard it—it's in there kicking something's butt, which is a good thing.

> SANITY TIP: Always start the Antimicrobial Rotation Schedule on a Friday. The worst of its effects will show up over the weekend and hopefully be gone by Monday morning in time for school.

First Four Weeks (Sac b)

Week 1: *Suggested dose is 1.5 billion CFUs S. boulardii every other day for one week.*

Weeks 2, 3, and 4: *Take 3 billion CFUs daily in the mornings.*

Now for the Rotation

Week 5 and thereafter: *Discontinue the S. boulardii for now. Choose three or four other supplements (from the following suggested list) and use only one at a time. For example, use one antimicrobial daily in the mornings for one week. Then put that one away, and use the next one for a week. Continue to rotate through your choices on a weekly basis.*

I don't use a lot of antimicrobial blends. In fact, early on, I strongly prefer pure, single supplements because children with ASD often have sensitivities to medications, foods, and supplements. Let's get some gut healing on board first, and then your child will probably be able to tolerate herbal blends better.

Suggested Antimicrobials

To start, I am suggesting only pure, single antimicrobial agents. You can branch out to using blends later on in the Maintenance Schedule:

- ☐ Artemisia
- ☐ Berberine
- ☐ Black walnut
- ☐ Caprylic acid
- ☐ Clove
- ☐ Cranberry
- ☐ Garlic

> *HOW MUCH DOES IT COST? Natural supplements are relatively inexpensive. Your initial average monthly cost will vary from about $30 to $60 and will cost far less once you are on a Maintenance Schedule.*

- ☐ Goldenseal
- ☐ Grapefruit seed extract
- ☐ Olive leaf extract
- ☐ Oregano
- ☐ Oregon grape
- ☐ Pau d'arco
- ☐ Quinic acid (cat's claw)
- ☐ Saccharomyces boulardii
- ☐ Thymol (oil of thyme)
- ☐ Undecylenic acid
- ☐ Usnea
- ☐ Uva ursi

Note: Only take one type of antimicrobial each week. Do not take them all at once.

The "Slow" Antimicrobial Rotation Schedule
Begin with half doses every other day or even every third day. Gradually increase to the suggested dose as your child can tolerate it.

The "Modified School Year" Antimicrobial Rotation Schedule
Use only on weekends during the school year (two days a week instead of seven days a week).

The "Detective" Antimicrobial Rotation Schedule
Use mere specks or partial drops every other day and mix with food or drink. Gradually increase to the suggested dose as your child can tolerate it.

The "Already on an Antimicrobial Rotation" Schedule
If your child is already on antifungals or antimicrobials, just expand into a wide-ranging weekly rotation.

The Maintenance Schedule
How long should I do this rotation for? When do I cut back?

- ☐ When a stool test comes back negative for yeast or bacterial overgrowth, you can cut back.

☐ No stool test? Try the rotation for a few months, then cut back to every other day for a month or two. If no GI symptoms return, try using antimicrobials only on weekends. For my patients who struggle with chronic dysbiosis, the most I ever suggest to cut back to is every other weekend. I always continue to rotate and use different antimicrobial agents. Once we get good "gut control," I like to stay off the merry-go-round and avoid dysbiotic relapses.

☐ Once on a Maintenance Schedule, try an antimicrobial blend, as opposed to a single pure agent.

What does this entire three-step Basic GI Support Protocol look like when it's all put together, week by week? Chapter 9 and its digital companion, the Online Action Plan, give you a year's worth of protocol suggestions, from the basics and beyond. The free basic version of my calendar app, *The Un-Prescription for Autism*, will help with scheduling these protocols in your calendar.

In Chapter 7 I'll explore how the immune system may be different in autism spectrum disorder, and strategies for immune support. Turn the page for some great tips.

7

Why Is My Child Always Sick?: How to Stop Catching Colds Right Away

You are so brave and quiet I forget you are suffering.
Ernest Hemingway

"Hi, Mrs. Grayling, I'm calling from Dr. Smith's office. I was just wondering how Emmy is. We haven't seen her lately. In fact, we're wondering if you changed pediatricians."

Emmy Grayling's pediatrician was pleased to learn she hadn't switched doctors in the last few months, and even more pleased to learn she wasn't getting sick much anymore.

Emmy was an active six-year-old on the autism spectrum when she first came to see me in April 2009. She was a pale, wispy little ghost, with deep, dark circles under her eyes, cold sores around her mouth, and a thick crust of warts on her tiny fingers and hands. She had stomachaches "all the time" and complained of headaches as well. Her mother joked they were "frequent flyers" at the pediatrician's office, with several visits a month. Emmy missed a lot of school, and when she was there, she didn't feel her best.

Research suggests some children on the spectrum may have what is called a "TH1 to TH2 shift," an alteration in the immune system that may leave them more vulnerable to viral and fungal entities. Was Emmy's immune system showing this pattern?

I could tell this young child had tummy troubles: She was gassy, constipated, and had a history of thrush. She put off going to sleep and woke up frequently in the night. Emmy draped her abdomen over furniture and chewed on her clothing. She exhibited very disruptive and aggressive behaviors such as hitting, biting, pinching hard enough to draw blood, throwing objects, and having huge meltdowns. More than two dozen large warts covered her fingers. These were refractive to treatment and had been burned off, frozen off, and peeled off with caustic acid several times.

My goal was for Emmy's immune system to balance out and begin fending off viruses, thrush, cold sores, and all those warts.

Immune health starts in the GI tract. A simple handful of digestive enzymes, probiotics, and antimicrobials took on the job of balancing Emmy's gastrointestinal system. I added Vitamin D3 and a touch of selenium for added immune support. Emmy immediately quit catching so many colds, and her bowel habits and sleep patterns began to straighten out. Her color improved, her under-eye circles faded, and her mom felt like throwing a party!

Within two months, Emmy's mom received that friendly call from the pediatrician's office to see if she had switched to another doctor since Emmy had abruptly stopped coming by. Nope, she just quit getting sick so much!

I noticed she still had all those warts, and I added monolaurin to her daily regimen. Monolaurin, made from coconut oil, is known to have antiviral, antifungal, and some antibacterial properties. Mrs. Grayling worked on cleaning up Emmy's diet.

At the end of 2009, we looked back over Emmy's record: Emmy caught a "slight cold" in August and had an ear infection in October. Her behavior had significantly improved, and she was missing school less often and getting more out of her education and therapies.

Since then, Emmy continues to have glowingly good health and only occasionally catches a cold. Her warts gradually resolved without further treatment and have not returned. I can't remember the last time I saw a cold sore around her mouth. Her behavior, cognition, and language have blossomed, although as she approaches her teen years, she has been a handful (as teenagers often are). Whatever challenges Emmy faces now, poor health, rampant warts, and frequent colds are not on the list.

Immune Dysfunction on the Autism Spectrum

Global research is strongly suggestive that those on the spectrum have immune system disturbances. There is even talk of the possibility of immune, autoimmune, and inflammatory subsets of autism. Let's look at some of these immune system problems. (I'll translate as I go.)

☐ A shift in the Th1 to Th2 ratio in the immune system, with a Th2 predominance[1]

☐ A disproportionate response to stress *(duh!)*[2]

> TRANSLATION: This means your child may catch more colds and viral infections, be more prone to fungal infections, and have more allergies and asthma than other children.[3]

☐ Pro-inflammatory immune state with:
  ○ Increased levels of pro-inflammatory cytokines[4]
  ○ Disregulated levels of anti-inflammatory cytokines[5]

> TRANSLATION: Those with ASD may be in a state of chronic inflammation throughout their body.

  ○ Increased level of pro-inflammatory neurotensin[6]
  ○ Elevated plasma neopterin levels[7]

☐ Neuroinflammation[8]

☐ Mast cell activation in the brain[9]

☐ Neurotoxic microglia activation[10]

☐ Increased levels of extracellular mitochondrial DNA, which triggers an autoimmune response in the brain[12]

> TRANSLATION: Mast cell activation contributes to brain inflammation. Prolonged microglia activation can lead to loss of connections (underconnectivity) in the brain.[11]

☐ Autoantibodies to brain tissues[13]:
  ○ Myelin basic protein (MBP)[14]
  ○ Hypothalamus[15]
  ○ Thalamus[16]
  ○ Cerebellum[17]

> TRANSLATION: The immune system is attacking various tissues in the brain.

- ○ Brain endothelial cells[18]
- ○ Brain nuclei cells[19]
- □ Low natural killer cell activity[20]
- □ Altered T-cell response[21]
- □ Elevated monocyte counts[22]
- □ Elevated levels of measles antibodies[23]

> *TRANSLATION: These are all types of cells from the immune system that are different in ASD.*

- □ Non-IgE-mediated food allergies:
  - ○ Aberrant innate immune response (inflammation), which may predispose children with ASD to sensitization to common

> *TRANSLATION: This means food really can cause inflammation in your child's GI tract and affect his behavior.*

dietary proteins and lead to inflammation of the GI tract and an increase in behavioral symptoms[24]

That's a lot of technospeak, but the translation is that the immune system may be out of whack in ASD, leaving your child more prone to colds, allergies, and asthma, and that his immune system may even turn on him and attack tissues in his own brain. Inflammation, which is a tool of the immune system, may be left in the "on" position, leaving a child in a state of chronic systemic inflammation, including brain inflammation. A child may become sensitive to common foods, which may further inflame the GI tract and create an increase in difficult behaviors. All of this is completely invisible to the naked eye and is a big part of why I say, "What you see isn't what you get with ASD." Research is increasingly suggestive that immune dysfunction in ASD may affect neurodevelopment and play a role in neurological dysfunction. Studies also allude to the possibility that immune dysfunction may affect behavior, thanks to the strong connection between the brain and the immune system.

These are not spoiled brats with bad parents; these are children with real medical problems and health challenges that affect their behavior and learning. Instead of medicating these children until they shut up, we need to find ways to naturally cool and put out these fires and bring balance to dysfunctional body systems.

What Does the Immune System Have to Do with the GI Tract?

Let's connect the dots here. It's no secret by now that many children and adults with ASD struggle with poor GI health. And where does the bulk of the immune system live? It's the GI tract—that amazing living tube that starts in your mouth and stretches all the way to your hind end. In fact, it houses about 70 percent of the immune system, so it's no leap of faith to draw a connection between poor GI health and immune dysfunction on the spectrum.

So, let's get this straight: We already learned that GI dysfunction can create difficult behaviors. And now we learn that immune dysfunction might affect behavior. So, could restoring, supporting, and maintaining optimal GI and immune health result in our children being medicated less for challenging behaviors? Sounds like a win-win-win to me.

Thank you, Captain Obvious!

Allergies and asthma, chronic congestion, and the ever-running nose can hit our spectrum children particularly hard. You've seen that bleary and droopy-eyed, mouth-breathing look on your child's face. It's a sign of congestion and allergies. And how about the "allergic salute," the upward swipe of the nose with the palm? It can leave a telltale horizontal crease across the tip of the nose if it's done frequently enough. Headaches, snoring, and seasonal misery in the spring and fall are common, too.

Consequences of Frequent Illnesses

When children don't feel well, they are miserable and whiny, and who can blame them? They require a lot of tender loving care, which we parents are happy to provide, but it sure takes a toll on the family dynamic. We usually have to cancel appointments, errands, and lessons and be a magician to get dinner on the table when our children are sick.

When our children miss school, especially if it's over and over again, it can create gaps in learning and understanding of the material covered in class. It interrupts mastering a goal in applied behavioral analysis (ABA), speech, occupational therapy (OT), or an activity of daily living (ADL). Your child is then left struggling to keep up when he returns to school, plus he'll be buried in makeup work, which can take a toll on grades. All that can leave any child feeling discouraged and overwhelmed.

Sometimes our children are not sick enough to miss school, but they aren't as vibrantly healthy as they could be. Children with autism might be *there* that day in the classroom, but they struggle with congestion, fatigue, brain fog, malaise, or headaches.

Vicious Cycle of Antibiotic Overuse

Like Ron Weasley's broken wand in *Harry Potter and the Chamber of Secrets*, antibiotics are a useful tool that can have unwelcome side effects on the gastrointestinal system. No, you won't cough up any giant slugs, but the price of antibiotic use in these children can be a gut ghetto and a battered immune system.

Despite the educational efforts of the American Academy of Pediatrics (AAP) to reduce the use of antibiotics, many parents still expect one when their child has an ear infection, and many doctors still hand them out. Some children experience one ear infection after another and get round after round of antibiotics. They often end up with bilateral tympanostomies, or "tubes" in their eardrums. When I ask how many rounds of antibiotics a child has had, some parents reply, "Too many to count!" (One parent replied, "Less than a hundred!" *Yikes.*)

Even appropriate use of antibiotics can damage the good bacteria in our gut and thus strike a blow to the immune system. It's like a merry-go-round you can't get off. You should support GI health *during* and *after* a round of antibiotics, or your child may go from ear infection to ear infection or even develop urinary tract infections.

Early antibiotic use seems to set off a cascade of gastrointestinal problems in autistic children and, for that matter, in children *without* autism. It's like the good bacteria never get off to a good start, and we usually see colic, gassiness, sleep problems, and recurrent ear infections, which lead to more antibiotics and finally tubes in the ears.

Vicious Cycle of Urinary Tract Infections

More bad news: Research suggests that overuse of antibiotics may lead to recurrent urinary tract infections, or UTIs. Overuse can also create drug-resistant bacterial UTIs.[25] Antibiotic overuse isn't the only thing that leads to urinary tract infections. Microbial imbalance, or dysbiosis in the GI tract, can lead to UTIs, which can lead to antibiotic use, which can lead to . . . microbial imbalance in the gut. Can you hear the merry-go-round music?

I'm not against antibiotics; my family uses them but only sparingly and when absolutely necessary. *How* our society uses antibiotics has created this generation's problems. Let me show you what I mean in Figure 7-1.

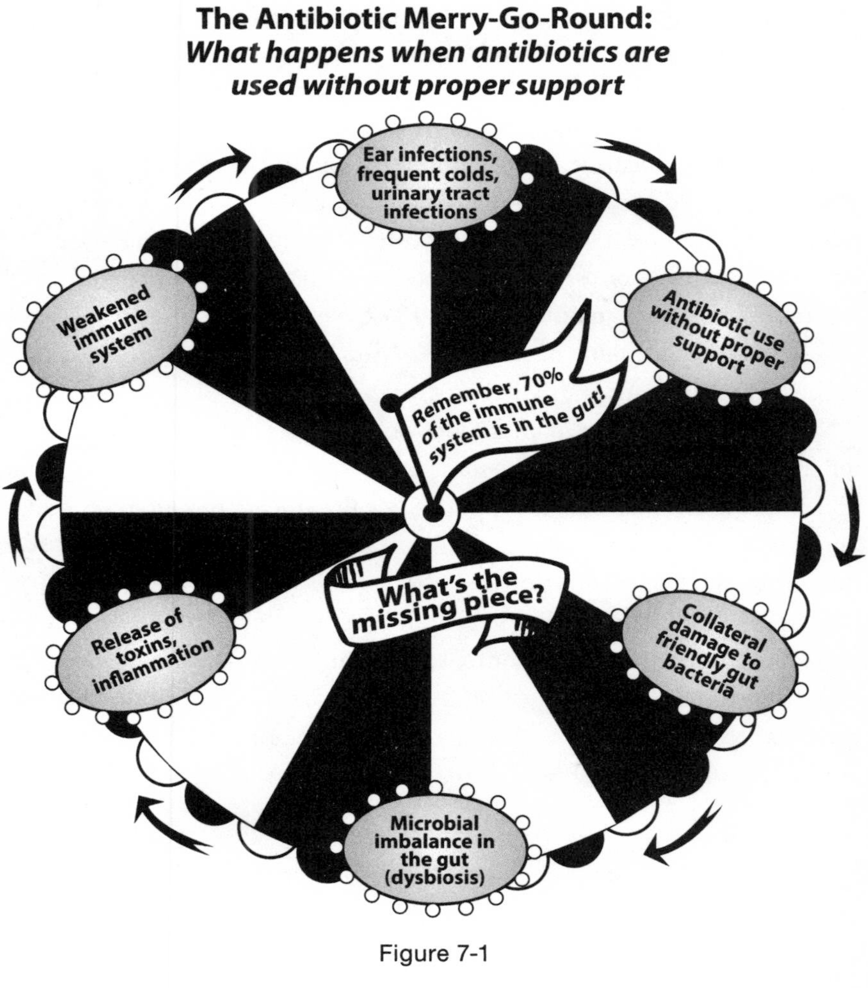

Figure 7-1

Is your child on the antibiotic merry-go-round? Let's look at Figure 7-2 and see how to break this cycle, reduce and prevent frequent ear infections and UTIs, and keep our children from catching so many colds.

Using antibiotics appropriately

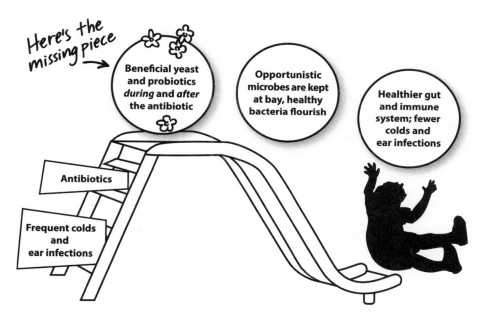

Figure 7-2

Replace the vicious cycle of antibiotic overuse with a virtuous one of support. You will need to provide probiotics and S. boulardii during rounds of antibiotics and follow with a gentle, natural rotation of effective antimicrobials that won't tax the liver or harm the child. You'll be following the Antibiotic Support Protocol that I use in my center, so your child can get off, and stay off, the antibiotic merry-go-round. (See Week 6 in the Chapter 9 Online Action Plan.)

Take a look at Sophia's struggle with chronic urinary tract infections.

Sophia's Story

Sophia was a twelve-year-old girl with autism and intellectual impairment who came to see me one December. Sophia had several UTIs per month and was on antibiotics almost constantly. During her initial visit, she had poor impulse control and created some pretty amazing graffiti all around the office. The rest of the time, Sophia kept a big goofy grin on her face and giggled and rolled around on the couch and floor like a rag doll. She couldn't even sit up in her chair properly. I wondered if some of this conduct was due to the by-products of microbial imbalance in her intestinal tract.

There were a number of ways to support vibrant health for Sophia, but I could not do much without first restoring balance to her gastrointestinal system. We started with the Basic GI Support Protocol.

When the family brought her back eight weeks later, they had barely been able to get even the enzymes in her. She was still giggly, goofy, and rolling around. And they brought bad news with them: Sophia's UTIs were so frequent that she had been put on antibiotics prophylactically, meaning she was on an antibiotic all the time with the hope that would prevent her from getting another UTI. Even worse, there was only one antibiotic left that she had not developed resistance to. What was going to happen when her UTIs became resistant to that one?

The family redoubled their efforts and began to get the supplements into Sophia. By her next visit, she was not catching UTIs and her goofy demeanor was diminished. Five months after her original visit, Sophia was off of all antibiotics and was UTI-free. She now comes to her appointments and sits daintily in her chair without giggling, looking goofy, or rolling around on the floor. Dignity restored!

In an attempt to treat Sophia, the constant antibiotics prescribed by her doctor actually began to cause her more problems. They created a vicious cycle to the point where she became resistant to almost all of them, without the original problem (UTIs) being resolved. A simple natural rotation of Sac b, antimicrobials, plus probiotics became the answer. We were able to balance her gastrointestinal and immune systems and then go on to other supportive therapies. Sophia could now take full advantage of social and learning opportunities and live up to her true potential.

The Basic Immune Support Protocol

You can break the cycle of your child getting sick all the time. I am going to share the basics for restoring and maintaining vibrant immune health on the spectrum.

Where should you start? The gut, the gut, the gut . . . . Got it? The gut! Any more questions? Use the Basic GI Support Protocol (Chapter 6) to get started, especially if your child is constipated. It also helps restore good sleep patterns—and getting a good night's sleep is essential for immune health. Then flow right into the Basic Protocol to support immune system health.

My Basic Immune Support Protocol is so simple you won't believe it. It has three ingredients—probiotics, Vitamin D3, and a touch of selenium—and it has helped hundreds of children and adults on the spectrum have a more balanced and robust immune system.

> *HOW MUCH DOES IT COST? Vitamin D3 is a bargain. Prices on the Internet run as low as $8 to $10 for a year's worth of the drops. Selenium is pretty cheap at less than $5 per year. Yay—for once, something our children need that doesn't break the bank.*

Week 1 and thereafter: *Give a daily probiotic with the evening meal.*
Week 2 and thereafter: *Give Vitamin D3 twice a day (400 to 2,000 International Units [IU]).*

The third ingredient is optional (for the most frequent of flyers):

Week 3 and for the next month: *Add selenium every other day (50 to 100 micrograms).*

See Table 7-1 to calculate how much selenium to give your child. I give 50 to 100 micrograms of selenium every other day, not daily, and I never give more than 100 micrograms, as selenium has a narrow window of safety.

Tolerable upper intake levels (ULs) for selenium.*				
AGE	**MALE**	**FEMALE**	**PREGNANCY**	**LACTATION**
Birth to 6 months	45 mcg	45 mcg		
7–12 months	60 mcg	60 mcg		
1–3 years	90 mcg	90 mcg		
4–8 years	150 mcg	150 mcg		
9–13 years	280 mcg	280 mcg		
14–18 years	400 mcg	400 mcg	400 mcg	400 mcg
19+ years	400 mcg	400 mcg	400 mcg	400 mcg

Table 7-1

Source: Institute of Medicine, Food, and Nutrition Board. Dietary Reference Intakes: Vitamin C, Vitamin E, Selenium, and Carotenoids. Washington, D.C.: National Academy Press, 2000; cited at the National Institutes of Health, Office of Dietary Supplements (https://ods.od.nih .gov/factsheets/Selenium-HealthProfessional/#en6).

* Breast milk, formula, and food should be the only sources of selenium for infants.

Why I Use Vitamin D3 and Not D2

Most of the world is low in Vitamin D.[26] It shouldn't have been named as a vitamin, because it behaves more like a hormone and is vitally important for not just our bone and immune health but also for cell growth, neurological health and mood, and reduction of inflammation, to name a few conditions. It's called the "sunshine vitamin" because we make it when sunlight hits our skin. It's a good idea to let your child get twenty to thirty minutes of direct sun exposure daily, *without* sunscreen, so she can make this vitamin naturally.

There are two forms of Vitamin D, commonly called Vitamin D2 and Vitamin D3.[27] Don't be fooled: The prescription form is nearly always in the form of D2, which is said to be over 200 times less active than the D3 form. That's why when you take the prescription form of Vitamin D you are usually given about 50,000 IU several times a week. The really good news is that your child's Vitamin D level can be tested using a completely painless finger prick—something I didn't believe was possible until I tried it myself! (See Week 44 in the Chapter 9 Online Action Plan.)

Don't be fooled by the results of the Vitamin D test, either. Most lab companies and doctors will tell you that any test value above 32 ng/mL is considered "adequate" for bone and overall health. Research into Vitamin D is ongoing, but I suggest you aim for an "optimal level" of 60–80 ng/mL. Many doctors and researchers believe that the daily recommended intake for Vitamin D is woefully inadequate. That does not mean you should give your child mega doses—Vitamin D is a fat-soluble vitamin and care must be taken with supplementation. I can get results using just 1,000 to 2,000 IU of D3 once or twice a day, and the entire dose can be delivered in one tiny drop of liquid. For young children, I use 400 IU twice a day.

Why I Use Just a Touch of Selenium

Research suggests selenium has a positive effect on the immune system,[28] even in subjects who were not deficient in selenium.[29] It may also have anti-oxidant and anti-inflammatory effects.

Selenium has a narrow window of toxicity, so more is not better in this case. I use it cautiously, and it's also the first supplement I drop when a child shows improved immune health. Monitor selenium intake, and don't forget to include the amounts in multivitamins and other supplements your child is taking. Table 7-1 shows maximum dosing limits.

If your child is a "frequent flyer"—that is, gets sick all the time and misses too much school—you'll want to drop this immune protocol into your Action Plan pretty early on. But how do you accomplish that if you're slogging through four weeks or more of an Enzyme Schedule? Our ASD children are often so sensitive to new things that you should never start more than one new supplement or medication at a time. Remember my rule of thumb? *Leave at least three days in between starting new supplements* so that you can keep an eye out for a sensitivity reaction.

There is a way to start the Enzyme Schedule *and* work in the immune protocol. We can layer in the immune protocol starting the first week of the Basic GI Support Protocol—that's when you're just getting started with everything—and you can begin to support immune health right away. Here's how it goes:

Week 1 of Basic GI Support Protocol: *Give enzymes with one meal a day this week. On Day 4 of this week: Begin giving Vitamin D3 twice a day.*

Week 2: *Give enzymes with two meals a day this week. On Day 4 of this week, begin giving selenium every other day.*

But what about the probiotic, you say? We have to wait until constipation is gone, so continue with the rest of your child's particular Enzyme Schedule and *then* go right into the Probiotic Schedule you have chosen.

If it's hard to picture what I mean, then Figure 7-3 gives you a simple visual explanation.

How to start Immune Support and enzymes at the same time

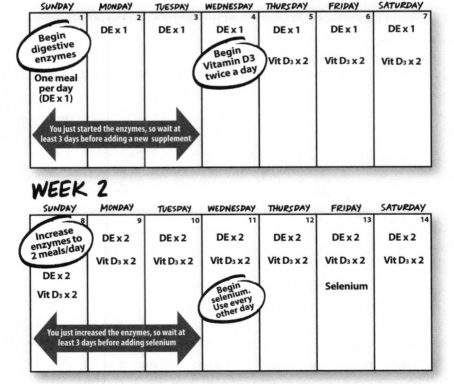

Figure 7-3

If you've already done the Basic GI Support Protocol in Chapter 6, then your child is already on a probiotic. Just add a little Vitamin D3 and selenium (three days apart) and your child will usually respond right away. You don't need to use large doses. See how well Hallie responded.

Hallie's Story

"I can't believe it; she always has some kind of runny nose all the time!" Hallie's mother was incredulous that for the two months since her first visit to my center, her daughter hadn't had any colds, runny noses, or sinus or strep infections—or, for that matter, any visits to the pediatrician's office. "She has better color, and I'm noticing a little more sassiness lately," she laughed.

Hallie's frequent absences at school had taken a toll on her grades, even though she was a bright little girl. Again, we used a few basics like digestive enzymes, probiotics, Sac b, Vitamin D3, and selenium. Her grades improved after her immune system became stronger, and she became the vibrant, happy little girl she was meant to be. She got off the antibiotic merry-go-round. With time, she moved from a daily dependence on allergy medications to using them on an as-needed basis only.

At most of her subsequent visits, her mother would tell me, "I can't remember the last time I took her to the pediatrician!"

MORE IMMUNE SUPPORT TIPS

Immune support doesn't always come in a bottle. Lifestyle choices have a significant impact. It's all connected.

- ☐ Reduce sugar in the diet. 100 grams of sugar (a pack of Skittles and a pint of apple juice or chocolate milk) is known to negatively impact the immune system within thirty minutes after eating it. The effects last for up to five hours.
- ☐ Green the diet. I know our children can be picky eaters, but do your best to work in whole, fresh, colorful organic foods. Make deals with your child for more computer time if he'll eat green beans or winter squash. Stay away from highly processed foods

like prepackaged snack items with no real nutritional value. (See Week 7 in the Chapter 9 Online Action Plan for more ideas on cleaning up the diet.)

☐ Exercise! Go for walks or visit the playground and get some sunshine.

☐ Stick with good old-fashioned hand washing. Hand sanitizers are not a good daily substitute for hand washing.

☐ Get in shape for school. Do the Basic Immune Support Protocol for a few weeks before class starts each fall.

☐ Minimize antibiotics: Take a conservative "wait and see" approach to fluid in the ears and ear infections. (See Week 29 in the Chapter 9 Online Action Plan for what to do if you suspect your child has an ear infection.) Because 97 percent of colds are viral in nature, an antibiotic is useless.

Avoid hand sanitizers, as they are thought to be endocrine disrupters. The common antibacterial ingredient triclosan may weaken mitochondria, something 60 percent of children with autism are thought to struggle with already. And a researcher at the University of California, Davis, suspects it may alter genetic expression that can increase susceptibility to autism.[30]

What's in Your Toolbox?

Every website you look at has its own approach to immune support. There are many herbs and nutrients that support immune health, and you're probably wondering why I don't use more of them. One reason is that young children don't always know how to swallow capsules, which means we have to resort to hiding bad-tasting supplements in their food or drinks. Second, they can usually tell we've hidden something in there and refuse it instantly. Third, I am a huge fan of using the least "stuff" to get results.

For those of you whose children don't mind taking a few supplements or who need a little extra immune support, here are some of my other favorites.

Omega-3 Fatty Acids

Children with autism tend to be low in essential fatty acids.[31] Omega-3 fatty acids help support the immune system, reduce inflammation, and improve autoimmune disorders.[32] Bonus: They seem to help with ADHD, too. Purchase a high-quality children's supplement and follow the dosing suggestions on the package.

Zinc

Children on the spectrum tend to be low in zinc.[33] I learned a lot about zinc from my mentor, Dr. Elizabeth Mumper. Zinc is beneficial to the immune system, helps stimulate appetite, can reduce diarrhea, and is healing to the GI tract—all things our ASD children need. It's a busy little helper in the body, involved in close to 300 metabolic processes and reactions. Low zinc levels have even been associated with aggression and antisocial behavior.[34]

Too much zinc can inhibit the immune system, however. Avoid the common pitfall of "if a little is good, more must be better." Just 20 milligrams a day should do the job, unless testing indicates a need for more. Zinc is easy on the wallet as well.

Xylitol

I recommend xylitol for support of oral health, immune health,[35] and management of tic disorders. Research shows it is helpful against ear infections, too. Since sugar can depress the immune system, it's a great idea to start swapping out sugar in your child's diet for xylitol. Look for toothpaste, mouthwash, candy, gum, and nasal spray made with xylitol. You can also get it in packets or by the sack at the health food store.

THE IMMUNE SUPPORT TOOLBOX

- ☐ Basic GI Support Protocol
- ☐ Basic Immune Support Protocol
- ☐ Zinc
- ☐ Omega-3 fatty acids
- ☐ Antioxidants such as Vitamin C
- ☐ Antibiotic Support Protocol (to follow when on an antibiotic)

- ☐ Xylitol
- ☐ An organic, colorful diet rich in fruits and vegetables
- ☐ Chiropractic visits for regular care and for ear infections and immune support

Anecdotally, chiropractors and the parents of school-age children who receive chiropractic care report that children get sick less often.

TAKE-HOME MESSAGE

- ☐ Many parents assume their child does not have any gut issues—always start with the gut, even if you don't think your child has any GI problems. At least you will have looked under that rock and can move on with confidence.
- ☐ Use your Un-Prescription Organizer to keep track of all supplements and protocols.
- ☐ Avoid use of herbal blends early on. Stick with pure, single AM supplements.
- ☐ KISS—keep it simple, stupid!
- ☐ Use conservative amounts of supplements. More isn't always better.
- ☐ Transition to a Maintenance Plan protocol once your child's immune system bounces back.
- ☐ Stop giving selenium once your child stops catching frequent colds.

Frequently Asked Questions About the Immune Support Protocol

Q: *Do I have to do the entire protocol—probiotics, Vitamin D3, selenium—for my child to get better?*

A: *I am a fan of doing the least amount of anything to get the job done. Add this protocol in stages if you like; if your child's immune system rebounds with just the probiotic and he stops catching every cold coming and going, then that's all you need. Still getting sick? Layer in the D3. Still needs a boost? Add a little selenium. These protocols are just suggestions, and are infinitely variable.*

Q: *When will his allergies and congestion go away?*

A: *I do not claim to "treat" allergies with this suggested immune support, and I do not promise that allergies will resolve. However, I have observed that after fifteen to twenty-four months of good GI and immune support, many of my patients report that their child doesn't seem as bothered by seasonal allergies, or that he only takes allergy medications on an as-needed basis instead of daily. Some families report fewer or no asthma attacks. I can only assume that these conditions lessen as their child's immune system becomes stronger and more balanced.*

Want the Science?

For sources of information found in this chapter, turn to the Endnotes.

8

The Forgotten Ones:
Adults on the Spectrum

Most of the media attention on autism focuses on children. But 50,000 children with ASD turn eighteen every year in the United States alone, and less than 20 percent will live independently.[1] Adults with autism have symptoms that range from those who may have intellectual impairment and no spoken language, with a need for extensive support and services, to those who live independently, and everything in between.

Can we talk? Autistic adults are some of the coolest people I know, but the current prognosis for adulthood on the autism spectrum is not so sparkly. An article in the journal *Pediatrics* states that children with ASD become adults who, "regardless of their intellectual functioning, continue to experience problems with independent living, employment, social relationships, and mental health."[2] The vast majority remain dependent on their families for support, and there never seem to be enough services after they turn eighteen.

The article further states, "Optimization of healthcare is likely to have a positive effect on habilitative progress, functional outcome, and quality of life."[3] If restoring and maintaining vibrant health increases the level of function, it makes sense that it also increases the odds of independence as an adult. I passionately believe that if the unique health challenges of ASD were better understood and addressed, many more adults would be able to live more independently.

Adults on the spectrum live in a variety of settings[4]:

- □ With their parents or other family members
- □ A group home or other assisted living facility
- □ A multifamily home, apartment, or townhouse with a roommate
- □ Their own single-family home, apartment, or townhouse
- □ A planned community
- □ A regular community
- □ An institution

Assessing and addressing the unique health challenges of ASD will vary depending on the setting.

Children with Autism Grow Up to Be Adults with Autism

Chronic health problems only magnify and deepen when ignored. If the health challenges and medical difficulties of ASD have not been appropriately addressed in youth,

> *GI pain isn't responsible for all behaviors, but it is the first thing to consider and rule out before reaching for the heavy-duty antipsychotics to calm them down.*

these children can grow up to have chronic health problems as adults, with difficult behaviors to match the pain and discomfort they are in. This puts them at risk for being medicated for those behaviors. The more challenging the behaviors, the more medications they are on.[5] Medications to control behavior become a big part of "treatment," which we now know may simply be due in part to unaddressed health problems. Armed with the knowledge of ongoing research, and the protocols in this book, you can give your son or daughter a best shot at living independently, and it starts with appropriate health assessment and care.

In my personal experience at the clinic, it is sometimes more difficult to *begin* these health protocols as adults for several reasons:

- □ Adults can make their own decisions, and you can't *make* them take anything. Unless you have guardianship, doctors can't even share what is discussed during an office visit without your adult son or daughter's permission.

- They may be opposed to taking any type of medication or supplement, even natural ones.
- Many struggle with ADHD, disorganization, and a lack of internal structure. I have some adult patients who try these protocols and want to do them, but cannot remember to consistently take the pills on their own.
- Fifty-four percent of adults with autism say they need moderate to complete support just *seeking* help from a healthcare professional.[6]
- Seventy-nine percent of caregivers for an adult with autism ranked seeking healthcare as the number-one daily activity requiring support.[7]

Children and adults with ASD use more healthcare services than their neurotypical peers, so it is vital to go after good health proactively, rather than reactively.

The vast majority of adults with autism live in a family setting or with roommates. Those of you whose adult son or daughter still lives in your home or in a home nearby will have an easier time helping them strive for health and independence because you will be there to keep things on schedule if need be. You will have the full toolbox to choose from and can make adjustments to the health plan on the fly. It will be easier to try new things and note the results for those in a family setting. The elephant in the room, and our biggest fear, is that we won't always be there for them. Teach your child to be involved, if possible, in his health protocols, so that he has his best chance at managing them himself in adulthood.

The same generally goes for adults living in *privately owned* assisted living facilities—if you and your adult son or daughter wish to take enzymes or probiotics, no one is going to fight you on it.

What about those of you who have a minor or adult child whose care is managed by an agency or organization? Is it possible for those in such an assisted living situation to use the protocols I've shared in this book? The answer is sometimes, depending on the policies of the organization.

The good news is that it's never too late to start, and adults, no matter what their age, will respond to appropriate treatment.

Jo-Jo's Story

Jo-Jo was thirty-five when I met him and had been in a residential living setting for more than ten years. The director of Jo-Jo's facility made the appointment at my clinic, saying, "We're out of ideas on how to handle him." He had become increasingly violent and unpredictable and was starting to injure his staff, and no one wanted to work with him.

For our own safety and that of our patients we were advised to "close" the office for Jo-Jo's first visit. We were told to pull back our hair and wear no jewelry. Even though he arrived accompanied by three strong companions who used a harness to control him, Jo-Jo wreaked havoc in the office that day.

He presented with an alphabet soup of diagnoses. In addition to autistic disorder, his chart claimed he suffered from intermittent explosive disorder, mood disorder/bipolar disorder, moderate "mental retardation," seizure disorder, chronic sinusitis, chronic urinary tract infections, cystitis, severe gastritis, history of pancreatitis, and gastroesophageal reflux disease (GERD).

He looked ghastly. He did not have any teeth, his skin was a shockingly pale white, and he had deep, deep dark circles under his eyes. His nose ran constantly during the two-hour visit. He had no self-control; he ran and jumped around the office, grabbing anything and anyone who caught his attention.

The medical history from his first two years of life indicated recurrent diarrhea, foul-smelling bowel movements one to three times a day, frequent gas, rashes, runny nose, and strep throat. (Are you already thinking what I'm thinking—that his GI tract needed support and balance?) Things didn't get any better as I reviewed his childhood: He spoke only one or two words, exhibited a high tolerance for pain, had frequent colds and strep, sinus infections, urinary tract infections, bright red cheeks and ears, cracking peeling hands and feet, poor sleep patterns, aggression, and a habit of sideways glancing.

At age 35, he had a vocabulary for three things: "Dinki-dink" for any type of drink; "Nu-Nu" for any type of food or a snack; and the word "Hurt." His adult medical record revealed chronic severe constipation, very foul-smelling bowel movements and gas, frequent colds, chronic runny nose, chronic sinusitis, chronic severe gastritis, chronic urinary tract infections, cystitis, seizures two to three times a week, severe sleep disruptions, chronic medical crises, and multiple hospitalizations. He said "hurt" hundreds of times a day; staff did not know why. He was commonly observed sitting doubled over or draped over furniture, pressing on his abdomen. He was taking nineteen medications to make him poop, sleep, behave, control fungal infections and seizures, and manage allergies and acid reflux, and he made frequent trips to the doctor. Jo-Jo experienced nighttime voiding seven days a week that completely drenched his pajamas and bedsheets. The workers couldn't wake him up to change his clothes and sheets without risking an angry beating. It was a difficult choice of either waking him and being attacked, or leaving him to sleep in wet bedding and clothes.

His behavior was recorded as "very violent." As a result, he was not allowed to go to restaurants or to join holiday or birthday parties with the other residents. He was banned from the local park (he had once attacked a stranger there). He had injured his social companions; now most were reluctant to work with him. His caregivers reported there had been no changes in his behavior in ten years, despite their best efforts: They put him on a dairy-free diet and took him to a massage therapist, a chiropractor, and multiple medical doctors in an attempt to improve his health and quality of life.

Jo-Jo lived in a caring facility, had a carefully monitored diet, was on nineteen medications (many taken daily, some only as needed), and had a skilled medical team. What could I possibly offer this very ill, violent, unhappy man? What in our current understanding of autism could help me design an appropriate health program for him?

I started with the gut; it was a source of pain, plus it contained the bulk of his immune system, and this was a very ill man. We followed the same Basic GI Support Protocol that I use for any ASD patient who presents with constipation, night awakenings, and irritability.

With the use of digestive enzymes, probiotics, antifungals, and immune support supplements (Vitamin D3 and low-dose selenium), the improvement was dramatic. Jo-Jo responded rapidly, as if his body couldn't wait to heal. His runny nose stopped immediately and hasn't been seen since.

Jo-Jo's seizures decreased significantly (from two or three a week to one a month, at most). He no longer had urinary tract infections, rarely caught a cold, had no seasonal allergies, was constipation-free, and his pallor was gone. His sleep patterns were greatly improved, his disposition calm, and his aggressive behavior had disappeared. He no longer tried to injure his companions and could walk past my tiniest patients without causing any alarm. Jo-Jo was not an inherently violent man; he was in extreme pain and unable to express it. Once out of pain, his true gentle nature was revealed. He attended three large Christmas parties in one month, without incident, and had a blast. He was allowed to visit the park again and have a sit-down meal in a restaurant with only one social companion accompanying him— something unheard of for him in the last ten years! He remains intellectually disabled but is happy and enjoys a good quality of life. His nighttime voiding in the bed decreased to about three times a week; however, his companions can now safely awaken him to change his clothing and sheets without fear of being harmed, and he can sleep through the night in dry clothing and sheets like a real human being.

Best of all, Jo-Jo could now speak in a few full sentences. Although this language achievement was quite limited, it was a huge improvement. He used to just hit people when he was hungry, thirsty, or wanted to be left alone. His social companions used to randomly hold up food or drinks throughout the day to avoid being hit. Now he could say, "I would like lunch, please," or "Alone" when he wanted others to go away. He no longer said "hurt" hundreds of times a day (or even at all). He was happy. Perhaps most amazing, he had a sheltered job that he enjoyed.

I have presented Jo-Jo's case to rehabilitation professionals, social workers, teachers, doctors, and medical students. When I ask, "What would you do for this patient?" I am met by blank stares.

My message here is to continue the healthcare strategies you learn in this book into your child's adult life. Once Jo-Jo's physical conditions had been corrected with the proper approach, he was well enough to engage in social skills exercises and speech therapy—interventions that were formerly beyond his reach because of his aggressive, violent behavior. Maintenance protocols are essential. Nothing is going to cure Jo-Jo's ASD or cognitive impairment, but I feel he could have had a much better quality of life than he experienced, as described later in this chapter.

The "Medical Home" Model

I always focus on building a team of doctors, therapists, and specialists for my patients. In fact, I advise you to avoid any one doctor or type of therapy that claims to have all the answers for ASD.

In 1967, the American Academy of Pediatrics developed the concept of the "medical home," a central system for medical records and a team-based approach to lifelong care that considers *all* of a patient's medical needs under one umbrella.[8] Ideally, care under such a model is centered on the patient and family, led by a personal physician, and coordinates and integrates care among all doctors and specialists for all the health needs of the patient.

The medical home model is ideal for all children and adults, especially those with an array of health challenges such as seen with ASD.[9] When organizations that manage housing and medical care for adults in the community with ASD take charge, medical decisions are centralized and team-based. And this can be a good thing: When my adult patients whose care is managed by an agency or organization come for a visit, I have access to a comprehensive set of integrated health records and can coordinate my contribution as well. Care is detailed, structured, and comprehensive. The patient is regularly seen by his doctor, chiropractor, dentist, and other specialists, and no appointments are overlooked or forgotten.

In this type of situation, families usually cannot just say they would like their son or daughter to try these protocols or a special diet. A physician or other healthcare professional must give written orders. When I provide a health plan for a patient in a facility, I always type it out, and I always keep in mind that supplements are easiest to give at meal times in these facilities.

There is a drawback to this model: The team leader's medical training and biases will obviously influence care decisions, and sometimes that's not a good thing if the leader hasn't followed all the new information and research about ASD that is available these days. Look at Trey's story to see what I mean.

Coming Home: Trey's Story ————————————————

"Trey wants to come home, but no facility will take him."

Trey is a fifteen-year-old with autism spectrum disorder. He has spent the last four years in a facility for juvenile offenders.

I got a call from the local Department of Health and Human Resources asking if I could come to a meeting downtown and see if there was anything I could do to help this young man, and adding, "We have tried everything and don't know what else to do." No medication had been left untried in the quest to control Trey's behavior.

I arrived at the meeting and was the only person in the room without a lawyer. The juvenile facility and Trey were participating via conference call. I listened to Trey's story and asked questions about constipation, sleep, and eating patterns. Here is a snapshot of his story:

Trey suffers from poor sleep patterns, constipation, aggression, and irritability. He is restrained four to six times a day for outbursts of anger and aggression, and he has fecal smears in his pants up to four times a day. He is being medicated to poop, sleep, and behave.

Trey is still in high school, and the facility wants him out of there. His goal is to be near family, but he is so violent that no facility here will agree to accept him. Trey is "willing to do anything" to move back home.

I explained how nationally recognized autism doctors feel GI dysfunction and discomfort can cause or exacerbate aggressive behaviors. Everyone in the room, including Trey, was excited to give the Basic GI Support Protocol a go. A trip was arranged for Trey to see me in my office.

Trey was a sweet young man and on his best behavior. I could see he would likely benefit from some basic gastrointestinal and health support strategies. I typed up a plan for digestive enzymes, probiotics and S. boulardii, among other suggestions, included copies of the pertinent research for the medical director of his facility, and off they went.

Surprisingly, the facility's medical doctor refused to implement this simple, straightforward plan. He did not "believe" in natural supplements. A judge issued a court order to implement the plan. The facility again refused. Action was threatened, and the facility finally complied.

Two months later, the facility had recorded only four violent outbursts from

Trey for an entire month instead of the usual four to six incidents per day, and he had only soiled his pants four times in the month instead of several times a day. He was sleeping better and reported feeling happier than before. Years of prescription medications could not achieve what a few weeks of probiotics and other supplements did for Trey. He is back home: He can now poop, sleep, and behave on his own, is employed, and wants to learn to drive. The rest is up to him—balanced GI health is giving him his best chance.

Why was the facility so dead set against trying something as innocuous as over-the-counter digestive enzymes and probiotics? They were willing to experiment with powerful antipsychotics and other medications with significant risks and side effects. They had admittedly tried "every kind of medicine there is." You may run into this lack of flexibility from your son or daughter's medical team as well.

There are some situations where you will have no say in your adult child's care. If you do not have custody or guardianship, you cannot intervene. If your child is doing time in a correctional facility of some type (like Trey was), you will have no say in his medical care. Same goes if he is a ward of the state. The medical director of a facility can refuse your suggestions.

But if you can be involved, where should you start? First off, always be an active member of your child's healthcare team, if possible. Be involved, ask questions, and accompany your son or daughter to appointments. Ask around or make a few calls to find a physician who will use natural protocols like the ones presented in this book, someone who is knowledgeable about the health challenges facing those on the spectrum. Look for a physician trained by the Medical Academy of Pediatric Special Needs. Ask for a group meeting with the facility and nursing staff—whoever makes the decisions. Give them the name of the physician you would like your child to see, the reasons why, and what your goals are. See if you have any sympathy for this approach. If so, then the staff can schedule an appointment with the new physician for your son or daughter. Feel free to share this book with the staff and physician.

Here is another example of an inflexible medical home—the heartbreaking surprise twist to Jo-Jo's story:

After several years of health for Jo-Jo, we noticed he was no longer coming for follow-up visits. We called one day to check on him, only to learn there had been a change in the nursing and medical staff.

The new nurse we spoke with was sarcastic and cold. She informed us that Jo-Jo was no longer following our protocols since "none of that stuff works." Incredulous, we asked if she was familiar with his history and how well he had done since coming to our center. She said she was very aware of his history, and again repeated that none of our advice or supplements had ever worked. She hung up.

I was dumbfounded. Natural interventions can be powerful and effective additions to the toolbox, yet the new medical staff obviously felt they were the equivalent of witchcraft. I often wonder how Jo-Jo is doing and am saddened to think that he may return to his former state of pain, ill health, and overmedication.

My Suggestions for Adults with ASD

I passionately believe that every adult with ASD deserves to be a happy, productive, *integrated* member of our society (see Figure 8-1). Each person has value and a place. We have to take the time to assess and support optimal health for adults with ASD, and to do that, we have to understand the health challenges they face. The conventional model of using prescription medications for individual symptoms isn't bringing vibrant health for many of them so far. Giving them antipsychotics instead of relieving painful health conditions is not doing anything to increase their chances of success and independence (see Figure 8-2). They may still need medication after these health issues have been addressed, but it will at least be appropriate at that point.

Take Advantage of Transition Services

Thanks to the Workforce Innovation and Opportunity Act (WIOA), signed into law in July 2014, transition and preemployment training services will reach our youth starting in the tenth grade, instead of their senior year in high school. Doug Auten and Angela Walker of the West Virginia Division

Finding the "sweet spot" on the autism spectrum

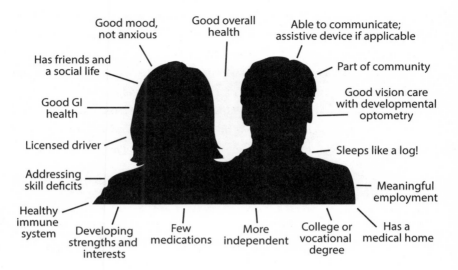

Good mood, not anxious

Good overall health

Able to communicate; assistive device if applicable

Has friends and a social life

Part of community

Good GI health

Good vision care with developmental optometry

Licensed driver

Sleeps like a log!

Addressing skill deficits

Meaningful employment

Healthy immune system

Developing strengths and interests

Few medications

More independent

College or vocational degree

Has a medical home

This is what we're aiming for

Figure 8-1

Suboptimal outcomes on the autism spectrum

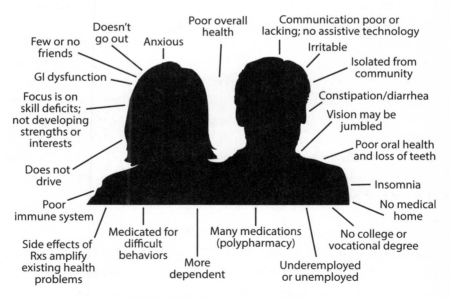

Doesn't go out

Poor overall health

Communication poor or lacking; no assistive technology

Few or no friends

Anxious

Irritable

Isolated from community

GI dysfunction

Focus is on skill deficits; not developing strengths or interests

Constipation/diarrhea

Vision may be jumbled

Poor oral health and loss of teeth

Does not drive

Insomnia

Poor immune system

No medical home

Side effects of Rxs amplify existing health problems

Medicated for difficult behaviors

Many medications (polypharmacy)

More dependent

Underemployed or unemployed

No college or vocational degree

This is what we want to avoid

Figure 8-2

of Rehabilitation Services point out that the benefits of this program include opportunities such as:

- ☐ Job readiness skills, including social skills and independent living skills
- ☐ Job exploration counseling
- ☐ Work-based learning, both in-school and after-school
- ☐ Job shadowing
- ☐ Apprenticeships
- ☐ On-the-job training
- ☐ Employment readiness
- ☐ Job clubs in schools
- ☐ Field trips to visit potential employers
- ☐ Counseling on post-secondary training
- ☐ Trips to visit colleges
- ☐ Self-advocacy instruction

> TIP: Schools can't single out and approach you or your child specifically for these transition and education services due to privacy issues, so make the first move and let your school know that you are interested while your child is still in school.

Every state and territory of the United States has a Division of Rehabilitation Services (DRS) in charge of implementing these services to youth. Contact your local office and get the ball rolling.

Include Them in the Conversation

If all my possessions were taken from me, with one exception,
I would choose to keep the power of communication, for by it,
I would soon regain all the rest.
Daniel Webster

"*Where* are her iPad and Proloquo2Go today?"

I was questioning the care team that had brought Dani, one of my nonverbal adult patients, for a visit. She couldn't connect or communicate with me that day since her assistive communication device had been left behind, and she spent the visit just silently looking at me and making occasional gestures that I could not interpret. Her caregivers looked sheepish, and one of them said she didn't have access to it every day because not everyone on the staff was trained in how to use it. Her mother was there for the visit and the surprised look on her face was priceless—she didn't even know her daughter had a communication device! Talk about a lack of communication.

Communication is essential for health, happiness, and everything in between. Clear communication is essential for safety, learning, and advocating. Social isolation and frustration increase without it. There are a slew of communication methods, apps, and devices, and I consider Proloquo2Go and Touch Chat HD-AAC with WordPower to be two of the best choices (see Week 33 in the Chapter 9 Online Action Plan). These devices can connect your son or daughter to the world and even speak aloud for them and be their voice. If they cannot or will not use such an app, consider the simple Picture Exchange Communication System (PECS). It's neither complicated nor expensive and is easily adapted to a variety of settings.

My nonverbal patients use a variety of communication styles, everything from high-tech apps to picture exchange systems and sign language, or even grunting and pointing. I'm excited about the new generation of assistive communication technology. Dani can even use hers to order in a restaurant. Her mother should have been included in the training, as well as all the staff members who work in Dani's home.

Just buying a device or app is not enough. Training and persistence is crucial to success. According to one study, up to 35 percent of those who had purchased an assistive communication device abandoned it, likely due to lack of training.[10]

Make Driving a Goal

In 2014, I was appointed by the governor to the West Virginia State Rehabilitation Council. It is one of the most rewarding and eye-opening experiences I have had. We were reviewing the budget and needs at one meeting, and transportation consistently ranked as one of the top concerns and expenses. There is always a greater need for transportation than the budget can accommodate.

Rehabilitation counselors and job coaches can prepare an adult for transition to college or a career he enjoys, and employers can offer job openings, but if the individual has no means of transportation to and from the college or job, well, that's a big problem. Nondrivers have trouble getting to work, classes, doctor's appointments, the grocery store, and recreational activities. Of great importance is that it can be *socially isolating* to be a nondriver.

Place Driving Goals in the IEP

One study indicated that actually having driving goals inserted in a teen's Individualized Education Plan (IEP) in high school was a predictor of driving status.[11] The study noted the majority of teens with ASD do not have driving goals in their IEPs and suggested this as an area of improvement we could all shoot for. When I discuss driving goals with the parents of my patients, I often hear that they just *assumed* their child would never drive. It may turn out that way, but you are *guaranteeing* it if you never do anything about it. Even if your child just audits the driver's ed class and rides along in the car as a passenger, she will be savvier about traffic and transportation as a result.

This same study should ease your fears about getting your teen behind the wheel: Only 12 percent of teens with ASD were reported to have gotten a ticket or been involved in an accident. Compare that to 31 percent of all teens who have gotten a ticket and 22 percent who have been in a crash. Turns out that we autism parents are more restrictive with the driving privileges, and our teens like to follow rules—and that's a good thing.

Indicators of functional status such as being in a mainstream classroom and planning to go to college and have a job increased the odds of being a driver, too.[12] The take-home message is to assume that your soon-to-be adult will drive, go to college, and have a career, and then plan accordingly. Talk the talk, or the walk will never happen. Aiming high never hurt anyone.

Get a Developmental Optometry Exam

As you saw in Chapter 1, individuals on the spectrum may not integrate and coordinate the visual input from both eyes correctly, so they may have problems with depth perception and coordination until it is corrected. Don't declare defeat on the learning to drive project until visual function has been checked out. In fact, get this developmental optometry exam first.

Get Oral Hygiene Under Control

Oral hygiene is of utmost importance for adult health. Several studies show children with autism have poorer oral hygiene and dental health than their neurotypical peers. I know, I know, your child cannot stand to have his teeth brushed and flossing is out of the question. That's why it's common for those with overwhelming sensory issues to be sedated for dental cleaning and procedures.

A fair number of my adult patients simply reply "no" when I ask if they brush or floss, which of course sets them up for gum disease and loss of teeth. That's why I have them use xylitol and probiotic oral care products at the very least. If they have to have sedation dentistry, let's try to prevent as many reasons for it as we can. Don't just throw up your hands and claim helplessness; this area of healthcare is important enough to fight for. Consult with a feeding specialist who may be able to help your son or daughter learn to tolerate the sensations associated with brushing and flossing.

Having good oral health contributes to overall health. Check out the dental hygiene tips in Week 48 of the Chapter 9 Online Action Plan to ensure maximum health and independence for your adult son or daughter.

Changing the Standards of Care

It will take years of trial and error for the standards of medical care for those on the autism spectrum to develop and change. Table 8-1 shows us what we know so far.

MINIMUM BASIC CATEGORIES FOR HEALTH ASSESSMENT
- ✓ GI dysfunction
- ✓ Microbial imbalance
- ✓ Immune dysfunction
- ✓ Neuroinflammation
- ✓ Oxidative stress
- ✓ Nutritional deficiencies
- ✓ Developmental optometry evaluation
- ✓ Mental health screening for anxiety, depression, and mood disorders

Changing the standards of care for those with ASD

Not Really Working	Better
Short medical appointments of 15–30 minutes	Scheduling 1–2 hours for initial intake, 1 hour for follow-up appointments
Giving prescriptions for constipation and poor sleep	Assessing and correcting underlying medical conditions of ASD that cause constipation and poor sleep
Giving antipsychotics for irritability, self-injuring, and aggression	Assessing and correcting underlying medical and environmental conditions that cause irritability, self-injuring, and aggression
Relying solely on prescriptions whose side effects contribute to symptoms patient already struggles with	Using natural supplements and therapies with fewer side effects and using prescriptions sparingly
The current disease-based model of healthcare (i.e., responding only when something is wrong)	A proactive preventive health-based model where our efforts are spent restoring, supporting, and maintaining vibrant health

Table 8-1

In addition to the basic health assessments, have a plan for aggression where medication is the last, not the first, thing we reach for. Irritability, self-injuring, poor sleep patterns and aggression should be evaluated in light of:

☐ Hidden pain and discomfort, especially in the GI tract
☐ Overstimulation by a noisy environment
☐ Frustration at not being able to communicate
☐ Mood disorders
☐ Side effects of medications and polypharmacy
☐ Gluten intolerance
☐ Food allergies and sensitivities

Basic needs should be met for optimal function and independence, dignity, and quality of life. These basics include:

- ☐ A form of communication that the adult and everyone around him is comfortable using
- ☐ Assistive communication devices, if applicable, with effective training for family members and all caregivers

> ON AUTISM.COM: "Keys to Successful Independent Living, Employment, and a Good Social Life for Individuals with Autism and Asperger's" by Temple Grandin

- ☐ Counseling for social skills and building relationships
- ☐ Social opportunities and inclusion in the community
- ☐ Driving goals in the young adult's high school IEP and transition plan
- ☐ A driver's license, if appropriate, or access to transportation
- ☐ Opportunity for college or vocational training
- ☐ Meaningful employment that the ASD adult enjoys and looks forward to
- ☐ A "medical home" for all medical records and coordination of care
- ☐ Basic GI and Immune Support Protocols
- ☐ Long-term Health Maintenance Protocols that adults with ASD can follow themselves, if possible
- ☐ Developmental optometry evaluation
- ☐ Excellent oral care, including probiotic and xylitol oral care products
- ☐ Occupational therapy and a sensory diet for managing sensory overload
- ☐ Management of anxiety
- ☐ Consideration given to natural supplements for residents on the autism spectrum, since so many of the helpful prescriptions have side effects that may amplify and worsen constipation, nausea, anxiety, and sleep problems

Not every adult in a group home has a parent still actively involved in his life. By being an activist and educating the facility's staff about the medical challenges of ASD, and how addressing them correctly can improve health, mood, sleep, language, and function, you will also be an advocate for those adults with ASD who have no one to speak for them.

Give your adult sons or daughters their best chance for an independent life by assessing and addressing the health challenges of the autism spectrum, no matter what their living arrangement. They will be healthier, happier, and cognitively at their best if you do.

9

A Sample Year of the Basic GI Support Protocol

Are you ready to get started, but still not quite sure how to proceed? This chapter gives you a month-by-month template for a year of the Basic GI Support Protocol including getting started, how to take enzyme holidays, what an antimicrobial (AM) rotation might look like over twelve months, and how to transition to an AM Maintenance Schedule. Think of it as "tech support."

All of these sample weeks and months are flexible and can be customized to suit your family. What I show are the basic "Go" schedules for enzymes, probiotics, and antimicrobials, but you can always substitute the variations of the schedules if your child needs to do the protocols a little differently. Don't forget, *The Un-Prescription for Autism* app found on the App Store will schedule the protocols for you, and the basic version is free, of course.

A Special Treat Just for You: The Online Action Plan

I've created some really fun bonus content for you: The *Online* Action Plan! You won't believe what a huge stash of ideas and resources this is. I've packed a virtual calendar with fifty-two weeks of information and tips on everything from travel and camps to service animals and Minecraft. I give you my best tips for calming, sleep, constipation, and anxiety, and share strategies for mixing supplements with food and which supplements to use for language support, inflammation, oxidative stress, and mitochondrial support. It is an amazing treasure trove of information and inspiration to keep you going for a full year.

You'll find all of my protocols there: Antibiotic Support, Xylitol Support, ideas to cool down inflammation and oxidative stress, the Fab Five, and more.

Let's get started! Here are the twelve monthly templates. We start the Basic GI Support Protocol with just the enzymes at first, just like I would if you came to my center. Be sure to check in with the Chapter 9 Online Action Plan each week for support tips.

Find the Online Action Plan at
www.amacombooks.org/go/AutismActionPlan.

❋ MONTH 1

SUNDAY	MONDAY	TUESDAY	WEDNESDAY	THURSDAY	FRIDAY	SATURDAY
Digestive Enzymes with DPP-IV With one meal per day (DE x 1)	DE x 1	DE x 1	DE x 1	DE x 1	DE x 1	DE x 1
Digestive Enzymes with DPP-IV With two meals per day (DE x 2)	DE x 2	DE x 2	DE x 2	DE x 2	DE x 2	DE x 2
Digestive Enzymes with DPP-IV With three meals per day (DE x 3)	DE x 3	DE x 3	DE x 3	DE x 3	DE x 3	DE x 3
Digestive Enzymes with DPP-IV With every meal & snack (DE x all)	DE x all	DE x all	DE x all	DE x all	DE x all	DE x all

Month 1: We are slowly introducing the enzymes over four weeks for the "Go" Schedule.

❀ MONTH 2

SUNDAY	MONDAY	TUESDAY	WEDNESDAY	THURSDAY	FRIDAY	SATURDAY
DE x all 1/2 capsule probiotic	DE x all	DE x all 1/2 capsule probiotic	DE x all	DE x all 1/2 capsule probiotic	DE x all	DE x all 1/2 capsule probiotic
DE x all 1 capsule probiotic	DE x all Probiotic	DE x all Probiotic	DE x all Probiotic	DE x all Probiotic	DE x all Probiotic	DE x all Probiotic
DE x all Probiotic 1.5 billion CFUs Sac B	DE x all Probiotic	DE x all Probiotic 1.5 billion CFUs Sac b	DE x all Probiotic	DE x all Probiotic 1.5 billion CFUs Sac b	DE x all Probiotic	DE x all Probiotic 1.5 billion CFUs Sac b
DE x all Probiotic 3 billion CFUs Sac B (1 SB)	DE x all Probiotic 1 SB	DE x all Probiotic 1 SB	DE x all Probiotic 1 SB	DE x all Probiotic 1 SB	DE x all Probiotic 1 SB	DE x all Probiotic 1 SB

Month 2: We are baby-stepping in the probiotics over two weeks, and then taking two more weeks to introduce Sac b.

MONTH 3 ✿

SUNDAY	MONDAY	TUESDAY	WEDNESDAY	THURSDAY	FRIDAY	SATURDAY
DE x all Probiotic 1 SB	DE x all Probiotic 1 SB	DE x all Probiotic 1 SB	DE x all Probiotic 1 SB	DE x all Probiotic 1 SB	DE x all Probiotic 1 SB	DE x all Probiotic 1 SB
DE x all Probiotic 1 SB	DE x all Probiotic 1 SB	DE x all Probiotic 1 SB	DE x all Probiotic 1 SB	DE x all Probiotic 1 SB	DE x all Probiotic 1 SB	DE x all Probiotic 1 SB
DE x all Probiotic AM#1	DE x all Probiotic AM#1	DE x all Probiotic AM#1	DE x all Probiotic AM#1	DE x all Probiotic AM#1	DE x all Probiotic AM#1	DE x all Probiotic AM#1
DE x all Probiotic AM#2	DE x all Probiotic AM#2	DE x all Probiotic AM#2	DE x all Probiotic AM#2	DE x all Probiotic AM#2	DE x all Probiotic AM#2	DE x all Probiotic AM#2

Month 3: We continue with Sac b for two more weeks, then we begin to rotate the AMs—a different one each week.

❁ MONTH 4

SUNDAY	MONDAY	TUESDAY	WEDNESDAY	THURSDAY	FRIDAY	SATURDAY
DE x all Probiotic AM#3	DE x all Probiotic AM#3	DE x all Probiotic AM#3	DE x all Probiotic AM#3	DE x all Probiotic AM#3	DE x all Probiotic AM#3	DE x all Probiotic AM#3
DE x all Probiotic AM#1	DE x all Probiotic AM#1	DE x all Probiotic AM#1	DE x all Probiotic AM#1	DE x all Probiotic AM#1	DE x all Probiotic AM#1	DE x all Probiotic AM#1
DE x all Probiotic AM#2	DE x all Probiotic AM#2	DE x all Probiotic AM#2	DE x all Probiotic AM#2	DE x all Probiotic AM#2	DE x all Probiotic AM#2	DE x all Probiotic AM#2
DE x all Probiotic AM#3	DE x all Probiotic AM#3	DE x all Probiotic AM#3	DE x all Probiotic AM#3	DE x all Probiotic AM#3	DE x all Probiotic AM#3	DE x all Probiotic AM#3

Month 4: Just continue to give digestive enzymes with DPP-IV with every meal and snack, a probiotic, and a different AM each week.

MONTH 5 ✿
✿

SUNDAY	MONDAY	TUESDAY	WEDNESDAY	THURSDAY	FRIDAY	SATURDAY
DE x all Probiotic Sac b (I SB)	DE x all Probiotic 1 SB	DE x all Probiotic 1 SB	DE x all Probiotic 1 SB	DE x all Probiotic 1 SB	DE x all Probiotic 1 SB	DE x all Probiotic 1 SB
DE x all Probiotic AM#1	DE x all Probiotic AM#1	DE x all Probiotic AM#1	DE x all Probiotic AM#1	DE x all Probiotic AM#1	DE x all Probiotic AM#1	DE x all Probiotic AM#1
DE x all Probiotic AM#2	DE x all Probiotic AM#2	DE x all Probiotic AM#2	DE x all Probiotic AM#2	DE x all Probiotic AM#2	DE x all Probiotic AM#2	DE x all Probiotic AM#2
DE x all Probiotic AM#3	DE x all Probiotic AM#3	DE x all Probiotic AM#3	DE x all Probiotic AM#3	DE x all Probiotic AM#3	DE x all Probiotic AM#3	DE x all Probiotic AM#3

Month 5: Steady as she goes—enzymes with everything, daily probiotics, and a weekly AM rotation.

MONTH 6

❀ Enzyme Holiday—Go GFCF Instead

SUNDAY	MONDAY	TUESDAY	WEDNESDAY	THURSDAY	FRIDAY	SATURDAY
GFCF	GFCF	GFCF	GFCF	GFCF	GFCF	GFCF
Probiotic	Probiotic	Probiotic	Probiotic	Probiotic	Probiotic	Probiotic
Sac b (I SB)	1 SB	1 SB	1 SB	1 SB	1 SB	1 SB
GFCF	GFCF	GFCF	GFCF	GFCF	GFCF	GFCF
Probiotic	Probiotic	Probiotic	Probiotic	Probiotic	Probiotic	Probiotic
AM#4	AM#4	AM#4	AM#4	AM#4	AM#4	AM#4
GFCF	GFCF	GFCF	GFCF	GFCF	GFCF	GFCF
Probiotic	Probiotic	Probiotic	Probiotic	Probiotic	Probiotic	Probiotic
AM#5	AM#5	AM#5	AM#5	AM#5	AM#5	AM#5
GFCF	GFCF	GFCF	GFCF	GFCF	GFCF	GFCF
Probiotic	Probiotic	Probiotic	Probiotic	Probiotic	Probiotic	Probiotic
AM#6	AM#6	AM#6	AM#6	AM#6	AM#6	AM#6

Month 6: Take an Enzyme Holiday. We are giving the enzymes a rest (to prevent developing a sensitivity), but only if you can manage to go GFCF. If you cannot pull off the GFCF diet, just keep using the enzymes with every meal, snack, and glass of milk.

I'm also branching out on the AM Rotation and adding a few new ones.

MONTH 7

SUNDAY	MONDAY	TUESDAY	WEDNESDAY	THURSDAY	FRIDAY	SATURDAY
DE x all	DE x all	DE x all	DE x all	DE x all	DE x all	DE x all
Probiotic	Probiotic	Probiotic	Probiotic	Probiotic	Probiotic	Probiotic
Sac b (l SB)	1 SB	1 SB	1 SB	1 SB	1 SB	1 SB
DE x all	DE x all	DE x all	DE x all	DE x all	DE x all	DE x all
Probiotic	Probiotic	Probiotic	Probiotic	Probiotic	Probiotic	Probiotic
AM#4	AM#4	AM#4	AM#4	AM#4	AM#4	AM#4
DE x all	DE x all	DE x all	DE x all	DE x all	DE x all	DE x all
Probiotic	Probiotic	Probiotic	Probiotic	Probiotic	Probiotic	Probiotic
AM#5	AM#5	AM#5	AM#5	AM#5	AM#5	AM#5
DE x all	DE x all	DE x all	DE x all	DE x all	DE x all	DE x all
Probiotic	Probiotic	Probiotic	Probiotic	Probiotic	Probiotic	Probiotic
AM#6	AM#6	AM#6	AM#6	AM#6	AM#6	AM#6

Month 7: Steady as she goes; you are just coasting this month. Check in with the Chapter 9 Online Action Plan for more great ideas!

212 | How—Taking Action

❀ MONTH 8

SUNDAY	MONDAY	TUESDAY	WEDNESDAY	THURSDAY	FRIDAY	SATURDAY
DE x all	DE x all	DE x all	DE x all	DE x all	DE x all	DE x all
Probiotic	Probiotic	Probiotic	Probiotic	Probiotic	Probiotic	Probiotic
Sac b (I SB)	1 SB	1 SB	1 SB	1 SB	1 SB	1 SB
DE x all	DE x all	DE x all	DE x all	DE x all	DE x all	DE x all
Probiotic	Probiotic	Probiotic	Probiotic	Probiotic	Probiotic	Probiotic
AM#7	AM#7	AM#7	AM#7	AM#7	AM#7	AM#7
DE x all	DE x all	DE x all	DE x all	DE x all	DE x all	DE x all
Probiotic	Probiotic	Probiotic	Probiotic	Probiotic	Probiotic	Probiotic
AM#8	AM#8	AM#8	AM#8	AM#8	AM#8	AM#8
DE x all	DE x all	DE x all	DE x all	DE x all	DE x all	DE x all
Probiotic	Probiotic	Probiotic	Probiotic	Probiotic	Probiotic	Probiotic
AM#9	AM#9	AM#9	AM#9	AM#9	AM#9	AM#9

Month 8: You're an old hand at this, and everything is much easier by now, so look for more fun ideas in the Chapter 9 Online Action Plan!

MONTH 9
Tapering off to an AM Maintenance Schedule ✳

SUNDAY	MONDAY	TUESDAY	WEDNESDAY	THURSDAY	✳ FRIDAY	SATURDAY
DE x all Probiotic Sac b (I SB)	DE x all Probiotic	DE x all Probiotic 1 SB	DE x all Probiotic	DE x all Probiotic 1 SB	DE x all Probiotic	DE x all Probiotic 1 SB
DE x all Probiotic AM#1	DE x all Probiotic	DE x all Probiotic AM#1	DE x all Probiotic	DE x all Probiotic AM#1	DE x all Probiotic	DE x all Probiotic AM#1
DE x all Probiotic AM#2	DE x all Probiotic	DE x all Probiotic AM#2	DE x all Probiotic	DE x all Probiotic AM#2	DE x all Probiotic	DE x all Probiotic AM#2
DE x all Probiotic AM#3	DE x all Probiotic	DE x all Probiotic AM#3	DE x all Probiotic	DE x all Probiotic AM#3	DE x all Probiotic	DE x all Probiotic AM#3

Month 9: Your child may or may not be ready to taper the AMs to a Maintenance Schedule, but this is just an example of how to do it when you are ready. Basically we're just using AMs every other day while continuing to maintain a weekly rotation. (If you try this and your child's GI symptoms return, go back to using the AMs daily and try again some other time.)

❋ MONTH 10

SUNDAY	MONDAY	TUESDAY	WEDNESDAY	THURSDAY	FRIDAY	SATURDAY
DE x all Probiotic Sac b (I SB)	DE x all Probiotic	DE x all Probiotic 1 SB	DE x all Probiotic	DE x all Probiotic 1 SB	DE x all Probiotic	DE x all Probiotic 1 SB
DE x all Probiotic AM#4	DE x all Probiotic	DE x all Probiotic AM#4	DE x all Probiotic	DE x all Probiotic AM#4	DE x all Probiotic	DE x all Probiotic AM#4
DE x all Probiotic AM#5	DE x all Probiotic	DE x all Probiotic AM#5	DE x all Probiotic	DE x all Probiotic AM#5	DE x all Probiotic	DE x all Probiotic AM#5
DE x all Probiotic AM#6	DE x all Probiotic	DE x all Probiotic AM#6	DE x all Probiotic	DE x all Probiotic AM#6	DE x all Probiotic	DE x all Probiotic AM#6

Month 10: Continue to use the AMs every other day for another month as you taper to a Maintenance Schedule.

MONTH 11

Cutting back to a Weekend AM Maintenance Schedule

SUNDAY	MONDAY	TUESDAY	WEDNESDAY	THURSDAY	FRIDAY	SATURDAY
DE x all Probiotic	DE x all Probiotic	DE x all Probiotic	DE x all Probiotic	DE x all Probiotic	DE x all Probiotic AM Blend #1	DE x all Probiotic AM Blend #1
DE x all Probiotic	DE x all Probiotic	DE x all Probiotic	DE x all Probiotic	DE x all Probiotic	DE x all Probiotic AM Blend #2	DE x all Probiotic AM Blend #2
DE x all Probiotic	DE x all Probiotic	DE x all Probiotic	DE x all Probiotic	DE x all Probiotic	DE x all Probiotic AM Blend #1	DE x all Probiotic AM Blend #1
DE x all Probiotic	DE x all Probiotic	DE x all Probiotic	DE x all Probiotic	DE x all Probiotic	DE x all Probiotic AM Blend #2	DE x all Probiotic AM Blend #2

Month 11: If you have successfully been able to use the AMs every other day for two months, you can try cutting back now to just two days a week on the weekends. I suggest that you use Friday and Saturday for your two weekend days, as this will let the bowels get back to normal on Sunday and reduce embarrassing gas at school on Monday. (If you try this and your child's GI symptoms return, go back to using the AMs every other day and try again some other time.)

MONTH 12
❀ Enzyme Holiday—Go GFCF Instead
❀

SUNDAY	MONDAY	TUESDAY	WEDNESDAY	THURSDAY	FRIDAY	SATURDAY
GFCF Probiotic	GFCF Probiotic	GFCF Probiotic	GFCF Probiotic	GFCF Probiotic	GFCF Probiotic AM Blend #1	GFCF Probiotic AM Blend #2
GFCF Probiotic	GFCF Probiotic	GFCF Probiotic	GFCF Probiotic	GFCF Probiotic	GFCF Probiotic AM Blend #1	GFCF Probiotic AM Blend #2
GFCF Probiotic	GFCF Probiotic	GFCF Probiotic	GFCF Probiotic	GFCF Probiotic	GFCF Probiotic AM Blend #1	GFCF Probiotic AM Blend #2
GFCF Probiotic	GFCF Probiotic	GFCF Probiotic	GFCF Probiotic	GFCF Probiotic	GFCF Probiotic AM Blend #1	GFCF Probiotic AM Blend #2

Month 12: Continue to use the AMs two days a week for another month as you taper to a Maintenance Schedule. The most I usually cut back to is every other weekend. I suggest another enzyme holiday if you can manage to go GFCF this month. If not, keep using the enzymes.

You are doing this! Remember to visit the Chapter 9 Online Action Plan each week—it is packed with a year of ideas, tips, and content to keep you going on your quest for a vibrant life on the autism spectrum. Read ahead to Chapter 10 so you can avoid the mistakes I've made along the way.

10

Oops, My Bad!:
How to Prevent and Handle Setbacks

Experience is simply the name we give our mistakes.
Oscar Wilde

When we were seeking help for our young sons, my husband and I went to some of the finest doctors in the country. The protocols were elaborate and usually involved up to fifteen or twenty different supplements daily. Invariably, we made mistakes. It seemed we took three steps forward and then two steps backward. The unexpected setbacks were disheartening.

You can avoid much of the distress my husband and I experienced at the beginning of our journey back to health with autism, all those years ago, by learning from my experiences and those of my patients. I want you to skip that sense of deep discouragement that makes you want to give up—or at least know how to handle it. When setbacks happen I want you to know it's perfectly acceptable to "circle the wagons and hunker down" for a while; just keep the essentials going while you catch your breath and get back your sense of direction.

These mistakes and setbacks are anything that sabotages your child's health plan, intentionally or accidently. Most are done without thinking, just innocent mistakes, but can have a long-lasting negative impact on your child's progress and health. The homes with an autistic child are often chaotic, and despite parents' best intentions, there are misunderstandings that must be tracked down and cleared up.

I've created some resources to help you implement my protocols with confidence and the least number of mistakes possible. On my website, www. LoveAutismHealth.com, I have a fun game called "Fact or Fart?" that helps you playfully explore FAQs and where things can go wrong. I also have an app named The Un-Prescription for Autism, which can be found on the App Store.

The following compilations are made from real discussions that I've had with patients' families. I hope they will help you avoid the same mistakes. I've created a few humorous categories like Magical Thinking, Head Slaps, the Hall of Shame, and "Oh Nos!" in an effort to get a few laughs. I offer them *humbly*, as I made many of the same mistakes early on in my own son's journey.

 Enzyme Errors

- *Not giving the enzymes time to work.* In their eagerness to help their child, many autism parents race through various interventions, barely giving them time to work before careening off to the next new therapy or intervention. (I call this Shiny Object Syndrome.) The enzyme plan takes time to work, and if you try it for a few days or a week and then abandon it, you will probably miss one of the biggest sources of improvement for your child. Relax, take a deep breath, and give this one a good six to eight weeks before moving on.

  ○ *Variation 1:* "Oh, we tried it for a few days and didn't see anything, so we stopped. . . ."

  ○ *Variation 2:* "We tried it for a week or two and didn't really see much change." If you were only giving the enzymes with a meal or two a day, for a few days, it makes sense that you didn't see anything yet. You just didn't do it long enough. Gluten is thought to take weeks to leave the body, so get back in there and give it a good go—100 percent—for at least eight weeks. This could be hugely beneficial for your child, so why would you give it a lukewarm effort for a few days?

  ○ *Variation 3:* "We tried it for a few days but it made him worse, so we stopped." Some parents drop the enzyme method at the first hint of irritability or grouchiness in their child. Grouchiness is actually a *good* sign; it likely means there is an opioid withdrawal going on and the protocol is working. You should redouble your efforts, not abandon them!

- Did you do the enzymes *100 percent strictly*? Answers:

  ○ *Variation 1:* "He gets them once a day."

  ○ *Variation 2:* "Well, not really . . . but he got them most of the time."

  ○ *Variation 3:* "He eats breakfast and lunch at school without enzymes, and we just give them at dinner at home, even on the weekends."

  ○ *Variation 4:* The parents tell me their child is taking them with every meal and snack, expecting me not to notice that a 180-capsule bottle "lasted" three or four months. These are not magic beans; they should be taken with every meal and snack for eight to twelve weeks before you can tell yourself that you gave them a good go.

- *Not using enough enzymes.* The dose of the enzymes is based on *the size of the meal*, not your child's age or weight. The more food that is eaten at a meal, the more enzymes are required in the dose. My favorite: Parents tell me the enzymes aren't working for their son, who happens to be six feet tall and weighs 225 pounds. I discover he is taking only one capsule of enzymes with his large, man-size meals. That one capsule doesn't have a chance of reaching every opioid peptide from his three plates of macaroni and cheese. Parents say, "He's still constipated, but that's his normal." Snacks and smaller meals count. Proper dosage counts.

- *How do you know the right dose?* You will know you are at the correct dose when your child is no longer constipated and is having daily bowel movements.

- *Thinking your child doesn't have to try the enzymes* because he doesn't have constipation, diarrhea, or any other GI symptoms. (Remember, many children on the spectrum don't make enough of their own digestive enzymes.)

- *Using an enzyme formulation that does not contain DPP-IV.* This may aid digestion, but it will not break down opioid neuropeptides. Papaya alone doesn't cut it.

- *Going too fast.* Whoa!

- *Going so slowly that you don't notice anything and quit.* I have a fair number of families who started the enzyme protocol, thought they weren't seeing any improvements, and quit, only to watch an explosive regression occur, which convinced them to start back up.

 Hoopla at Home

- Your child sneaks down at night and eats food without the enzymes. You may have to lock the cabinets and fridge or make the whole house GFCF.

- You don't give the enzymes with snacks.

- You thought a little milk or wheat without enzymes wouldn't hurt. For some children, molecules matter.

- *Oh No!* You ran out of enzymes! Be sure to order online ahead of time, or brace yourself for a spike in difficult behaviors. Keep an extra bottle in the freezer as a backup.

- *Head Slap!* You aren't giving the enzymes with glasses of milk.

> *"Oh, does that count?*
> *I thought it was just with solid food."*

  - *Variation 1:* Thinking raw or organic milk doesn't count.

  - *Variation 2:* Thinking chocolate milk doesn't count.

  - *Variation 3:* Thinking strawberry milk doesn't count.

  - *Variation 4:* Thinking goat's milk doesn't count.

  - *Variation 5:* Thinking 2 percent milk doesn't count.

- Your child is using gluten-based play doughs. The gluten is *absorbed through the skin* and the enzymes cannot help you here. Just switch to gluten-free play clays; they are available commercially and there are recipes on the Internet. (See Week 28 in the Chapter 9 Online Action Plan.)

- Your child is helping you bake, which poses the same risks. Flour can float through the air, be inhaled, or settle on kitchen surfaces and even your child's skin.

- You are starting, stopping, or changing more than one medicine or supplement at a time.

- Your child begins bouncing off the walls after starting a new supplement. Hyperactivity is common especially with the B vitamins, methyl B12 shots, cod liver oil, or hyperbaric oxygen therapy (HBOT). Start over, use a fraction of the dose, and try gradually building back up to the target dose. For HBOT, hyperactivity may occur in about 30 percent of children and will usually resolve after ten to twelve sessions. Just hang on.

- You stopped everything when your child got sick. Of course, everything must be stopped if he's throwing up, but for run-of-the-mill coughs and colds, try to keep the enzymes and probiotics on board. If he cannot take the enzymes, try to go GFCF until he can. It's okay to stop antimicrobials and other supplements until he feels better.

- You're giving activated charcoal along with your child's other supplements. Some doctors give activated charcoal to absorb microbial die-off products. The absorption powers of charcoal are amazing; it can absorb a deadly dose of narcotics in the case of a drug overdose, and it can absorb the expensive supplements you buy for your child. Give charcoal either two hours before or two hours after other supplements and prescriptions.

- You got complacent once your child felt better and became inconsistent with the protocols. Remember the story of my son at the dude ranch in Chapter 1? Stay vigilant and consistent.

- You are using stickers and envelopes with adhesive that contains gluten. Place stickers on your child's clothing, not her skin, and don't let her lick envelopes.

- You are wearing perfume and using scented personal care products. I know—they smell so good, how could it bother him? (But it does.) Be sure to use only fragrance-free and toxin-free laundry and cleaning supplies.

- *Oh No!* Get rid of artificially scented plug-ins, "tart warmers," candles, incense, and the like. Use real essential oils instead. Some children cannot tolerate even the natural ones. (Surprisingly, it's usually husbands who are passionate about the room fragrances!)

- You have a severely underweight child and the doctor wants to take away gluten, casein, and twenty-three foods from the IgG test. Remember Ava from Chapter 1? A child has to eat. Unless it's a true allergy, give these foods back and use the enzymes. Food sensitivities can be addressed at a later point in the Action Plan when your child's health is more stable.

- You don't have a Maintenance Plan. One pediatrician confided that some of her patients say that my methods seem to "wear off" after a year or two, and the previous gains fade away. These were patients without a Maintenance Plan. Sure, there can be regressions, but good health doesn't just "wear off." Don't expect to correct and support lifelong health challenges for a few months or even a few years and have the health gains last indefinitely. Some children may keep their gains, but for the majority, a Maintenance Plan is a must.

- Your child is taking antibiotics without an Antibiotic Support Protocol. See Week 6 in the Chapter 9 Online Action Plan.

- A major life event—divorce, death, moving—sidetracks your good health plan. It's okay to "circle your wagons," maintain *just the basics* like enzymes and probiotics, and then pick up again when life settles down. Stopping everything completely is usually a disaster.

- *Hall of Shame.* When your spouse eats forbidden foods in front of your child and makes him cry.

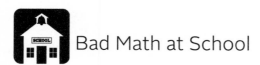 Bad Math at School

- *Head Slap!* At the follow-up visit, I review how and when the child is receiving enzymes, how consistently he gets them, and how many enzymes are given. Parents will insist they are doing everything exactly as specified. Then I ask, "Is Johnny getting the enzymes at school?" They pause, look at each other in surprise, then turn to me and say, "Is he supposed to?" or "Do those meals count?" Every meal and snack means *every meal and snack*, no matter where it is being consumed.

Phrase of the Day: "Does that count?"

- Don't ask the school to give anything other than the enzymes. It's just too complicated, and the other supplements can be given with breakfast, dinner, or after school.

- Your school won't give the enzymes. What then? You have a few options: Pack your child's lunch and either make it GFCF, so no enzymes are needed, or prepare food with the enzymes mixed in. Nut butters and frozen apple sauce are ideal food choices because they don't activate the enzymes. Or you can ask your pediatrician to order the GFCF diet at school.

- The cafeteria staff thinks Cheerios, pudding, and 2 percent milk are GFCF. One school was so kind and went to the effort of making homemade gluten-free rolls for one student. Detective work revealed they switched from "wheat flour" to "white flour," not understanding that white flour *is* wheat flour. Graciously direct them to the "Directory of Website" at GFCFDiet.com for a clickable list of acceptable and unacceptable foods. It's a great resource and teaching tool.

- Your child is trading snacks with classmates. As long as there have been schools, kids have traded lunch items and snacks. If your child is sensitive or allergic to various foods, or on the Feingold diet, you may have to ask if your child can sit with a teacher or an aide at lunch and block all trading. (Sorry, teachers and aides, it's that important!) Otherwise, as long as enzymes are on board, occasional trading of wheat and dairy-based snacks shouldn't hurt anything.

- Don't make an enzyme drink and expect it to last all day. Liquids activate the enzymes. Putting ice into the drink slows down and helps preserve the enzyme activity, but it cannot last forever. Four hours is the *maximum* you can count on when the drink is kept icy cold.

- Don't give the enzymes at the wrong time. Some well-meaning parents will have the child drink the enzyme drink right at the school bus stop and then eat breakfast at school an hour later. Based on the still-present constipation, fog, and behavior issues that I see in the child on the follow-up visit, I find this is not effective and can only assume the enzymes have passed through the stomach and into the intestinal tract before the child is able to get to breakfast. As for lunch, parents were just letting that meal go and then hoping that giving an enzyme as soon as he got home from school would do the job. (You can get away with it if your child is only on the bus for a very short ride, attends a half-day program, and eats lunch last thing before getting on the bus home.)

- School supplies such as paste, glue, stickers, markers, and play clays should all be gluten-free and toxin-free.

- Turnover of cafeteria staff is a problem. Revisit the cafeteria staff every year and make sure they are aware of your child's needs.

- The school may have made changes that you are unaware of. All you know is your child is upset, and the teacher is suggesting more medication for the behaviors. Ask questions before you medicate. It could be your child is reacting to a new student, a new aide or bus driver, an air freshener, forgotten enzymes . . . get your Sherlock on!

- Schools sometimes have surprise treats that are loaded with gluten and casein. Make sure the teacher knows to give enzymes with them. If your school cannot give the enzymes, ask the cafeteria to store some frozen GFCF treats for your child for just such occasions.

 Daycare Dang-Its

- *Head Slap!* "Oh, do meals and snacks at daycare and after-school programs count?"

Breaking Bad at Grandma's House

Many of you tell me that your parents watch your child after school. The grandparents' house is like the gingerbread house in Hansel and Gretel: a magical place loaded with hidden pitfalls.

- I've known a lot of grandparents who do not hesitate to sabotage a GFCF diet protocol. They are of a generation that is convinced a child who does not get a glass of milk will have some sort of nutritional damage and his growth will be stunted. You will have to convince them how important the enzymes are each and every time. Share this book with them.

- My favorite solution? One of my dads, a single father, could not get his parents to give his son the enzymes when they gave him forbidden foods such as milk and cookies. When he came to pick his son up one Friday evening after work, he could tell his son was wild and out of control again. He paused to take in the scene, then called out he would see them on Monday, closed the door, and drove off. The grandparents got to experience firsthand what a difference enzymes can make, and it never happened again.

- *Magical Thinking:*

  ○ *Variation 1:* "A cookie can't hurt!"

  ○ *Variation 2:* Anything in a drive-through doesn't count.

  ○ *Variation 3:* "Well, it was just some chicken nuggets." For some reason this one seems to be a grandparent thing. However, using the digestive enzymes removes any argument they may have. They can stop at the drive-through window and get the chicken nuggets, *with* a carton of milk, and still stay on track by using the enzymes.

- Keep a second set of supplements at the grandparents' house if you can.

- If you aren't sure if the grandparents are giving the supplements, use weekly pill organizers or one of those obnoxiously large Overnight Boards you learned to make in Chapter 2, so you can track at a glance if today's supplements were used.

Scary Stuff at the Ex's House

Communication with ex-spouses can be tricky and isn't always friendly.

- A parent will often say, "We don't send the enzymes to my ex-spouse's house." ("Oh, does that count?")

- Purchase an extra set of supplements just for the ex's house. It's less tricky than sending bottles back and forth between the two houses.

- Sometimes you just don't know if the ex is really giving the supplements like he or she should. Send along a transparent weekly pill organizer or an Overnight Board, and any skipped doses will be obvious at a glance.

- Pare it down to just the basics for the other house. If you can get just the enzymes with every meal and snack, consider it a victory. It won't kill your child to go without probiotics or essential fatty acids every other weekend.

 Restaurant Follies

- Your child grabs the bread basket before you can say "Bob's your uncle!"

- You forgot to bring enzymes. Try to order a GFCF meal in that case.

- Your server was uninformed about the ingredients and served your child a food she is sensitive to. Communicate clearly with waitstaff or ask to speak with the chef before food is prepared.

- Many restaurant staff do not understand what gluten or casein is. Except at Disney. Disney always knows. I want to marry them.

- Whatever was cooked on the grill before your food may have contained breading or cheese. As long as you didn't forget the enzymes, no problem.

- Different line cooks do their own thing, and just because a certain restaurant dish used to be GFCF or Feingold compliant doesn't mean it still is. Restaurants may change the ingredients. Always use the enzymes when eating out.

- Soy sauce is loaded with gluten. Bring your own GF soy sauce if your child is sensitive to gluten.

 # Drive-Through Dillies

- *Magical Thinking:* Anything gotten in a drive-through doesn't count!

- Don't have enzymes on you? Take a different way home and don't drive by the fast-food place.

- Food stays in the stomach for an hour and a half or more. Get the food if you have to, drive straight home, and immediately give an enzyme drink. (That way you won't have to wait another thirty minutes for the capsule to dissolve in the stomach.)

 # Party Poopers

- There is always ice cream, cake, and pizza at birthday parties, and special dinners always include dishes and desserts loaded with gluten and casein. It's almost impossible to refuse your adorable child a piece of cake or slice of pizza, so be sure to tuck a baggie of enzymes in your pocket, or bring food that's acceptable to your child's special diet.

- Between a rock and a hard place: Forgot to bring enzymes or your own food? Here's a tip to minimize the consequences of eating the party goodies: If I had to pick something for my child to eat without the enzymes, I would choose ice cream over cake, and eat only the toppings off the pizza. Why? Because the casein found in the dairy products will leave the body within forty-eight to seventy-two hours, but the effects of gluten may linger for weeks and weeks. *When there's no good choice, choose the dairy.* (Unless your child is allergic, of course.)

- Always carry enzymes with you. Leave some in the car (they can actually withstand heat up to about 130° Fahrenheit), some at Grandma's, some at the ex's house, some at the school—you get the idea.

- Plan ahead and keep frozen treats in the freezer for impromptu gatherings.

 ## Travel Shenanigans

- *Magical Thinking:* Not doing your child's enzyme protocol while on vacation.

"Oh, does that count?"

- Keep supplements in the hotel room, not the hot car. Probiotics and herbals won't do well in the heat.

- Disney theme parks make it very easy to eat out with a child on a special diet. I was pleasantly surprised to discover the chefs know every ingredient of every dish and they are familiar with many special diets.

- Keep supplements and prescriptions in their original containers for airline, cruise, and foreign travel.

- Triple up on taking probiotics during travel, especially foreign travel.

 ## Tips for Anxiety-Free Sleepovers

- A first sleepover should be with family or friends who understand your child's needs.

- Instructions should be printed out on an at-a-glance sheet.

- If your child wants to eat out with the host family, provide a list of acceptable foods to make ordering at restaurants easy for your son or daughter.

- Don't expect the host family to prepare foods for any special diet your child is on. Send your own food over, and try to match the host's menu if you can. Sometimes I simply provided all the food and snacks for my child for the weekend, and friends were grateful for that effort.

- Your child may want to eat what the host family is eating. Here is where enzymes make it easy!

- Send just the enzymes and any prescriptions. I really didn't want friends to know how many different supplements Evan was on, and it wasn't really their job to give them correctly. If your child *cannot* go without any of his supplements, here is where the true beauty of the Overnight Board comes in handy. Friends could easily tell at a glance when to give Evan his pills, and could also tell if they had forgotten anything.

- Agree on a quiet area where your child can go to recharge if necessary.

 ## Spooky Stories Around the Campfire

- For some camps, you will only need to fill out a medication log and turn over your bottles to a competent camp nurse. For others, like the Boy Scouts, you will have to fill their own system of sealed daily "bubble" compartments with your child's medications and supplements. For less organized camp situations, I like to use a Travel Board because it's big and obnoxious and hard to forget. Make time to stop and talk with the camp director and nurse. See Week 26 in the Chapter 9 Online Action Plan for how to find a camp for your child.

- Don't assume a camp will accommodate your child's special diet—speak with the camp staff ahead of time. For example, my boys went to many Boy Scout camps that did not provide specialized meals for any reason. I always gave detailed written instructions for how enzymes were to be given and skipped the probiotics and antimicrobials for camps. It also took a bit of planning ahead for camp meals. I always brought a week's worth of GFCF meals for my son at Boy Scout camps, labeled as to what the food was (spaghetti and meatballs, for example) and which meal it was for. The camp cooks were always very appreciative and gratefully slid my big cooler right into their walk-in cooler. I taped a list of what was available for each type of meal. For example: "Breakfasts can be eggs, GFCF toast, grits, oatmeal, fruit, or GFCF cereals. Almond milk is included for cereal," or for lunch "I have included enough sandwich fixings for three days, and the other two days are chili and GFCF spaghetti. They are in labeled glass containers that can be heated in the microwave," and so on for each meal. I always included GFCF chips and fruit for snacks. Surprisingly, the camp cooks told me that kids were dropped off every week where the parent would just announce "Billy can't have any gluten," and then drive off. The vast majority of camps do not accommodate special diets, and those poor Scouts ended up eating mostly lettuce and peanut butter by the spoonful all week.

- If you can't bring meals from home, speak with the camp nurse, the counselors, and any volunteers about making sure your son or daughter has the enzymes at every single meal and snack. I know of one ASD teenager who went off to a ten-day National Boy Scout Jamboree with enzymes, but the importance of administering the enzymes wasn't discussed with the group leaders, who didn't really make sure he was taking them. The lad began addictively eating breaded chicken strips and nuggets several times every day without the enzymes and, by the end of the first week, was acting bizarrely and frightening the other campers. He became surly and irrational, and his family was called to take him home.

 Therapy Bloopers

- *Head Slap!* Using gluten-laden snacks as a reward. We often forget about the rewards a therapist might use when we are doing detective work. Be sure to suggest some acceptable alternatives.

- The therapist is using a play dough made with gluten during therapy sessions. Request that gluten-free doughs be used instead.

- You neglect to use a feeding specialist. If your child doesn't branch out and eat new foods after the opiate effect is broken, he may not be able to tolerate the smell, taste, or texture of foods due to sensory issues. This may cause gagging or food refusal. A good feeding specialist can often teach a child to tolerate and accept new foods without gagging. See Week 19 of the Chapter 9 Online Action Plan.

- You aren't using a sensory diet. A sensory diet addresses your child's needs with sensory activities multiple times throughout the day. Have your occupational therapist (OT) help design one for your son or daughter.

 ## Holy Moly at the Church or Temple

- It is likely that different people are working the nursery each week who won't always be familiar with your child and won't know about enzymes. You may have to develop a handout that you personally distribute to the workers each week.

- You are mistaken if you think Vacation Bible School doesn't count. Send the enzymes everywhere!

- For church outings, see the next section on class and field trips.

 ## The Magic School Bust: Class and Field Trips

Most of Evan's class trips occurred before we knew about the digestive enzymes. I usually had to go on the trips to look out for his dietary needs.

- All-day and overnight class trips almost always include stops at a pancake house for breakfast, fast food for lunch, and a pasta or pizza place for dinner. If your child cannot tolerate gluten even with the enzymes, you had better make special arrangements ahead of time. My school was well aware of Evan's diet needs, yet didn't give them a second thought on class trips. I learned that lesson the hard way: At one restaurant my son had only lettuce to eat while everyone around him gaily ate a full Italian meal. When I questioned why unbreaded chicken hadn't been arranged for him, the principal just shrugged it off and said, "We can't deal with special diets on a trip!"

- The trip will likely have parent chaperones who will be unfamiliar with your child's supplements or protocols. Handouts might be helpful.

- Sometimes the class trips stretch over a long day, with the students going from activity to activity without an opportunity to go back to the bus or hotel for more enzymes. Your child will find himself at dinner without enzymes, and well-meaning chaperones will insist he eat the pizza or spaghetti without them, not realizing the dramatic change in behavior that may result. If you can't go on the trip, make sure you give two or three of the chaperones the enzymes, and make them promise to see your child has them with every meal and snack.

 Boo-Boos at the Doctor's Office

Unfortunately, I don't have any quick fixes for these clangers. Perhaps you can donate a copy of this book or Dr. Martha Herbert's book *Autism Revolution*, but don't hold your breath.

- The doctor is unaware of the research and science about the health challenges of the autism spectrum.

- *Magical Thinking:* The doctor tells you that your child isn't autistic because:

  - He can look you in the eye.

  - She has a sense of humor.

  - He likes to be hugged.

  - He can speak.

- *Hall of Shame:* The doctor has a tendency to "mansplain" things to you.

- *Head Slap!* The doctor or staff think constipation, diarrhea, stomachaches, and waking up all night are just part of autism.

- Doctors may be oblivious to the fact that food can significantly change behavior and attention in these kids.

- Doctors neglect to recommend a probiotic during an antibiotic.

- Doctors neglect to advise the use of Saccharomyces boulardii during an antibiotic.

- They tell parents their child doesn't have to do the GFCF diet because he's not allergic to gluten or casein, or because gluten doesn't cause autism.

- They tell parents their child only has to avoid gluten, but not casein (or vice versa), because of the results of his urinary peptide test.

- Your pediatrician will not cooperate. Consider switching doctors or at least *adding* one to the team who is willing to provide some oversight as you try the protocols in this book.

 ## Foolery at the Pharmacy

- Check with manufacturers and your pharmacist about ingredients and dyes used in prescriptions and over-the-counter medications.

- Ask your doctor for a prescription to have your child's medicines and supplements compounded in a GFCF, dye-free, allergen-free formula, if necessary.

- Always start with a fraction of the dose. These children often need a lower dose than their neurotypical peers.

- Watch out for paradoxical (i.e., opposite or unexpected) reactions to medications.

- Don't pry open the bottle of Vitamin D3 and use a larger dropper. A child can end up in the ER with Vitamin D toxicity.

- Only change one thing at a time!

 ## The Internet: Satan's Swamp of Misinformation

- *Hall of Shame:* Trying something crazy off the Internet like "the saltwater flush" or "the lemonade fast"

- Detoxing without a lab test indicating it is warranted

- Detoxing before you have "gut readiness"

- *Magical Thinking:* Treating yeast and detoxing at the same time

- *Head Slap!* Thinking *everything* your child does is due to yeast, PANDAS, metals, or toxins

 Food Flubs

- Food sensitivities are underestimated. I have seen many cases of ADHD, wild impulsivity, difficult behaviors, terrible handwriting, and learning difficulties clear up with:

  - The Feingold diet, which has an 80 percent success rate and is by far the number-one diet people try at my office (Week 41 in the Chapter 9 Online Action Plan)

  - The IgG food sensitivity four-day rotation diet (Week 39 in the Chapter 9 Online Action Plan)

  - No-Fenol enzymes from Houston Enzymes, which may help your child tolerate fruits and vegetables that are high in phenols

- Helpful tools here are a food journal that includes not just the foods your child eats, but symptoms such as red cheeks and ears, flushing of the neck or face, hyperactivity, difficulty paying attention or staying on task, difficulty falling asleep, or changes in bowel patterns or mood.

I wish you the best as you try the protocols and suggestions in this book. As Robert Frost said, "The best way out is always through."

Twenty Years on the Front Lines— Evan, Liam, and Eli

At the end of the day, the most overwhelming key to a child's success is the positive involvement of parents.
Jane D. Hull

These days, our house is peaceful and upbeat. We listen to music, laugh, goof off, and make plans for the weekend, all things that used to be missing in our lives. Alan and I work too much, but we focus on the delightful, ordinary challenges of everyday life: studying for the ACT or a driver's test, deciding what to make for dinner, taking care of pets, and cleaning out the car. We go to movies and campouts and can even go on vacation without obsessively planning and worrying about it ahead of time. I enjoy going to the grocery store without having to hire two babysitters.

Our friends and families think we're doing a great job of parenting. Strangers no longer suggest that we medicate our children or slap them harder. More often than not, we are congratulated on what awesome, courteous, delightful young men our sons are.

Evan made us work for it every inch of the way, of course, but over the years his neurological, immunological, metabolic, gastrointestinal, and emotional health saw more and more healing and balance. There are long periods of time now where life is like a float trip on the sunny, peaceful section of the river. Our boys are growing up into the young men they are meant to be. I have learned not to be lulled and think, "We've made it. I can stop now." Let me bastardize a quote and say eternal vigilance is the price of health and balance on the autism spectrum.

Evan graduated from high school in the top 5 percent of his class and was offered several scholarships. He's an Eagle Scout and assistant Scoutmaster. His Eagle project, a "bat condo" with room for 10,000 bug-eating bats, graces Little Beaver State Park. Evan organized over sixty volunteers who put in 750 man-hours to build it. I was really pleased when he went to the Boy Scout World Jamboree in Sweden and was elected (yes, *elected!*) Patrol Leader.

Evan's in college now. He loves business, finance, and politics and has an almost native accent in French. He writes beautiful thank-you notes without any prompting from me, has a driver's license, and drives to and from college over three hours away. No tickets or accidents yet!

Evan's had a girlfriend now and then, and has a few good friends, but social skills and relationships remain a challenge. The smallest disagreement or criticism sets off an urge to escape the conversation. He is exploring the Dale Carnegie courses, and we just made the decision to find a good counselor to fine-tune his social skills. He struggles with organization, but has been finding external systems and structure that works for him. External structure in the form of wall calendars, iPhone alerts, and lists are essentials.

He's no longer hyperactive, but a restlessness remains, and he loves to exercise and go for walks. He is off of all prescription medications but still takes his enzymes, probiotics, GABA, and other supplements religiously. He hasn't been irritable or destructive in years. The term "gentle giant" comes to mind. *All* of that behavior was due to discomfort and pain from underlying medical issues the world was only just learning about when he was born.

What makes me really optimistic is Evan's "get up and go." He is an early-morning riser and tackles all projects with energy and optimism. He'll make phone calls, run errands, and can get more tasks checked off his list by breakfast than I do all day sometimes.

His biggest challenge is ADHD. We find that meditation, neurofeedback, the Feingold diet, Pycnogenol, and hyperbaric oxygen therapy (HBOT) help, but they aren't the complete answers.

Life is smoother for our other two boys as well. Autism families and siblings of an individual with autism have higher rates of GI troubles, anxiety, and tic disorders, among other challenges, but we stay vigilant and keep life on as even a keel as possible for everyone. I am the mother of two Eagle Scouts and will have my third one soon. Liam has headed off to college and life is quiet with only Eli at home. I hope to get back to my African violets and spend more time with my wonderful husband. It is so good to focus on the regular challenges and joys of life these days. I'm no longer afraid of getting a ticket from the "Normal Police."

Our youngest son can't even remember the difficult, chaotic, depressing years; he thinks we've always been this calm and happy in our home. And that's as good as it gets!

Autism is always with us, but it's the quiet, sedate wallpaper of our life now, not the flashing lights and sirens of nonstop yelling, chaos, and tension that used to be the heartbeat of our home.

I've never quite gotten back to being that carefree, waggy-tail chick I was before my children were born, but what parent ever does? I am blessed and give thanks for all things, including autism. We are looking forward to many more happy years with our sons, and my dearest hope is that other families will find this peace, too. Love and blessings to you as you find your child's path back to health on the autism spectrum.

ENDNOTES

Chapter 1: The Rules of Tack Sitting

1. Myers, S. M., C. P. Johnson, and Council on Children with Disabilities, "Management of Children with Autism Spectrum Disorders," *Pediatrics* 120, no. 5 (Nov. 2007): 1162–82.

2. Ibid.

3. Buie, T., D. B. Campbell, G. J. Fuchs III, G. T. Furuta, J. Levy, J. Vandewater, A. H. Whitaker et al., "Evaluation, Diagnosis, and Treatment of Gastrointestinal Disorders in Individuals with ASDs: A Consensus Report," supplement, *Pediatrics* 125, no. S1 (Jan. 2010): S1–18.

4. American Psychiatric Association, *Diagnostic and Statistical Manual of Mental Disorders*, 5th ed. (Arlington, VA: American Psychiatric Publishing), xliv, 947.

5. "Side Effects of Abilify," *Internet Drug Database*, www.drugs.com/sfx/abilify-side-effects.html; "Side Effects of Risperdal," www.drugs.com/sfx/clonidine-side-effects.html; "Side Effects of Clonidine," www.drugs.com/sfx/clonidine-side-effects.html.

6. Finegold, S. M., D. Molitoris, Y. Song, C. Liu, M. L. Vaisanen, E. Bolte, M. McTeague, et al., "Gastrointestinal Microflora Studies in Late-Onset Autism," supplement, *Clinical Infectious Diseases* 35, no. S1 (Sept. 1, 2002): S6–16; Horvath, K., J. C. Papadimitriou, A. Rabsztyn, C. Drachenberg, and J. T. Tildon, "Gastrointestinal Abnormalities in Children with Autistic Disorder," *Journal of Pediatrics* 135, no. 5 (Nov. 1999): 559–63; Reichelt, K. L., K. Hole, A. Hamberger, G. Saelid, P. D. Edminson, C. B. Braestrup, O. Lingjaerde, P. Ledaal, and H. Orbeck, "Biologically Active Peptide-Containing Fractions in Schizophrenia and Childhood Autism," *Advances in Biochemical Psychopharmacology* 28 (1981): 627–43; Reichelt, K. L., and A. M. Knivsberg, "Can the Pathophysiology of Autism Be Explained by the Nature of the Discovered Urine Peptides?" *Nutritional Neuroscience* 6, no. 1 (Feb. 2003): 19–28; Reichelt, K. L., D. Tveiten, A. M. Knivsberg, and G. Bronstad, "Peptides' Role in Autism with Emphasis on

Exorphins," *Microbial Ecology in Health and Disease* 23 (2012); Shaw, W., "Increased Urinary Excretion of a 3-(3-Hydroxyphenyl)-3-Hydroxypropionic Acid (HPHPA), an Abnormal Phenylalanine Metabolite of Clostridia Spp. in the Gastrointestinal Tract, in Urine Samples from Patients with Autism and Schizophrenia," *Nutritional Neuroscience* 13, no. 3 (June 2010): 135–43; Wasilewska, J., E. Jarocka-Cyrta, and M. Kaczmarski, "Gastrointestinal Abnormalities in Children with Autism" [in Polish], *Polski Merkuriusz Lekarski* 27, no. 157 (July 2009): 40–43.

7. Penders, J., et al., "Factors Influencing the Composition of the Intestinal Microbiota in Early Infancy," *Pediatrics* 118, no. 2 (2006): 511–21.

8. Biasucci, G., et al., "Cesarean Delivery May Affect the Early Biodiversity of Intestinal Bacteria," *Journal of Nutrition* 138, no. 9 (2008): 1796S–1800S; Penders et al., "Factors Influencing the Composition of the Intestinal Microbiota in Early Infancy."

9. Jimenez, J., et al., "Isolation of Commensal Bacteria from Umbilical Cord Blood of Healthy Neonates Born by Cesarean Section," *Current Microbiology* 51, no. 4 (2005): 270–74.

10. Munyaka, P. M., E. Khafipour, and J. E. Ghia, "External Influence of Early Childhood Establishment of Gut Microbiota and Subsequent Health Implications," *Frontiers in Pediatrics* 2 (2014): 109; Kostic, A. D. et al., "The Dynamics of the Human Infant Gut Microbiome in Development and in Progression Toward Type 1 Diabetes," *Cell Host and Microbe* 17, no. 2 (2015): 260–73; Schippa, S., et al., "A Distinctive 'Microbial Signature' in Celiac Pediatric Patients," *BMC Microbiology* 10 (2010): 175; Wold, A. E., and I. Adlerberth, "Breast Feeding and the Intestinal Microflora of the Infant: Implications for Protection Against Infectious Diseases," *Advances in Experimental Medicine and Biology* 478 (2000): 77–93; West, C. E., et al., "Gut Microbiome and Innate Immune Response Patterns in IgE-Associated Eczema," *Clinical and Experimental Allergy* (2015); Manzoni, P., "Use of Lactobacillus Casei Subspecies Rhamnosus GG and Gastrointestinal Colonization by Candida Species in Preterm Neonates," supplement, *Journal of Pediatric Gastroenterology and Nutrition* 45, no. S3 (2007): S190–94; Bik, E. M., and D. A. Relman, "Unrest at Home: Diarrheal Disease and Microbiota Disturbance," *Genome Biology* 15, no. 6 (2014): 120.

11. Munasinghe, S. A., C. Oliff, J. Finn, and J. A. Wray, "Digestive Enzyme Supplementation for Autism Spectrum Disorders: A Double-Blind Randomized Controlled Trial," *Journal of Autism and Developmental Disorders* 40, no. 9 (Sept. 2010): 1131–38.

12. Bradstreet, J. J., S. Smith, M. Baral, and D. A. Rossignol, "Biomarker-Guided Interventions of Clinically Relevant Conditions Associated with Autism Spectrum Disorders and Attention Deficit Hyperactivity Disorder," *Alternative Medicine Review* 15, no. 1 (Apr. 2010): 15–32; Frye, R. E., S. Rose, J. Slattery, and D. F. MacFabe, "Gastrointestinal Dysfunction in Autism Spectrum Disorder: The Role of the Mitochondria and the Enteric Microbiome," *Microbial Ecology in Health and Disease* 26 (2015): 27458; Gupta, S., S. Aggarwal, B. Rashanravan, and T. Lee, "Th1- and Th2-Like Cyto-

kines in Cd4+ and Cd8+ T Cells in Autism," *Journal of Neuroimmunology* 85, no. 1 (May 1, 1998): 106–9; Horvath et al., "Gastrointestinal Abnormalities in Children with Autistic Disorder"; Horvath, K., and J. A. Perman, "Autism and Gastrointestinal Symptoms," *Current Gastroenterology Reports* 4, no. 3 (June 2002): 251–58; Jyonouchi, H., L. Geng, D. L. Streck, and G. A. Toruner, "Children with Autism Spectrum Disorders (ASD) Who Exhibit Chronic Gastrointestinal (GI) Symptoms and Marked Fluctuation of Behavioral Symptoms Exhibit Distinct Innate Immune Abnormalities and Transcriptional Profiles of Peripheral Blood (Pb) Monocytes," *Journal of Neuroimmunology* 238, no. 1–2 (Sept. 15, 2011): 73–80.

13. Wold, A. E., and I. Adlerberth, "Breast Feeding and the Intestinal Microflora of the Infant."

14. Gupta, S., S. Aggarwal, B. Rashanravan, and T. Lee, "Th1- and Th2-Like Cytokines in Cd4+ and Cd8+ T Cells in Autism"; Lavrnja, I., A. Parabucki, P. Brkic, T. Jovanovic, S. Dacic, D. Savic, I. Pantic, M. Stojiljkovic, and S. Pekovic, "Repetitive Hyperbaric Oxygenation Attenuates Reactive Astrogliosis and Suppresses Expression of Inflammatory Mediators in the Rat Model of Brain Injury," *Mediators of Inflammation* 2015 (2015): 498405; Mead, J., and P. Ashwood, "Evidence Supporting an Altered Immune Response in ASD," *Immunolology Letters* 163, no. 1 (Jan. 2015): 49–55; Wasilewska et al., "Gastrointestinal Abnormalities in Children with Autism" [in Polish]; Williams, B. L., M. Hornig, T. Buie, M. L. Bauman, M. Cho Paik, I. Wick, A. Bennett, et al., "Impaired Carbohydrate Digestion and Transport and Mucosal Dysbiosis in the Intestines of Children with Autism and Gastrointestinal Disturbances," *PLOS One* 6, no. 9 (2011): e24585.

15. Ashwood, P., S. Wills, and J. Van de Water, "The Immune Response in Autism: A New Frontier for Autism Research," *Journal of Leukocyte Biology* 80, no. 1 (July 2006): 1–15; Mead, J., and P. Ashwood, "Evidence Supporting an Altered Immune Response in ASD"; Papageorgiou, N., D. Tousoulis, T. Psaltopoulou, A. Giolis, C. Antoniades, E. Tsiamis, A. Miliou, et al., "Divergent Anti-Inflammatory Effects of Different Oil Acute Consumption on Healthy Individuals," *European Journal of Clinical Nutrition* 65, no. 4 (Apr. 2011): 514–19; Song, Y., C. Liu, and S. M. Finegold, "Real-Time Pcr Quantitation of Clostridia in Feces of Autistic Children," *Applied and Environmental Microbiology* 70, no. 11 (Nov. 2004): 6459–65; Zerbo, O., A. Leong, L. Barcellos, P. Bernal, B. Fireman, and L. A. Croen, "Immune Mediated Conditions in Autism Spectrum Disorders," *Brain, Behavior, and Immunity* 46 (May 2015): 232–36.

16. Centers for Disease Control, "Majority of U.S. Hospitals Do Not Fully Support Breastfeeding," news release, Aug. 2, 2011, www.cdc.gov/media/releases/2011/p0802 _breastfeeding.html.

17. UC Davis MIND Institute, "Autism Phenome Project (APP)," UC Davis MIND (Medical Investigation of Neurodevelopmental Disorders) Institute, www.ucdmc.ucdavis .edu/mindinstitute/research/app/.

18. Jyonouchi, H., S. Sun, and H. Le, "Proinflammatory and Regulatory Cytokine Production Associated with Innate and Adaptive Immune Responses in Children with Autism Spectrum Disorders and Developmental Regression," *Journal of Neuroimmunology* 120, no. 1–2 (Nov. 1, 2001): 170–79.

19. Pardo, C. A., D. L. Vargas, and A. W. Zimmerman, "Immunity, Neuroglia, and Neuroinflammation in Autism," *International Review of Psychiatry* 17, no. 6 (Dec. 2005): 485–95; Vargas, D. L., C. Nascimbene, C. Krishnan, A. W. Zimmerman, and C. A. Pardo, "Neuroglial Activation and Neuroinflammation in the Brain of Patients with Autism," *Annals of Neurology* 57, no. 1 (Jan. 2005): 67–81.

20. Meguid, N. A., A. A. Dardir, E. R. Abdel-Raouf, and A. Hashish, "Evaluation of Oxidative Stress in Autism: Defective Antioxidant Enzymes and Increased Lipid Peroxidation," *Biological Trace Element Research* 143, no. 1 (Oct. 2011): 58–65; Zoroglu, S. S., F. Armutcu, S. Ozen, A. Gurel, E. Sivasli, O. Yetkin, and I. Meram, "Increased Oxidative Stress and Altered Activities of Erythrocyte Free Radical Scavenging Enzymes in Autism," *European Archives of Psychiatry and Clinical Neuroscience* 254, no. 3 (June 2004): 143–47.

21. Shmaya, Y., S. Eilat-Adar, Y. Leitner, S. Reif, and L. Gabis, "Nutritional Deficiencies and Overweight Prevalence Among Children with Autism Spectrum Disorder," *Research in Developmental Disabilities* 38 (Mar. 2015): 1–6.

22. Chen, L. F., Y. F. Tian, C. H. Lin, L. Y. Huang, K. C. Niu, and M. T. Lin, "Repetitive Hyperbaric Oxygen Therapy Provides Better Effects on Brain Inflammation and Oxidative Damage in Rats with Focal Cerebral Ischemia," *Journal of the Formosan Medical Association* 113, no. 9 (Sept. 2014): 620–28; Chen, X., X. S. Duan, L. J. Xu, J. J. Zhao, Z. F. She, W. W. Chen, Z. J. Zheng, and G. D. Jiang, "Interleukin-10 Mediates the Neuroprotection of Hyperbaric Oxygen Therapy Against Traumatic Brain Injury in Mice," *Neuroscience* 266 (Apr. 25, 2014): 235–43; Das, U. N., "Essential Fatty Acids and Their Metabolites Could Function as Endogenous HMG-CoA Reductase and ACE Enzyme Inhibitors, Anti-Arrhythmic, Anti-Hypertensive, Anti-Atherosclerotic, Anti-Inflammatory, Cytoprotective, and Cardioprotective Molecules," *Lipids in Health and Disease* 7 (2008): 37; DeMio, P. C., and E. Finley-Belgrad, "A Clinical Study of Effects of Enhansa® (Enhanced Absorption Curcumin) on Immunologic and Cognitive/Metabolic Disorders: An Overview of Results," www.leesilsby.com/wp-content/uploads/2012/05/Enhansa_project_study_results___LATEST.pdf; Papageorgiou et al., "Divergent Anti-Inflammatory Effects of Different Oil Acute Consumption on Healthy Individuals."

23. Bradstreet et al., "Biomarker-Guided Interventions of Clinically Relevant Conditions Associated with Autism Spectrum Disorders and Attention Deficit Hyperactivity Disorder."

24. Bradstreet et al., "Biomarker-Guided Interventions"; Jyonouchi et al., "Children with Autism Spectrum Disorders (ASD) Who Exhibit Chronic Gastrointestinal (GI)

Symptoms"; Jyonouchi, H., L. Geng, A. Ruby, and B. Zimmerman-Bier, "Dysregu-lated Innate Immune Responses in Young Children with Autism Spectrum Disor-ders: Their Relationship to Gastrointestinal Symptoms and Dietary Intervention," *Neuropsychobiology* 51, no. 2 (2005): 77–85; Maenner, M. J., C. L. Arneson, S. E. Levy, R. S. Kirby, J. S. Nicholas, and M. S. Durkin, "Brief Report: Association Between Behavioral Features and Gastrointestinal Problems Among Children with Autism Spectrum Disorder," *Journal of Autism and Developmental Disorders* 42, no. 7 (July 2012): 1520–25; Mazefsky, C. A., D. R. Schreiber, T. M. Olino, and N. J. Minshew, "The Association Between Emotional and Behavioral Problems and Gastrointestinal Symptoms Among Children with High-Functioning Autism," *Autism* 18, no. 5 (July 2014): 493–501; Reichelt, K. L., K. Hole, A. Hamberger, G. Saelid, P. D. Edminson, C. B. Braestrup, O. Lingjaerde, P. Ledaal, and H. Orbeck, "Biologically Active Peptide-Containing Fractions in Schizophrenia and Childhood Autism," *Advances in Bio-chemical Psychopharmacology* 28 (1981): 627–43; Reichelt et al., "Can the Pathophys-iology of Autism Be Explained by the Nature of the Discovered Urine Peptides?"; Reichelt et al., "Peptides' Role in Autism with Emphasis on Exorphins."

25. Stenstrom, R., P. A. Bernard, and H. Ben-Simhon, "Exposure to Environmental Tobacco Smoke as a Risk Factor for Recurrent Acute Otitis Media in Children Under the Age of Five Years," *International Journal of Pediatric Otorhinolaryngology* 27, no. 2 (Aug. 1993): 127–36.

26. Levy, D. E., J. Winickoff, and N. Rigotti, "School Absenteeism Among Children Liv-ing with Smokers," *Pediatrics* (Sept. 2, 2011), doi: 10.1542/peds. 2011-1067; Parracho, H. M., M. O. Bingham, G. R. Gibson, and A. L. McCartney, "Differences Between the Gut Microflora of Children with Autistic Spectrum Disorders and That of Healthy Children," *Journal of Medical Microbiology* 54, pt. 10 (Oct. 2005): 987–91.

27. Singh, K., S. L. Connors, E. A. Macklin, K. D. Smith, J. W. Fahey, P. Talalay, and A. W. Zimmerman, "Sulforaphane Treatment of Autism Spectrum Disorder (ASD)," *Proceedings of the National Academy of Sciences USA* 111, no. 43 (Oct. 28, 2014): 15550–55.

28. Gupta et al., "Th1- and Th2-Like Cytokines in Cd4+ and Cd8+ T Cells in Autism."

29. Finegold et al., "Gastrointestinal Microflora Studies in Late-Onset Autism"; Parracho et al., "Differences Between the Gut Microflora of Children"; Shaw, "Increased Uri-nary Excretion of a 3-(3-Hydroxyphenyl)-3-Hydroxypropionic Acid (HPHPA)."

30. Castagliuolo, I., M. F. Riegler, L. Valenick, J. T. LaMont, and C. Pothoulakis, "Sac-charomyces Boulardii Protease Inhibits the Effects of Clostridium Difficile Toxins A and B in Human Colonic Mucosa," *Infection and Immunity* 67, no. 1 (Jan. 1999): 302–7; Castex, F., G. Corthier, S. Jouvert, G. W. Elmer, F. Lucas, and M. Bastide, "Pre-vention of Clostridium Difficile–Induced Experimental Pseudomembranous Colitis by Saccharomyces Boulardii: A Scanning Electron Microscopic and Microbiological Study," *Journal of General Microbiology* 136, no. 6 (June 1990): 1085–89; Qamar, A., S.

Aboudola, M. Warny, P. Michetti, C. Pothoulakis, J. T. LaMont, and C. P. Kelly, "Sac-charomyces Boulardii Stimulates Intestinal Immunoglobulin A Immune Response to Clostridium Difficile Toxin A in Mice," *Infection and Immunity* 69, no. 4 (Apr. 2001): 2762–65.

31. Adachi, A., T. Horikawa, M. Ichihashi, T. Takashima, and A. Komura, "Role of Candida Allergen in Atopic Dermatitis and Efficacy of Oral Therapy with Various Antifungal Agents" [in Japanese], *Arerugi* 48, no. 7 (July 1999): 719–25; Khosravi, A. R., A. N. Bandghorai, M. Moazzeni, H. Shokri, P. Mansouri, and M. Mahmoudi, "Evaluation of Candida Albicans Allergens Reactive with Specific IgE in Asthma and Atopic Eczema Patients," *Mycoses* 52, no. 4 (July 2009): 326–33; Kimura, M., S. Tsuruta, and T. Yoshida, "Measurement of Candida-Specific Lymphocyte Proliferation by Flow Cytometry in Children with Atopic Dermatitis" [in Japanese], *Arerugi* 47, no. 4 (Apr. 1998): 449–56; Morita, E., M. Hide, Y. Yoneya, M. Kannbe, A. Tanaka, and S. Yamamoto, "An Assessment of the Role of Candida Albicans Antigen in Atopic Dermatitis," *Journal of Dermatology* 26, no. 5 (May 1999): 282–87; Savolainen, J., K. Lammintausta, K. Kalimo, and M. Viander, "Candida Albicans and Atopic Dermatitis," *Clinical and Experimental Allergy* 23, no. 4 (Apr. 1993): 332–39.

32. Buie et al., "Evaluation, Diagnosis, and Treatment of Gastrointestinal Disorders in Individuals with ASDs"; Elrod, M. G., and B. S. Hood, "Sleep Differences Among Children with Autism Spectrum Disorders and Typically Developing Peers: A Meta-Analysis," *Journal of Developmental and Behavioral Pediatrics* 36, no. 3 (Apr. 2015): 166–77; Humphreys, J. S., P. Gringras, P. S. Blair, N. Scott, J. Henderson, P. J. Fleming, and A. M. Emond, "Sleep Patterns in Children with Autistic Spectrum Disorders: A Prospective Cohort Study," *Archives of Disease in Childhood* 99, no. 2 (Feb. 2014): 114–18.

33. Bradstreet et al., "Biomarker-Guided Interventions"; Leyfer, O. T., S. E. Folstein, S. Bacalman, N. O. Davis, E. Dinh, J. Morgan, H. Tager-Flusberg, and J. E. Lainhart, "Comorbid Psychiatric Disorders in Children with Autism: Interview Development and Rates of Disorders," *Journal of Autism and Developmental Disorders* 36, no. 7 (Oct. 2006): 849–61.

34. Munasinghe, S. A., C. Oliff, J. Finn, and J. A. Wray, "Digestive Enzyme Supplementation for Autism Spectrum Disorders: A Double-Blind Randomized Controlled Trial," *Journal of Autism and Developmental Disorders* 40, no. 9 (Sept. 2010): 1131–38.

35. Chaidez, V., R. L. Hansen, and I. Hertz-Picciotto, "Gastrointestinal Problems in Children with Autism, Developmental Delays, or Typical Development," *Journal of Autism and Developmental Disorders* 44, no. 5 (May 2014): 1117–27; Chandler, S., I. Carcani-Rathwell, T. Charman, A. Pickles, T. Loucas, D. Meldrum, E. Simonoff, P. Sullivan, and G. Baird, "Parent-Reported Gastro-Intestinal Symptoms in Children with Autism Spectrum Disorders," *Journal of Autism and Developmental Disorders*

43, no. 12 (Dec. 2013): 2737–47; Horvath et al., "Gastrointestinal Abnormalities in Children with Autistic Disorder"; Wasilewska et al., "Gastrointestinal Abnormalities in Children with Autism" [in Polish].

36. Krigsman, A., "Gastrointestinal Pathology in Autism: Description and Treatment," *Medical Veritas* 4 (2007): 1528–36.

37. Buie et al., "Evaluation, Diagnosis, and Treatment of Gastrointestinal Disorders in Individuals with ASDs."

38. Kushak, R. I., G. Y. Lauwers, H. S. Winter, and T. M. Buie, "Intestinal Disaccharidase Activity in Patients with Autism: Effect of Age, Gender, and Intestinal Inflammation," *Autism* 15, no. 3 (May 2011): 285–94.

39. Canitano, R., and G. Vivanti, "Tics and Tourette Syndrome in Autism Spectrum Disorders," *Autism* 11, no. 1 (Jan. 2007): 19–28; Leyfer et al., "Comorbid Psychiatric Disorders in Children with Autism."

40. Rossignol, D. A., and R. E. Frye, "Mitochondrial Dysfunction in Autism Spectrum Disorders: A Systematic Review and Meta-Analysis," *Molecular Psychiatry* 17, no. 3 (Mar. 2012): 290–314.

41. Yasuda, H., K. Yoshida, Y. Yasuda, and T. Tsutsui, "Infantile Zinc Deficiency: Association with Autism Spectrum Disorders," *Scientific Reports* 1 (2011): 129.

42. Khademian, M., N. Farhangpajouh, A. Shahsanaee, M. Bahreynian, M. Mirshamsi, and R. Kelishadi, "Effects of Zinc Supplementation on Subscales of Anorexia in Children: A Randomized Controlled Trial," *Pakistan Journal of Medical Science* 30, no. 6 (Nov./Dec. 2014): 1213–17.

43. Bradstreet et al., "Biomarker-Guided Interventions."

44. Brigandi, S. A., H. Shao, S. Y. Qian, Y. Shen, B. L. Wu, and J. X. Kang, "Autistic Children Exhibit Decreased Levels of Essential Fatty Acids in Red Blood Cells," *International Journal of Molecular Sciences* 16, no. 5 (2015): 10061–76; Das, "Essential Fatty Acids and Their Metabolites Could Function as Endogenous HMG-CoA Reductase and ACE Enzyme Inhibitors."

45. Chandler, S., P. Howlin, E. Simonoff, T. O'Sullivan, E. Tseng, J. Kennedy, T. Charman, and G. Baird, "Emotional and Behavioural Problems in Young Children with Autism Spectrum Disorder," *Developmental Medicine and Child Neurology* (June 16, 2015).

46. White, S. W., D. Oswald, T. Ollendick, and L. Scahill, "Anxiety in Children and Adolescents with Autism Spectrum Disorders," *Clinical Psychology Review* 29, no. 3 (Apr. 2009): 216–29.

47. Partty, A., M. Kalliomaki, P. Wacklin, S. Salminen, and E. Isolauri, "A Possible Link Between Early Probiotic Intervention and the Risk of Neuropsychiatric Disorders Later in Childhood: A Randomized Trial," *Pediatric Research* 77, no. 6 (June 2015): 823–28.

Chapter 3: You Are What You Don't Poop

1. Canty, S. L., "Constipation as a Side Effect of Opioids," *Oncology Nursing Forum* 21, no. 4 (May 1994): 739–45; De Luca, A., and I. M. Coupar, "Insights into Opioid Action in the Intestinal Tract," *Pharmacology and Therapeutics* 69, no. 2 (1996): 103–15; LeFort, S. M., "Review: Intravenous and Oral Opioids Reduce Chronic Non-Cancer Pain but Are Associated with High Rates of Constipation, Nausea, and Sleepiness," *Evidence-Based Nursing* 8, no. 3 (July 2005): 88.

2. Myers, S. M., C. P. Johnson, and Council on Children with Disabilities, "Management of Children with Autism Spectrum Disorders," *Pediatrics* 120, no. 5 (Nov. 2007): 1162–82.

3. Buie, T., D. B. Campbell, G. J. Fuchs III, G. T. Furuta, J. Levy, J. Vandewater, A. H. Whitaker et al., "Evaluation, Diagnosis, and Treatment of Gastrointestinal Disorders in Individuals with ASDs: A Consensus Report," supplement, *Pediatrics* 125, no. 1 (Jan. 2010): S1–18.

4. Ibid.

5. "Side Effects of Abilify," *Internet Drug Database*, www.drugs.com/sfx/abilify-side-effects.html; "Side Effects of Clonidine," www.drugs.com/sfx/clonidine-side-effects.html; "Side Effects of Risperdal," www.drugs.com/sfx/clonidine-side-effects.html.

6. Jinsmaa, Y., and M. Yoshikawa, "Enzymatic Release of Neocasomorphin and Beta-Casomorphin from Bovine Beta-Casein," *Peptides* 20, no. 8 (1999): 957–62; Sokolov, O., N. Kost, O. Andreeva, E. Korneeva, V. Meshavkin, Y. Tarakanova, A. Dadayan, et al., "Autistic Children Display Elevated Urine Levels of Bovine Casomorphin-7 Immunoreactivity," *Peptides* 56 (June 2014): 68–71.

7. Fukudome, S., Y. Jinsmaa, T. Matsukawa, R. Sasaki, and M. Yoshikawa, "Release of Opioid Peptides, Gluten Exorphins by the Action of Pancreatic Elastase," *FEBS Letters* 412, no. 3 (Aug. 4, 1997): 475–79.

8. Sun, Z., and R. Cade, "Findings in Normal Rats Following Administration of Gliadorphin-7 (Gd-7)," *Peptides* 24, no. 2 (Feb. 2003): 321–23.

9. Johnson, B., S. Ulberg, S. Shivale, J. Donaldson, B. Milczarski, and S. V. Faraone, "Fibromyalgia, Autism, and Opioid Addiction as Natural and Induced Disorders of the Endogenous Opioid Hormonal System," *Discovery Medicine* 18, no. 99 (Oct. 2014): 209–20; Koch, G., K. Wiedemann, and H. Teschemacher, "Opioid Activities of Human Beta-Casomorphins," *Naunyn-Schmiedeberg's Archives of Pharmacology* 331, no. 4 (Dec. 1985): 351–54; Kost, N. V., O. Y. Sokolov, O. B. Kurasova, A. D. Dmitriev, J. N. Tarakanova, M. V. Gabaeva, Y. A. Zolotarev, et al., "Beta-Casomorphins-7 in Infants on Different Type of Feeding and Different Levels of Psychomotor Development," *Peptides* 30, no. 10 (Oct. 2009): 1854–60; Reichelt, K. L., D. Tveiten, A. M. Knivsberg, and G. Bronstad, "Peptides' Role in Autism with Emphasis on Exorphins," *Microbial Ecology in Health and Disease* 23 (2012); Reichelt, K. L., and A. M. Knivsberg, "Can the Pathophysiology of Autism Be Explained by the Nature of the

Discovered Urine Peptides?" *Nutritional Neuroscience* 6, no. 1 (Feb. 2003): 19–28; Sun, Z., and R. Cade, "A Peptide Found in Schizophrenia and Autism Causes Behavioral Changes in Rats," *Autism* 3, no. 1 (1999): 85–95; Sun and Cade, "Findings in Normal Rats Following Administration of Gliadorphin-7"; Trivedi, M. S., J. S. Shah, S. Al-Mughairy, N. W. Hodgson, B. Simms, G. A. Trooskens, W. Van Criekinge, and R. C. Deth, "Food-Derived Opioid Peptides Inhibit Cysteine Uptake with Redox and Epigenetic Consequences," *Journal of Nutritional Biochemistry* 25, no. 10 (Oct. 2014): 1011–18; White, J. F., "Intestinal Pathophysiology in Autism," *Experimental Biology and Medicine (Maywood)* 228, no. 6 (June 2003): 639–49.

10. Brigandi, S. A., H. Shao, S. Y. Qian, Y. Shen, B. L. Wu, and J. X. Kang, "Autistic Children Exhibit Decreased Levels of Essential Fatty Acids in Red Blood Cells," *International Journal of Molecular Sciences* 16, no. 5 (2015): 10061–76; Rautava, S., "Early Microbial Contact, the Breast Milk Microbiome, and Child Health," *Journal of Developmental Origins of Health and Disease* (June 8, 2015): 1–10; Sun and Cade, "A Peptide Found in Schizophrenia and Autism Causes Behavioral Changes in Rats."

11. Sun and Cade, "A Peptide Found in Schizophrenia and Autism Causes Behavioral Changes in Rats"; Sun and Cade, "Findings in Normal Rats Following Administration of Gliadorphin-7."

12. Lionetti E., Leonardi S., Franzonello C., Mancardi M., Ruggieri M., Catassi C. "Gluten Psychosis: Confirmation of a New Clinical Entity," *Nutrients* (July 8, 2015): 5532–9.

13. Hyman, S., Stewart, P., Foley, J., Cain, U., Peck, R., Morris, D., Wang, H., Smith, T. "The Gluten-Free/Casein-Free Diet: A Double-Blind Challenge Trial in Children with Autism," *Journal of Autism and Developmental Disorders* 7, no. 7 (July 8, 2015): 1–16

14. Hyman, S. "Diet Free of Gluten and Casein Has No Effect on Autism Symptoms," 9th Annual International Meeting for Autism Research (IMFAR), reported by Keller, D. M., *Medscape Medical News* (May 24, 2010), http://www.medscape.com/viewarticle/722283.

15. Hartrodt, B., K. Neubert, G. Fischer, H. Schulz, and A. Barth, "Synthesis and Enzymatic Degradation of Beta-Casomorphin-5 (Author's Trans.)," [in German] *Die Pharmazie* 37, no. 3 (Mar. 1982): 165–69.

16. Brudnak, M. A., B. Rimland, R. E. Kerry, M. Dailey, R. Taylor, B. Stayton, F. Waickman, et al., "Enzyme-Based Therapy for Autism Spectrum Disorders: Is It Worth Another Look?" *Medical Hypotheses* 58, no. 5 (May 2002): 422–28.

17. "Children with ASD May Be Deficient in Digestive Enzymes," www.klaire.com/enzymesforgi_vz.htm; Horvath, K., J. C. Papadimitriou, A. Rabsztyn, C. Drachenberg, and J. T. Tildon, "Gastrointestinal Abnormalities in Children with Autistic Disorder," *Journal of Pediatrics* 135, no. 5 (Nov. 1999): 559–63; Horvath, K., and J. A. Perman, "Autism and Gastrointestinal Symptoms," *Current Gastroenterology*

Reports 4, no. 3 (June 2002): 251–58; Kushak, R. I., G. Y. Lauwers, H. S. Winter, and T. M. Buie, "Intestinal Disaccharidase Activity in Patients with Autism: Effect of Age, Gender, and Intestinal Inflammation," *Autism* 15, no. 3 (May 2011): 285–94; Williams, B. L., M. Hornig, T. Buie, M. L. Bauman, M. Cho Paik, I. Wick, A. Bennett, et al., "Impaired Carbohydrate Digestion and Transport and Mucosal Dysbiosis in the Intestines of Children with Autism and Gastrointestinal Disturbances," *PLOS One* 6, no. 9 (2011): e24585.

18. Horvath, K., et al., "Gastrointestinal Abnormalities in Children with Autistic Disorder"; Horvath, K., and J. A. Perman, "Autism and Gastrointestinal Symptoms"; Kang, V., G. C. Wagner, and X. Ming, "Gastrointestinal Dysfunction in Children with Autism Spectrum Disorders," *Autism Research* 7, no. 4 (Aug. 2014): 501–6; Samsam, M., R. Ahangari, and S. A. Naser, "Pathophysiology of Autism Spectrum Disorders: Revisiting Gastrointestinal Involvement and Immune Imbalance," *World Journal of Gastroenterology* 20, no. 29 (Aug. 2014): 9942–51.

19. "Children with ASD May Be Deficient in Digestive Enzymes," www.klaire.com/ enzymesforgi_vz.htm; Horvath, K., et al., "Gastrointestinal Abnormalities in Children with Autistic Disorder"; Kushak, R. I., et al., "Intestinal Disaccharidase Activity in Patients with Autism"; Munasinghe, S. A., C. Oliff, J. Finn, and J. A. Wray, "Digestive Enzyme Supplementation for Autism Spectrum Disorders: A Double-Blind Randomized Controlled Trial," *Journal of Autism and Developmental Disorders* 40, no. 9 (Sept. 2010): 1131–38; Williams, B. L., et al., "Impaired Carbohydrate Digestion and Transport and Mucosal Dysbiosis."

20. Horvath, K., and J. A. Perman, "Autism and Gastrointestinal Symptoms"; Munasinghe, S. A., et al., "Digestive Enzyme Supplementation for Autism Spectrum Disorders"; Williams, B. L., et al., "Impaired Carbohydrate Digestion and Transport and Mucosal Dysbiosis."

21. Myers, S. M., C. P. Johnson, and Council on Children with Disabilities, "Management of Children with Autism Spectrum Disorders."

Chapter 4: Dirty Jobs

1. Baquero, F., and C. Nombela, "The Microbiome as a Human Organ," supplement, *Clinical Microbiology and Infection* 18, no. S4 (July 2012): 2–4.

2. Mueller, N. T., E. Bakacs, J. Combellick, Z. Grigoryan, and M. G. Dominguez-Bello, "The Infant Microbiome Development: Mom Matters," *Trends in Molecular Medicine* 21, no. 2 (Feb. 2015): 109–17.

3. Biasucci, G., B. Benenati, L. Morelli, E. Bessi, and G. Boehm, "Cesarean Delivery May Affect the Early Biodiversity of Intestinal Bacteria," *Journal of Nutrition* 138, no. 9 (2008): 1796S–800S; Hendricks-Munoz, K. D., J. Xu, H. I. Parikh, P. Xu, J. M. Fettweis, Y. Kim, M. Louie, et al., "Skin-to-Skin Care and the Development of the Preterm Infant Oral Microbiome," *American Journal of Perinatology* (May 22, 2015);

Penders, J., C. Thijs, C. Vink, F. F. Stelma, B. Snijders, I. Kummeling, P. A. van den Brandt, and E. E. Stobberingh, "Factors Influencing the Composition of the Intestinal Microbiota in Early Infancy," *Pediatrics* 118, no. 2 (Aug. 2006): 511–21; Rautava, S., "Early Microbial Contact, the Breast Milk Microbiome, and Child Health," *Journal of Developmental Origins of Health and Disease* (June 8, 2015): 1–10.

4. Adams, J. B., L. J. Johansen, L. D. Powell, D. Quig, and R. A. Rubin, "Gastrointestinal Flora and Gastrointestinal Status in Children with Autism: Comparisons to Typical Children and Correlation with Autism Severity," *BMC Gastroenterology* 11 (2011): 22; Cao, X., P. Lin, P. Jiang, and C. Li, "Characteristics of the Gastrointestinal Microbiome in Children with Autism Spectrum Disorder: A Systematic Review," *Shanghai Archives of Psychiatry* 25, no. 6 (Dec. 2013): 342–53; De Angelis, M., R. Francavilla, M. Piccolo, A. De Giacomo, and M. Gobbetti, "Autism Spectrum Disorders and Intestinal Microbiota," *Gut Microbes* 6, no. 3 (May 2015): 207–13; Finegold, S. M., D. Molitoris, Y. Song, C. Liu, M. L. Vaisanen, E. Bolte, M. McTeague, et al., "Gastrointestinal Microflora Studies in Late-Onset Autism," *Clinical Infectious Diseases* 35, no. S1 (Sept. 1, 2002): S6–S16; Horvath, K., J. C. Papadimitriou, A. Rabsztyn, C. Drachenberg, and J. T. Tildon, "Gastrointestinal Abnormalities in Children with Autistic Disorder," *Journal of Pediatrics* 135, no. 5 (Nov. 1999): 559–63; Horvath, K., and J. A. Perman, "Autism and Gastrointestinal Symptoms," *Current Gastroenterology Reports* 4, no. 3 (June 2002): 251–58; Hsiao, E. Y., "Gastrointestinal Issues in Autism Spectrum Disorder," *Harvard Review of Psychiatry* 22, no. 2 (Mar./Apr. 2014): 104–11; Kang, V., G. C. Wagner, and X. Ming, "Gastrointestinal Dysfunction in Children with Autism Spectrum Disorders," *Autism Research* 7, no. 4 (Aug. 2014): 501–6; Reddy, B. L., and M. H. Saier, "Autism and Our Intestinal Microbiota," *Journal of Molecular Microbiology and Biotechnology* 25, no. 1 (2015): 51–55.

5. Aiba, Y., N. Suzuki, A. M. Kabir, A. Takagi, and Y. Koga, "Lactic Acid–Mediated Suppression of Helicobacter Pylori by the Oral Administration of Lactobacillus Salivarius as a Probiotic in a Gnotobiotic Murine Model," *American Journal of Gastroenterology* 93, no. 11 (Nov. 1998): 2097–101; Yamano, T., H. Iino, M. Takada, S. Blum, F. Rochat, and Y. Fukushima, "Improvement of the Human Intestinal Flora by Ingestion of the Probiotic Strain Lactobacillus Johnsonii La1," *British Journal of Nutrition* 95, no. 2 (Feb. 2006): 303–12.

6. Foster, J. A., and K. A. McVey Neufeld, "Gut-Brain Axis: How the Microbiome Influences Anxiety and Depression," *Trends in Neurosciences* 36, no. 5 (May 2013): 305–12; Luna, R. A., and J. A. Foster, "Gut Brain Axis: Diet Microbiota Interactions and Implications for Modulation of Anxiety and Depression," *Current Opinion in Biotechnology* 32 (Apr. 2015): 35–41; Maenner, M. J., C. L. Arneson, S. E. Levy, R. S. Kirby, J. S. Nicholas, and M. S. Durkin, "Brief Report: Association Between Behavioral Features and Gastrointestinal Problems Among Children with Autism Spectrum Disorder," *Journal of Autism and Developmental Disorders* 42, no. 7 (July

2012): 1520–25; Mazefsky, C. A., D. R. Schreiber, T. M. Olino, and N. J. Minshew, "The Association Between Emotional and Behavioral Problems and Gastrointestinal Symptoms Among Children with High-Functioning Autism," *Autism* 18, no. 5 (July 2014): 493–501; Rao, A. V., A. C. Bested, T. M. Beaulne, M. A. Katzman, C. Iorio, J. M. Berardi, and A. C. Logan, "A Randomized, Double-Blind, Placebo-Controlled Pilot Study of a Probiotic in Emotional Symptoms of Chronic Fatigue Syndrome," *Gut Pathogens* 1, no. 1 (2009): 6; Saulnier, D. M., Y. Ringel, M. B. Heyman, J. A. Foster, P. Bercik, R. J. Shulman, J. Versalovic, et al., "The Intestinal Microbiome, Probiotics and Prebiotics in Neurogastroenterology," *Gut Microbes* 4, no. 1 (Jan./Feb. 2013): 17–27.

7. Logan, A. C., and M. Katzman, "Major Depressive Disorder: Probiotics May Be an Adjuvant Therapy," *Medical Hypotheses* 64, no. 3 (2005): 533–38.

8. Dinan, T. G., C. Stanton, and J. F. Cryan, "Psychobiotics: A Novel Class of Psychotropic," *Biological Psychiatry* 74, no. 10 (Nov. 15, 2013): 720–26; Saulnier et al., "Intestinal Microbiome, Probiotics and Prebiotics in Neurogastroenterology."

9. Galland, L., "The Gut Microbiome and the Brain," *Journal of Medicinal Food* 17, no. 12 (Dec. 2014): 1261–72.

10. Gilbert, J. A., R. Krajmalnik-Brown, D. L. Porazinska, S. J. Weiss, and R. Knight, "Toward Effective Probiotics for Autism and Other Neurodevelopmental Disorders," *Cell* 155, no. 7 (Dec. 19, 2013): 1446–48.

11. Dinan, Stanton, and Cryan, "Psychobiotics: A Novel Class of Psychotropic"; Forsythe, P., N. Sudo, T. Dinan, V. H. Taylor, and J. Bienenstock, "Mood and Gut Feelings," *Brain, Behavior, and Immunity* 24, no. 1 (Jan. 2010): 9–16; Saulnier et al., "Intestinal Microbiome, Probiotics and Prebiotics in Neurogastroenterology"; Tillisch, K., J. Labus, L. Kilpatrick, Z. Jiang, J. Stains, B. Ebrat, D. Guyonnet, et al., "Consumption of Fermented Milk Product with Probiotic Modulates Brain Activity," *Gastroenterology* 144, no. 7 (June 2013): 1394–401; Wall, R., J. F. Cryan, R. P. Ross, G. F. Fitzgerald, T. G. Dinan, and C. Stanton, "Bacterial Neuroactive Compounds Produced by Psychobiotics," *Advances in Experimental Medicine and Biology* 817 (2014): 221–39.

12. Al-Asmakh, M., F. Anuar, F. Zadjali, J. Rafter, and S. Pettersson, "Gut Microbial Communities Modulating Brain Development and Function," *Gut Microbes* 3, no. 4 (July/Aug. 2012): 366–73.

13. Dinan, Stanton, and Cryan, "Psychobiotics: A Novel Class of Psychotropic"; Patterson, E., J. F. Cryan, G. F. Fitzgerald, R. P. Ross, T. G. Dinan, and C. Stanton, "Gut Microbiota, the Pharmabiotics They Produce, and Host Health," *Proceedings of the Nutrition Society* 73, no. 4 (Nov. 2014): 477–89; Wall et al., "Bacterial Neuroactive Compounds Produced by Psychobiotics."

14. Foster and McVey Neufeld, "Gut-Brain Axis: How the Microbiome Influences Anxiety and Depression."

15. Ibid.

16. Groeger, D., L. O'Mahony, E. F. Murphy, J. F. Bourke, T. G. Dinan, B. Kiely, F. Sha-

nahan, and E. M. Quigley, "Bifidobacterium Infantis 35624 Modulates Host Inflammatory Processes Beyond the Gut," *Gut Microbes* 4, no. 4 (July/Aug. 2013): 325–39; Guigoz, Y., J. Dore, and E. J. Schiffrin, "The Inflammatory Status of Old Age Can Be Nurtured from the Intestinal Environment," *Current Opinion in Clinical Nutrition and Metabolic Care* 11, no. 1 (Jan. 2008): 13–20.

17. Partty, A., M. Kalliomaki, P. Wacklin, S. Salminen, and E. Isolauri, "A Possible Link Between Early Probiotic Intervention and the Risk of Neuropsychiatric Disorders Later in Childhood: A Randomized Trial," *Pediatric Research* 77, no. 6 (June 2015): 823–28.

18. Diaz Heijtz, R., S. Wang, F. Anuar, Y. Qian, B. Bjorkholm, A. Samuelsson, M. L. Hibberd, H. Forssberg, and S. Pettersson, "Normal Gut Microbiota Modulates Brain Development and Behavior," *Proceedings of the National Academy of Sciences USA* 108, no. 7 (Feb. 15, 2011): 3047–52.

19. Foster and McVey Neufeld, "Gut-Brain Axis: How the Microbiome Influences Anxiety and Depression"; Luna, R. A., and J. A. Foster, "Gut Brain Axis: Diet Microbiota Interactions and Implications for Modulation of Anxiety and Depression," *Current Opinion in Biotechnology* 32 (Apr. 2015): 35–41.

20. Bibiloni, R., R. N. Fedorak, G. W. Tannock, K. L. Madsen, P. Gionchetti, M. Campieri, C. De Simone, and R. B. Sartor, "VSL#3 Probiotic-Mixture Induces Remission in Patients with Active Ulcerative Colitis," *American Journal of Gastroenterology* 100, no. 7 (July 2005): 1539–46; Groeger et al., "Bifidobacterium Infantis 35624 Modulates Host Inflammatory Processes Beyond the Gut"; Guigoz, Dore, and Schiffrin, "Inflammatory Status of Old Age Can Be Nurtured from the Intestinal Environment"; Kuhbacher, T., S. J. Ott, U. Helwig, T. Mimura, F. Rizzello, B. Kleessen, P. Gionchetti, et al., "Bacterial and Fungal Microbiota in Relation to Probiotic Therapy (VSL#3) in Pouchitis," *Gut* 55, no. 6 (June 2006): 833–41; Mimura, T., F. Rizzello, U. Helwig, G. Poggioli, S. Schreiber, I. C. Talbot, R. J. Nicholls, et al., "Once Daily High Dose Probiotic Therapy (VSL#3) for Maintaining Remission in Recurrent or Refractory Pouchitis," *Gut* 53, no. 1 (Jan. 2004): 108–14.

21. De Milliano, I., M. M. Tabbers, J. A. van der Post, and M. A. Benninga, "Is a Multispecies Probiotic Mixture Effective in Constipation During Pregnancy?: A Pilot Study," *Nutrition Journal* 11 (2012): 80; Kim, S. E., S. C. Choi, K. S. Park, M. I. Park, J. E. Shin, T. H. Lee, K. W. Jung, et al., "Change of Fecal Flora and Effectiveness of the Short-Term VSL#3 Probiotic Treatment in Patients with Functional Constipation," *Journal of Neurogastroenterology and Motility* 21, no. 1 (Jan. 1, 2015): 111–20; Koebnick, C., I. Wagner, P. Leitzmann, U. Stern, and H. J. Zunft, "Probiotic Beverage Containing Lactobacillus Casei Shirota Improves Gastrointestinal Symptoms in Patients with Chronic Constipation," *Canadian Journal of Gastroenterology* 17, no. 11 (Nov. 2003): 655–59.

22. De Milliano et al., "Is a Multispecies Probiotic Mixture Effective in Constipation

During Pregnancy?"; Nobaek, S., M. L. Johansson, G. Molin, S. Ahrne, and B. Jeppsson, "Alteration of Intestinal Microflora Is Associated with Reduction in Abdominal Bloating and Pain in Patients with Irritable Bowel Syndrome," *American Journal of Gastroenterology* 95, no. 5 (May 2000): 1231–38.

23. Nobaek et al., "Alteration of Intestinal Microflora Is Associated with Reduction in Abdominal Bloating and Pain"; Kim et al., "Change of Fecal Flora and Effectiveness of the Short-Term VSL#3 Probiotic Treatment."

24. Ait-Belgnaoui, A., H. Durand, C. Cartier, G. Chaumaz, H. Eutamene, L. Ferrier, E. Houdeau, et al., "Prevention of Gut Leakiness by a Probiotic Treatment Leads to Attenuated HPA Response to an Acute Psychological Stress in Rats," *Psychoneuroendocrinology* 37, no. 11 (Nov. 2012): 1885–95.

25. Guo, J., B. Brosnan, A. Furey, E. Arendt, P. Murphy, and A. Coffey, "Antifungal Activity of Lactobacillus Against Microsporum Canis, Microsporum Gypseum, and Epidermophyton Floccosum," *Bioengeered Bugs* 3, no. 2 (Mar./Apr. 2012): 104–13; Kohler, G. A., S. Assefa, and G. Reid, "Probiotic Interference of Lactobacillus Rhamnosus Gr-1 and Lactobacillus Reuteri Rc-14 with the Opportunistic Fungal Pathogen Candida Albicans," *Infectious Diseases in Obstetics and Gynecology* 2012 (2012): 636474; Roy, A., J. Chaudhuri, D. Sarkar, P. Ghosh, and S. Chakraborty, "Role of Enteric Supplementation of Probiotics on Late-Onset Sepsis by Candida Species in Preterm Low Birth Weight Neonates: A Randomized, Double Blind, Placebo-Controlled Trial," *North American Journal of Medical Sciences* 6, no. 1 (Jan. 2014): 50–57; Shekh, R. M., and U. Roy, "Biochemical Characterization of an Anti-Candida Factor Produced by Enterococcus Faecalis," *BMC Microbiology* 12 (2012): 132.

26. Yamano et al., "Improvement of the Human Intestinal Flora by Ingestion of the Probiotic Strain Lactobacillus Johnsonii La1."

27. Sherman, P. M., K. C. Johnson-Henry, H. P. Yeung, P. S. Ngo, J. Goulet, and T. A. Tompkins, "Probiotics Reduce Enterohemorrhagic Escherichia Coli O157:H7- and Enteropathogenic E. Coli O127:H6-Induced Changes in Polarized T84 Epithelial Cell Monolayers by Reducing Bacterial Adhesion and Cytoskeletal Rearrangements," *Infection and Immunity* 73, no. 8 (Aug. 2005): 5183–88.

28. Shokryazdan, P., C. C. Sieo, R. Kalavathy, J. B. Liang, N. B. Alitheen, M. Faseleh Jahromi, and Y. W. Ho, "Probiotic Potential of Lactobacillus Strains with Antimicrobial Activity Against Some Human Pathogenic Strains," *BioMed Research International* 2014 (2014): 927268.

29. Travers, M. A., I. Florent, L. Kohl, and P. Grellier, "Probiotics for the Control of Parasites: An Overview," *Journal of Parasitology Research* 2011 (2011): 610769.

30. Patel, R. M., L. S. Myers, A. R. Kurundkar, A. Maheshwari, A. Nusrat, and P. W. Lin, "Probiotic Bacteria Induce Maturation of Intestinal Claudin 3 Expression and Barrier Function," *American Journal of Pathology* 180, no. 2 (Feb. 2012): 626–35.

31. Van Zanten, G. C., A. Knudsen, H. Roytio, S. Forssten, M. Lawther, A. Blennow,

S. J. Lahtinen et al., "The Effect of Selected Synbiotics on Microbial Composition and Short-Chain Fatty Acid Production in a Model System of the Human Colon," *PLOS One* 7, no. 10 (2012): e47212.

32. Patterson et al., "Gut Microbiota, the Pharmabiotics They Produce, and Host Health"; Zhang, W., M. S. Azevedo, K. Wen, A. Gonzalez, L. J. Saif, G. Li, A. E. Yousef, and L. Yuan, "Probiotic Lactobacillus Acidophilus Enhances the Immunogenicity of an Oral Rotavirus Vaccine in Gnotobiotic Pigs," *Vaccine* 26, no. 29–30 (July 4 2008): 3655–61.

33. Messaoudi, S., M. Manai, G. Kergourlay, H. Prevost, N. Connil, J. M. Chobert, and X. Dousset, "Lactobacillus Salivarius: Bacteriocin and Probiotic Activity," *Food Microbiology* 36, no. 2 (Dec. 2013): 296–304; Patterson et al., "Gut Microbiota, the Pharmabiotics They Produce, and Host Health."

34. Da Silva, S., C. Robbe-Masselot, A. Ait-Belgnaoui, A. Mancuso, M. Mercade-Loubiere, C. Salvador-Cartier, M. Gillet, et al., "Stress Disrupts Intestinal Mucus Barrier in Rats Via Mucin O-Glycosylation Shift: Prevention by a Probiotic Treatment," *American Journal of Physiology-Gastrointestinal and Liver Physiology* 307, no. 4 (Aug. 15, 2014): G420–29.

35. Imani Fooladi, A. A., M. H. Yazdi, M. R. Pourmand, A. Mirshafiey, Z. M. Hassan, T. Azizi, M. Mahdavi, and M. M. Soltan Dallal, "Th1 Cytokine Production Induced by Lactobacillus Acidophilus in Balb/C Mice Bearing Transplanted Breast Tumor," *Jundishapur Journal of Microbiology* 8, no. 4 (Apr. 2015): e17354; Sharma, R., R. Kapila, G. Dass, and S. Kapila, "Improvement in Th1/Th2 Immune Homeostasis, Antioxidative Status, and Resistance to Pathogenic E. Coli on Consumption of Probiotic Lactobacillus Rhamnosus Fermented Milk in Aging Mice," *Age (Dordrecht, Netherlands)* 36, no. 4 (2014): 9686; Yeom, M., B. J. Sur, J. Park, S. G. Cho, B. Lee, S. T. Kim, K. S. Kim, H. Lee, and D. H. Hahm, "Oral Administration of Lactobacillus Casei Variety Rhamnosus Partially Alleviates TMA-Induced Atopic Dermatitis in Mice Through Improving Intestinal Microbiota," *Journal of Applied Microbiology* 119, no. 2 (Aug. 2015): 560–70.

36. Garaiova, I., J. Muchova, Z. Nagyova, D. Wang, J. V. Li, Z. Orszaghova, D. R. Michael, S. F. Plummer, and Z. Durackova, "Probiotics and Vitamin C for the Prevention of Respiratory Tract Infections in Children Attending Preschool: A Randomised Controlled Pilot Study," *European Journal of Clinical Nutrition* 69, no. 3 (Mar. 2015): 373–79.

37. Garaiova et al., "Probiotics and Vitamin C for the Prevention of Respiratory Tract Infections in Children Attending Preschool"; Grandy, G., M. Medina, R. Soria, C. G. Teran, and M. Araya, "Probiotics in the Treatment of Acute Rotavirus Diarrhoea: A Randomized, Double-Blind, Controlled Trial Using Two Different Probiotic Preparations in Bolivian Children," *BMC Infectious Diseases* 10 (2010): 253; Harata, G., F. He, N. Hiruta, M. Kawase, A. Kubota, M. Hiramatsu, and H. Yausi, "Intranasal

Administration of Lactobacillus Rhamnosus Gg Protects Mice from H1n1 Influenza Virus Infection by Regulating Respiratory Immune Responses," *Letters in Applied Microbiology* 50, no. 6 (June 1, 2010): 597–602.

38. Travers, M. A., I. Florent, L. Kohl, and P. Grellier, "Probiotics for the Control of Parasites: An Overview," *Journal of Parasitology Research* 2011 (2011): 610769.

39. Casey, P. G., G. E. Gardiner, G. Casey, B. Bradshaw, P. G. Lawlor, P. B. Lynch, F. C. Leonard, et al., "A Five-Strain Probiotic Combination Reduces Pathogen Shedding and Alleviates Disease Signs in Pigs Challenged with Salmonella Enterica Serovar Typhimurium," *Applied and Environmental Microbiology* 73, no. 6 (Mar. 2007): 1858–63; Eom, J. S., J. Song, and H. S. Choi, "Protective Effects of a Novel Probiotic Strain of Lactobacillus Plantarum JSA22 from Traditional Fermented Soybean Food Against Infection by Salmonella Enterica Serovar Typhimurium," *Journal of Microbiology and Biotechnology* 25, no. 4 (Apr. 28, 2015): 479–91.

40. Bruce, A. W., and G. Reid, "Probiotics and the Urologist," *Canadian Journal of Urology* 10, no. 2 (Apr. 2003): 1785–89; Reid, G, "Probiotic Lactobacilli for Urogenital Health in Women," supplement, *Journal of Clinical Gastroenterology* 42, no. S3 pt. 2 (Sept. 2008): S234–36.

41. Aiba et al., "Lactic Acid–Mediated Suppression of Helicobacter Pylori by the Oral Administration of Lactobacillus Salivarius as a Probiotic"; Emara, M. H., S. A. Elhawari, S. Yousef, M. I. Radwan, and H. R. Abdel-Aziz, "Emerging Role of Probiotics in the Management of Helicobacter Pylori Infection: Histopathologic Perspectives," *Helicobacter* (May 22, 2015); Lesbros-Pantoflickova, D., I. Corthesy-Theulaz, and A. L. Blum, "Helicobacter Pylori and Probiotics," supplement, *Journal of Nutrition* 137, no. 3 (Mar. 2007): 812S–18S.

42. Goldenberg, J. Z., S. S. Ma, J. D. Saxton, M. R. Martzen, P. O. Vandvik, K. Thorlund, G. H. Guyatt, and B. C. Johnston, "Probiotics for the Prevention of Clostridium Difficile–Associated Diarrhea in Adults and Children," *Cochrane Database of Systematic Reviews* 5 (2013): CD006095; McFarland, L. V., "Meta-Analysis of Probiotics for the Prevention of Antibiotic-Associated Diarrhea and the Treatment of Clostridium Difficile Disease," *American Journal of Gastroenterology* 101, no. 4 (Apr. 2006): 812–22.

43. Zhang, M., X. Fan, B. Fang, C. Zhu, J. Zhu, and F. Ren, "Effects of Lactobacillus Salivarius Ren on Cancer Prevention and Intestinal Microbiota in 1, 2-Dimethylhydrazine-Induced Rat Model," *Journal of Microbiology* 53, no. 6 (June 2015): 398–405; Zhu, J., C. Zhu, S. Ge, M. Zhang, L. Jiang, J. Cui, and F. Ren, "Lactobacillus Salivarius Ren Prevent the Early Colorectal Carcinogenesis in 1, 2-Dimethylhydrazine-Induced Rat Model," *Journal of Applied Microbiology* 117, no. 1 (July 2014): 208–16.

44. D'Souza, A. L., C. Rajkumar, J. Cooke, and C. J. Bulpitt, "Probiotics in Prevention of Antibiotic-Associated Diarrhoea: Meta-Analysis," *BMJ* 324, no. 7350 (June 8 2002): 1361; Hickson, M., "Probiotics in the Prevention of Antibiotic-Associated Diarrhoea and Clostridium Difficile Infection," *Therapeutic Advances in Gastroenterology* 4, no.

3 (May 2011): 185–97; McFarland, "Meta-Analysis of Probiotics for the Prevention of Antibiotic-Associated Diarrhea and the Treatment of Clostridium Difficile Disease."

45. Goldenberg et al., "Probiotics for the Prevention of Clostridium Difficile–Associated Diarrhea in Adults and Children"; McFarland, "Meta-Analysis of Probiotics for the Prevention of Antibiotic-Associated Diarrhea and the Treatment of Clostridium Difficile Disease."

46. Bisson, J. F., S. Hidalgo, P. Rozan, and M. Messaoudi, "Preventive Effects of Different Probiotic Formulations on Travelers' Diarrhea Model in Wistar Rats: Preventive Effects of Probiotics on TD," *Digestive Diseases and Sciences* 55, no. 4 (Apr. 2010): 911–19.

47. Grandy et al., "Probiotics in the Treatment of Acute Rotavirus Diarrhoea: A Randomized, Double-Blind, Controlled Trial Using Two Different Probiotic Preparations in Bolivian Children"; Lee do, K., J. E. Park, M. J. Kim, J. G. Seo, J. H. Lee, and N. J. Ha, "Probiotic Bacteria, B. Longum and L. Acidophilus Inhibit Infection by Rotavirus in Vitro and Decrease the Duration of Diarrhea in Pediatric Patients," *Clinics and Research in Hepatology and Gastroenterology* 39, no. 2 (Apr. 2015): 237–44.

48. Nowak, A., S. Kuberski, and Z. Libudzisz, "Probiotic Lactic Acid Bacteria Detoxify N-Nitrosodimethylamine," *Food Additives and Contaminants: Part A, Chemistry, Analysis, Control, Exposure, and Risk Assessment* 31, no. 10 (2014): 1678–87.

49. Brudnak, M. A., "Probiotics as an Adjuvant to Detoxification Protocols," *Medical Hypotheses* 58, no. 5 (May 2002): 382–85; Zoghi, A., K. Khosravi-Darani, and S. Sohrabvandi, "Surface Binding of Toxins and Heavy Metals by Probiotics," *Mini-Reviews in Medicinal Chemistry* 14, no. 1 (Jan. 2014): 84–98.

50. Heikkila, J. E., S. M. Nybom, S. J. Salminen, and J. A. Meriluoto, "Removal of Cholera Toxin from Aqueous Solution by Probiotic Bacteria," *Pharmaceuticals (Basel, Switzerland)* 5, no. 6 (2012): 665–73; Nybom, S. M., S. J. Salminen, and J. A. Meriluoto, "Removal of Microcystin-Lr by Strains of Metabolically Active Probiotic Bacteria," *FEMS Microbiology Letters* 270, no. 1 (May 2007): 27–33.

51. Patterson et al., "Gut Microbiota, the Pharmabiotics They Produce, and Host Health."

52. Adam, E., L. Delbrassine, C. Bouillot, V. Reynders, A. C. Mailleux, E. Muraille, and A. Jacquet, "Probiotic Escherichia Coli Nissle 1917 Activates DC and Prevents House Dust Mite Allergy Through a TLR4-Dependent Pathway," *European Journal of Immunology* 40, no. 7 (July 2010): 1995–2005; Costa, D. J., P. Marteau, M. Amouyal, L. K. Poulsen, E. Hamelmann, M. Cazaubiel, B. Housez, et al., "Efficacy and Safety of the Probiotic Lactobacillus Paracasei LP-33 in Allergic Rhinitis: A Double-Blind, Randomized, Placebo-Controlled Trial (GA2LEN Study)," *European Journal of Clinical Nutrition* 68, no. 5 (May 2014): 602–7; Gorissen, D. M., N. B. Rutten, C. M. Oostermeijer, L. E. Niers, M. O. Hoekstra, G. T. Rijkers, and C. K. van der Ent, "Preventive Effects of Selected Probiotic Strains on the Development of Asthma and Allergic Rhinitis in Childhood: The Panda Study," *Clinical and Experimental Allergy* 44, no.

11 (Nov. 2014): 1431–33; Zajac, A. E., A. S. Adams, and J. H. Turner, "A Systematic Review and Meta-Analysis of Probiotics for the Treatment of Allergic Rhinitis," *International Forum of Allergy and Rhinology* 5, no. 6 (June 2015): 524–32.

53. Hatab, S., T. Yue, and O. Mohamad, "Removal of Patulin from Apple Juice Using Inactivated Lactic Acid Bacteria," *Journal of Applied Microbiology* 112, no. 5 (May 2012): 892–99; Nowak et al., "Probiotic Lactic Acid Bacteria Detoxify N-Nitrosodimethylamine."

54. Furrie, E., "Probiotics and Allergy," *Proceedings of the Nutrition Society* 64, no. 4 (Nov. 2005): 465–69.

55. Gorissen et al., "Preventive Effects of Selected Probiotic Strains on the Development of Asthma and Allergic Rhinitis in Childhood: The Panda Study"; Wu, C. T., P. J. Chen, Y. T. Lee, J. L. Ko, and K. H. Lue, "Effects of Immunomodulatory Supplementation with Lactobacillus Rhamnosus on Airway Inflammation in a Mouse Asthma Model," *Journal of Microbiology, Immunology, and Infection* (Nov. 11, 2014).

56. Costa et al., "Efficacy and Safety of the Probiotic Lactobacillus Paracasei LP-33 in Allergic Rhinitis"; Zajac, Adams, and Turner, "Systematic Review and Meta-Analysis of Probiotics for the Treatment of Allergic Rhinitis."

57. Cao, L., L. Wang, L. Yang, S. Tao, R. Xia, and W. Fan, "Long-Term Effect of Early-Life Supplementation with Probiotics on Preventing Atopic Dermatitis: A Meta-Analysis," *Journal of Dermatological Treatment* (May 5, 2015): 1–4; Kim, S. O., Y. M. Ah, Y. M. Yu, K. H. Choi, W. G. Shin, and J. Y. Lee, "Effects of Probiotics for the Treatment of Atopic Dermatitis: A Meta-Analysis of Randomized Controlled Trials," *Annals of Allergy, Asthma, and Immunology* 113, no. 2 (Aug. 2014): 217–26; Panduru, M., N. M. Panduru, C. M. Salavastru, and G. S. Tiplica, "Probiotics and Primary Prevention of Atopic Dermatitis: A Meta-Analysis of Randomized Controlled Studies," *Journal of the European Academy of Dermatology and Venereology* 29, no. 2 (Feb. 2015): 232–42.

58. Gungor, O. E., Z. Kirzioglu, E. Dincer, and M. Kivanc, "Who Will Win the Race in Childrens' Oral Cavities? Streptococcus Mutans or Beneficial Lactic Acid Bacteria?" *Beneficial Microbes* 4, no. 3 (Sept. 2013): 237–45; Gungor, O. E., Z. Kirzioglu, and M. Kivanc, "Probiotics: Can They Be Used to Improve Oral Health?" *Beneficial Microbes* (June 30, 2015): 1–10.

59. Anderson, M. H., and W. Shi, "A Probiotic Approach to Caries Management," *Pediatric Dentistry* 28, no. 2 (Mar./Apr. 2006): 151–53, discussion 92–98; Gungor, Kirzioglu, and Kivanc, "Probiotics: Can They Be Used to Improve Oral Health?"

60. Hong, S. N., and P. L. Rhee, "Unraveling the Ties Between Irritable Bowel Syndrome and Intestinal Microbiota," *World Journal of Gastroenterology* 20, no. 10 (Mar. 14, 2014): 2470–81; Lee, K. N., and O. Y. Lee, "Intestinal Microbiota in Pathophysiology and Management of Irritable Bowel Syndrome," *World Journal of Gastroenterology* 20, no. 27 (July 21, 2014): 8886–97.

61. Bedaiwi, M. K., and R. D. Inman, "Microbiome and Probiotics: Link to Arthritis," *Cur-*

rent Opinion in Rheumatology 26, no. 4 (July 2014): 410–15; Pineda, M. de L.A., S. F. Thompson, K. Summers, F. de Leon, J. Pope, and G. Reid, "A Randomized, Double-Blinded, Placebo-Controlled Pilot Study of Probiotics in Active Rheumatoid Arthritis," *Medical Science Monitor* 17, no. 6 (June 2011): CR347–54.

62. Dominici, L., M. Villarini, F. Trotta, E. Federici, G. Cenci, and M. Moretti, "Protective Effects of Probiotic Lactobacillus Rhamnosus IMC501 in Mice Treated with PhIP," *Journal of Microbiology and Biotechnology* 24, no. 3 (Mar. 28, 2014): 371–78; Khalil, A. A., A. E. Abou-Gabal, A. A. Abdellatef, and A. E. Khalid, "Protective Role of Probiotic Lactic Acid Bacteria Against Dietary Fumonisin B1-Induced Toxicity and DNA-Fragmentation in Sprague-Dawley Rats," *Preparative Biochemistry and Biotechnology* 45, no. 6 (Aug. 18, 2015): 530–50.

63. Patterson et al., "Gut Microbiota, the Pharmabiotics They Produce, and Host Health."

64. Ibid.

65. Penders, J., K. Gerhold, E. E. Stobberingh, C. Thijs, K. Zimmermann, S. Lau, and E. Hamelmann, "Establishment of the Intestinal Microbiota and Its Role for Atopic Dermatitis in Early Childhood," *Journal of Allergy and Clinical Immunology* 132, no. 3 (Sept. 2013): 601–7 e8; Penders, J., C. Thijs, P. A. van den Brandt, I. Kummeling, B. Snijders, F. Stelma, H. Adams, R. van Ree, and E. E. Stobberingh, "Gut Microbiota Composition and Development of Atopic Manifestations in Infancy: The Koala Birth Cohort Study," *Gut* 56, no. 5 (May 2007): 661–67.

Chapter 5: Sh!ts and Giggles

1. Buie, T., D. B. Campbell, G. J. Fuchs III, G. T. Furuta, J. Levy, J. Vandewater, A. H. Whitaker, et al., "Evaluation, Diagnosis, and Treatment of Gastrointestinal Disorders in Individuals with ASDs: A Consensus Report," supplement, *Pediatrics* 125, no. S1 (Jan. 2010): S1–18; Myers, S. M., C. P. Johnson, and Council on Children with Disabilities, "Management of Children with Autism Spectrum Disorders," *Pediatrics* 120, no. 5 (Nov. 2007): 1162–82.

2. Bradstreet, J. J., S. Smith, M. Baral, and D. A. Rossignol, "Biomarker-Guided Interventions of Clinically Relevant Conditions Associated with Autism Spectrum Disorders and Attention Deficit Hyperactivity Disorder," *Alternative Medicine Review* 15, no. 1 (Apr. 2010): 15–32; De Angelis, M., R. Francavilla, M. Piccolo, A. De Giacomo, and M. Gobbetti, "Autism Spectrum Disorders and Intestinal Microbiota," *Gut Microbes* 6, no. 3 (May 2015): 207–13; Rescigno, M., "Intestinal Microbiota and Its Effects on the Immune System," *Cell Microbiology* 16, no. 7 (July 2014): 1004–13; Samsam, M., R. Ahangari, and S. A. Naser, "Pathophysiology of Autism Spectrum Disorders: Revisiting Gastrointestinal Involvement and Immune Imbalance," *World Journal of Gastroenterology* 20, no. 29 (Aug. 2014): 9942–51; Wasilewska, J., E. Jarocka-Cyrta, and M. Kaczmarski, "Gastrointestinal Abnormalities in Children with Autism" [in Polish], *Polski Merkuriusz Lekarski* 27, no. 157 (July 2009): 40–43.

3. Frye, R. E., S. Rose, J. Slattery, and D. F. MacFabe, "Gastrointestinal Dysfunction in Autism Spectrum Disorder: The Role of the Mitochondria and the Enteric Microbiome," *Microbial Ecology in Health and Disease* 26 (2015): 27458; MacFabe, D. F., "Short-Chain Fatty Acid Fermentation Products of the Gut Microbiome: Implications in Autism Spectrum Disorders," *Microbial Ecology in Health and Disease* 23 (2012:19260); Shaw, W., "Increased Urinary Excretion of a 3-(3-Hydroxyphenyl)-3-Hydroxypropionic Acid (HPHPA), an Abnormal Phenylalanine Metabolite of Clostridia Spp. in the Gastrointestinal Tract, in Urine Samples from Patients with Autism and Schizophrenia," *Nutritional Neuroscience* 13, no. 3 (June 2010): 135–43.

4. Bradstreet et al., "Biomarker-Guided Interventions of Clinically Relevant Conditions Associated with Autism Spectrum Disorders and Attention Deficit Hyperactivity Disorder"; Samsam, Ahangari, and Naser, "Pathophysiology of Autism Spectrum Disorders: Revisiting Gastrointestinal Involvement and Immune Imbalance"; Wasilewska, Jarocka-Cyrta, and Kaczmarski, "Gastrointestinal Abnormalities in Children with Autism."

5. Compare, D., L. Pica, A. Rocco, F. De Giorgi, R. Cuomo, G. Sarnelli, M. Romano, and G. Nardone, "Effects of Long-Term PPI Treatment on Producing Bowel Symptoms and SIBO," *European Journal of Clinical Investigation* 41, no. 4 (Apr. 2011): 380–86.

6. Miazga, A., M. Osinski, W. Cichy, and R. Zaba, "Current Views on the Etiopathogenesis, Clinical Manifestation, Diagnostics, Treatment, and Correlation with Other Nosological Entities of SIBO," *Advances in Medical Sciences* 60, no. 1 (Mar. 2015): 118–24.

7. Khalighi, A. R., M. R. Khalighi, R. Behdani, J. Jamali, A. Khosravi, Sh. Kouhestani, H. Radmanesh, S. Esmaeelzadeh, and N. Khalighi, "Evaluating the Efficacy of Probiotic on Treatment in Patients with Small Intestinal Bacterial Overgrowth (SIBO): A Pilot Study," *Indian Journal of Medical Research* 140, no. 5 (Nov. 2014): 604–8.

8. Jawhara, S., and D. Poulain, "Saccharomyces Boulardii Decreases Inflammation and Intestinal Colonization by Candida Albicans in a Mouse Model of Chemically Induced Colitis," *Medical Mycology* 45, no. 8 (Dec. 2007): 691–700.

9. Qamar, A., S. Aboudola, M. Warny, P. Michetti, C. Pothoulakis, J. T. LaMont, and C. P. Kelly, "Saccharomyces Boulardii Stimulates Intestinal Immunoglobulin A Immune Response to Clostridium Difficile Toxin in Mice," *Infection and Immunity* 69, no. 4 (Apr. 2001): 2762–65; Rodrigues, A. C., D. C. Cara, S. H. Fretez, F. Q. Cunha, E. C. Vieira, J. R. Nicoli, and L. Q. Vieira, "Saccharomyces Boulardii Stimulates sIgA Production and the Phagocytic System of Gnotobiotic Mice," *Journal of Applied Microbiology* 89, no. 3 (Sept. 2000): 404–14.

10. Jawhara and Poulain, "Saccharomyces Boulardii Decreases Inflammation and Intestinal Colonization by Candida Albicans in a Mouse Model."

11. Szajewska, H., A. Horvath, and M. Kolodziej, "Systematic Review with Meta-

Analysis: Saccharomyces Boulardii Supplementation and Eradication of Helicobacter Pylori Infection," *Alimentary Pharmacology and Therapeutics* 41, no. 12 (June 2015): 1237–45.

12. Castex, F., G. Corthier, S. Jouvert, G. W. Elmer, F. Lucas, and M. Bastide, "Prevention of Clostridium Difficile–Induced Experimental Pseudomembranous Colitis by Saccharomyces Boulardii: A Scanning Electron Microscopic and Microbiological Study," *Journal of General Microbiology* 136, no. 6 (June 1990): 1085–89.

13. Kelesidis, T., and C. Pothoulakis, "Efficacy and Safety of the Probiotic Saccharomyces Boulardii for the Prevention and Therapy of Gastrointestinal Disorders," *Therapeutic Advances in Gastroenterology* 5, no. 2 (Mar. 2012): 111–25; Linday, L. A., "Saccharomyces Boulardii: Potential Adjunctive Treatment for Children with Autism and Diarrhea," *Journal of Child Neurology* 16, no. 5 (May 2001): 387.

14. Castex et al., "Prevention of Clostridium Difficile–Induced Experimental Pseudomembranous Colitis by Saccharomyces Boulardii"; Jawhara and Poulain, "Saccharomyces Boulardii Decreases Inflammation and Intestinal Colonization by Candida Albicans in a Mouse Model"; Szajewska, Horvath, and Kolodziej, "Systematic Review with Meta-Analysis: Saccharomyces Boulardii Supplementation and Eradication of Helicobacter Pylori Infection."

15. Castagliuolo, I., M. F. Riegler, L. Valenick, J. T. LaMont, and C. Pothoulakis, "Saccharomyces Boulardii Protease Inhibits the Effects of Clostridium Difficile Toxins A and B in Human Colonic Mucosa," *Infection and Immunity* 67, no. 1 (Jan. 1999): 302–7.

16. Jawhara and Poulain, "Saccharomyces Boulardii Decreases Inflammation and Intestinal Colonization by Candida Albicans in a Mouse Model."

17. Li, M., L. Zhu, A. Xie, and J. Yuan, "Oral Administration of Saccharomyces Boulardii Ameliorates Carbon Tetrachloride–Induced Liver Fibrosis in Rats Via Reducing Intestinal Permeability and Modulating Gut Microbial Composition," *Inflammation* 38, no. 1 (Feb. 2015): 170–79.

18. Micklefield, G., "Saccharomyces Boulardii in the Treatment and Prevention of Antibiotic-Associated Diarrhea" [in German], supplement, *MMW Fortschritte der Medizin* 156, no. S1 (Apr. 17, 2014): 18–22.

19. McFarland, L. V., "Systematic Review and Meta-Analysis of Saccharomyces Boulardii in Adult Patients," *World Journal of Gastroenterology* 16, no. 18 (May 14, 2010): 2202–22.

20. Fitzpatrick, L. R., "Probiotics for the Treatment of Clostridium Difficile Associated Disease," *World Journal of Gastrointestinal Pathophysiology* 4, no. 3 (Aug. 15, 2013): 47–52.

21. Dinleyici, E. C., A. Kara, N. Dalgic, Z. Kurugol, V. Arica, O. Metin, E. Temur, et al., "Saccharomyces Boulardii CNCM I-745 Reduces the Duration of Diarrhoea, Length of Emergency Care, and Hospital Stay in Children with Acute Diarrhoea," *Beneficial Microbes* 6, no. 4 (Jan. 2015): 415–21.

22. McFarland, "Systematic Review and Meta-Analysis of Saccharomyces Boulardii in Adult Patients."
23. Jawhara and Poulain, "Saccharomyces Boulardii Decreases Inflammation and Intestinal Colonization by Candida Albicans in a Mouse Model."
24. Schneider, S. M., F. Girard-Pipau, J. Filippi, X. Hebuterne, D. Moyse, G. C. Hinojosa, A. Pompei, and P. Rampal, "Effects of Saccharomyces Boulardii on Fecal Short-Chain Fatty Acids and Microflora in Patients on Long-Term Total Enteral Nutrition," *World Journal of Gastroenterology* 11, no. 39 (Oct. 21, 2005): 6165–69.
25. Qamar et al., "Saccharomyces Boulardii Stimulates Intestinal Immunoglobulin A Immune Response to Clostridium Difficile Toxin in Mice"; Rodrigues et al., "Saccharomyces Boulardii Stimulates sIgA Production and the Phagocytic System of Gnotobiotic Mice."
26. McFarland, "Systematic Review and Meta-Analysis of Saccharomyces Boulardii in Adult Patients."
27. Ibid.
28. Linday, L. A., "Saccharomyces Boulardii: Potential Adjunctive Treatment for Children with Autism and Diarrhea."
29. Kelesidis and Pothoulakis, "Efficacy and Safety of the Probiotic Saccharomyces Boulardii for the Prevention and Therapy of Gastrointestinal Disorders."

Chapter 7: Why Is My Child Always Sick?

1. Ashwood, P., S. Wills, and J. Van de Water, "The Immune Response in Autism: A New Frontier for Autism Research," *Journal of Leukocyte Biology* 80, no. 1 (July 2006): 1–15; Gupta, S., S. Aggarwal, B. Rashanravan, and T. Lee, "Th1- and Th2-Like Cytokines in CD4+ and CD8+ T Cells in Autism," *Journal of Neuroimmunology* 85, no. 1 (May 1 1998): 106–9; Molloy, C. A., A. L. Morrow, J. Meinzen-Derr, K. Schleifer, K. Dienger, P. Manning-Courtney, M. Altaye, and M. Wills-Karp, "Elevated Cytokine Levels in Children with Autism Spectrum Disorder," *Journal of Neuroimmunology* 172, no. 1–2 (Mar. 2006): 198–205.
2. Theoharides, T. C., "Is a Subtype of Autism an Allergy of the Brain?" *Clinical Therapeutics* 35, no. 5 (May 2013): 584–91.
3. Chandler, S., I. Carcani-Rathwell, T. Charman, A. Pickles, T. Loucas, D. Meldrum, E. Simonoff, P. Sullivan, and G. Baird, "Parent-Reported Gastro-Intestinal Symptoms in Children with Autism Spectrum Disorders," *Journal of Autism and Developmental Disorders* 43, no. 12 (Dec. 2013): 2737–47; Gupta et al., "Th1- and Th2-Like Cytokines in CD4+ and CD8+ T Cells in Autism."
4. Jyonouchi, H., S. Sun, and H. Le, "Proinflammatory and Regulatory Cytokine Production Associated with Innate and Adaptive Immune Responses in Children with Autism Spectrum Disorders and Developmental Regression," *Journal of Neuroimmunology* 120, no. 1–2 (Nov. 1, 2001): 170–79.
5. Molloy et al., "Elevated Cytokine Levels in Children with Autism Spectrum Disorder."

6. Tsilioni, I., N. Dodman, A. I. Petra, A. Taliou, K. Francis, A. Moon-Fanelli, L. Shuster, and T. C. Theoharides, "Elevated Serum Neurotensin and CRH Levels in Children with Autistic Spectrum Disorders and Tail-Chasing Bull Terriers with a Phenotype Similar to Autism," *Translational Psychiatry* 4 (2014): e466.

7. Messahel, S., A. E. Pheasant, H. Pall, J. Ahmed-Choudhury, R. S. Sungum-Paliwal, and P. Vostanis, "Urinary Levels of Neopterin and Biopterin in Autism," *Neuroscience Letters* 241, no. 1 (Jan. 23, 1998): 17–20; Zhao, H. X., S. S. Yin, and J. G. Fan, "High Plasma Neopterin Levels in Chinese Children with Autism Spectrum Disorders," *International Journal of Developmental Neuroscience* 41 (Apr. 2015): 92–97.

8. Pardo, C. A., D. L. Vargas, and A. W. Zimmerman, "Immunity, Neuroglia, and Neuroinflammation in Autism," *International Review of Psychiatry* 17, no. 6 (Dec. 2005): 485–95; Theoharides, T. C., J. M. Stewart, S. Panagiotidou, and I. Melamed, "Mast Cells, Brain Inflammation, and Autism," *European Journal of Pharmacology* (May 1, 2015); Vargas, D. L., et al., "Neuroglial Activation and Neuroinflammation in the Brain of Patients with Autism," *Annals of Neurology* 57 (Jan. 2005): 67–81.

9. Theoharides et al., "Mast Cells, Brain Inflammation, and Autism."

10. Theoharides et al., "Mast Cells, Brain Inflammation, and Autism"; Vargas et al., "Neuroglial Activation and Neuroinflammation in the Brain of Patients with Autism."

11. Rodriguez, J. I., and J. K. Kern, "Evidence of Microglial Activation in Autism and Its Possible Role in Brain Underconnectivity," *Neuron Glia Biology* 7, no. 2–4 (May 2011): 205–13.

12. Zhang, B., A. Angelidou, K. D. Alysandratos, M. Vasiadi, K. Francis, S. Asadi, A. Theoharides, et al., "Mitochondrial DNA and Anti-Mitochondrial Antibodies in Serum of Autistic Children," *Journal of Neuroinflammation* 7 (2010): 80.

13. Vojdani, A., A. W. Campbell, E. Anyanwu, A. Kashanian, K. Bock, and E. Vojdani, "Antibodies to Neuron-Specific Antigens in Children with Autism: Possible Cross-Reaction with Encephalitogenic Proteins from Milk, Chlamydia Pneumoniae, and Streptococcus Group A," *Journal of Neuroimmunology* 129, no. 1–2 (Aug. 2002): 168–77.

14. Singh, V. K., R. P. Warren, J. D. Odell, W. L. Warren, and P. Cole, "Antibodies to Myelin Basic Protein in Children with Autistic Behavior," *Brain, Behavior, and Immunity* 7, no. 1 (Mar. 1993): 97–103.

15. Cabanlit, M., S. Wills, P. Goines, P. Ashwood, and J. Van de Water, "Brain-Specific Autoantibodies in the Plasma of Subjects with Autistic Spectrum Disorder," *Annals of the New York Academy of Sciences* 1107 (June 2007): 92–103.

16. Ibid.

17. Wills, S., C. C. Rossi, J. Bennett, V. Martinez Cerdeno, P. Ashwood, D. G. Amaral, and J. Van de Water, "Further Characterization of Autoantibodies to GABAergic Neurons in the Central Nervous System Produced by a Subset of Children with Autism," *Molecular Autism* 2 (2011): 1–15.

18. Connolly, A. M., M. G. Chez, A. Pestronk, S. T. Arnold, S. Mehta, and R. K. Deuel,

"Serum Autoantibodies to Brain in Landau-Kleffner Variant, Autism, and Other Neurologic Disorders," *Journal of Pediatrics* 134, no. 5 (May 1999): 607–13.

19. Ibid.

20. Singh, V. K., and R. L. Jensen, "Elevated Levels of Measles Antibodies in Children with Autism," *Pediatric Neurology* 28, no. 4 (Apr. 2003): 292–94.

21. Mead, J., and P. Ashwood, "Evidence Supporting an Altered Immune Response in ASD," *Immunology Letters* 163, no. 1 (Jan. 2015): 49–55.

22. Ashwood, Wills, and J Van de Water, "The Immune Response in Autism: A New Frontier for Autism Research."

23. Singh and Jensen, "Elevated Levels of Measles Antibodies in Children with Autism."

24. Jyonouchi, H., L. Geng, A. Ruby, C. Reddy, and B. Zimmerman-Bier, "Evaluation of an Association Between Gastrointestinal Symptoms and Cytokine Production Against Common Dietary Proteins in Children with Autism Spectrum Disorders," *Journal of Pediatrics* 146, no. 5 (May 2005): 605–10; Jyonouchi, H., L. Geng, A. Ruby, and B. Zimmerman-Bier, "Dysregulated Innate Immune Responses in Young Children with Autism Spectrum Disorders: Their Relationship to Gastrointestinal Symptoms and Dietary Intervention," *Neuropsychobiology* 51, no. 2 (2005): 77–85; Jyonouchi, H., S. Sun, and N. Itokazu, "Innate Immunity Associated with Inflammatory Responses and Cytokine Production Against Common Dietary Proteins in Patients with Autism Spectrum Disorder," *Neuropsychobiology* 46, no. 2 (2002): 76–84.

25. Edlin, R. S., D. J. Shapiro, A. L. Hersh, and H. L. Copp, "Antibiotic Resistance Patterns of Outpatient Pediatric Urinary Tract Infections," *Journal of Urology* 190, no. 1 (July 2013): 222–27; Miranda, E. J., G. S. Oliveira, F. L. Roque, S. R. Santos, R. D. Olmos, and P. A. Lotufo, "Susceptibility to Antibiotics in Urinary Tract Infections in a Secondary Care Setting from 2005–2006 and 2010–2011, in Sao Paulo, Brazil: Data from 11,943 Urine Cultures," *Revista do Instituto de Medicina Tropical de Sao Paulo* 56, no. 4 (July/Aug. 2014): 313–24.

26. Gordon, C. M., K. C. DePeter, H. A. Feldman, E. Grace, and S. J. Emans, "Prevalence of Vitamin D Deficiency Among Healthy Adolescents," *Archives of Pediatrics and Adolescent Medicine* 158, no. 6 (June 2004): 531–37; Gordon, C. M., H. A. Feldman, L. Sinclair, A. L. Williams, P. K. Kleinman, J. Perez-Rossello, and J. E. Cox, "Prevalence of Vitamin D Deficiency Among Healthy Infants and Toddlers," *Archives of Pediatrics and Adolescent Medicine* 162, no. 6 (June 2008): 505–12; Huh, S. Y., and C. M. Gordon, "Vitamin D Deficiency in Children and Adolescents: Epidemiology, Impact, and Treatment," *Reviews in Endocrine and Metabolic Disorders* 9, no. 2 (June 2008): 161–70.

27. Tripkovic, L., H. Lambert, K. Hart, C. Smith, G. Bucca, S. Penson, G. Chope, E. Hyppönen, J. Berry, R. Vieth, and S. Lanham-New, "Comparison of Vitamin D2 and Vitamin D3 Supplementation in Raising Serum 25-Hydroxyvitamin D Status: A Systematic Review and Meta-Analysis," *American Journal of Clinical Nutrition* 95, no. 6 (June 2012): 1357–64.

28. Hoffmann, P. R., and M. J. Berry, "The Influence of Selenium on Immune Responses," *Molecular Nutrition and Food Research* 52, no. 11 (Nov. 2008): 1273–80.

29. Roy, M., L. Kiremidjian-Schumacher, H. I. Wishe, M. W. Cohen, and G. Stotzky, "Supplementation with Selenium and Human Immune Cell Functions: I. Effect on Lymphocyte Proliferation and Interleukin 2 Receptor Expression," *Biological Trace Element Resesearch* 41, no. 1–2 (Apr./May 1994): 103–14.

30. http://www.vetmed.ucdavis.edu/local_resources/pdfs/impact_sheets_pdfs/Autism PessahFormat2.pdf; Ahn, K. C., B. Zhao, J. Chen, G. Cherednichenko, E. Sanmarti, M. S. Denison, B. Lasley, I. N. Pessah, D. Kültz, D. P. Chang, S. J. Gee, and B. D. Hammock, "In Vitro Biologic Activities of the Antimicrobials Triclocarban, Its Analogs, and Triclosan in Bioassay Screens: Receptor-Based Bioassay Screens," *Environmental Health Perspectives* 116, no. 9 (Sept. 2008): 1203–10; Cherednichenko, G., R. Zhang, R. A. Bannister, V. Timofeyev, N. Li , E. B. Fritsch, W. Feng, G. C. Barrientos, N. H. Schebb, B. D. Hammock, K. G. Beam, N. Chiamvimonvat, and I. N. Pessah, "Triclosan Impairs Excitation-Contraction Coupling and Ca2+ Dynamics in Striated Muscle," *Proceedings of the National Academy of Sciences* 109, no. 35 (Aug. 28, 2012): 14158–63.

31. Brigandi, S. A., H. Shao, S. Y. Qian, Y. Shen, B. L. Wu, and J. X. Kang, "Autistic Children Exhibit Decreased Levels of Essential Fatty Acids in Red Blood Cells," *International Journal of Molecular Sciences* 16, no. 5 (2015): 10061–76.

32. Das, U. N., "Essential Fatty Acids and Their Metabolites Could Function as Endogenous HMG-CoA Reductase and ACE Enzyme Inhibitors, Anti-Arrhythmic, Anti-Hypertensive, Anti-Atherosclerotic, Anti-Inflammatory, Cytoprotective, and Cardioprotective Molecules," *Lipids in Health and Disease* 7 (2008): 1–18.

33. Yasuda, H., K. Yoshida, Y. Yasuda, and T. Tsutsui, "Infantile Zinc Deficiency: Association with Autism Spectrum Disorders," *Scientific Reports* 1 (2011): 129.

34. Liu, J., A. Hanlon, C. Ma, S. R. Zhao, S. Cao, and C. Compher, "Low Blood Zinc, Iron, and Other Sociodemographic Factors Associated with Behavior Problems in Preschoolers," *Nutrients* 6, no. 2 (2014): 530–45.

35. Yin, S. Y., H. J. Kim, and H. J. Kim, "Protective Effect of Dietary Xylitol on Influenza A Virus Infection," *PLOS One* 9, no. 1 (2014): e84633.

Chapter 8: The Forgotten Ones

1. Autism Speaks, "National Housing and Residential Supports Survey"; Billstedt, E., I. C. Gillberg, and C. Gillberg, "Autism After Adolescence: Population-Based 13- to 22-Year Follow-up Study of 120 Individuals with Autism Diagnosed in Childhood," *Journal of Autism and Developmental Disorders* 35, no. 3 (June 2005): 351–60; Seltzer, M. M., P. Shattuck, L. Abbeduto, and J. S. Greenberg, "Trajectory of Development in Adolescents and Adults with Autism," *Mental Retardation and Developmental Disabilities Research Reviews* 10, no. 4 (2004): 234–47.

2. Myers, S. M., C. P. Johnson, and Council on Children with Disabilities, "Management of Children with Autism Spectrum Disorders," *Pediatrics* 120, no. 5 (Nov. 2007): 1162–82.

3. Ibid.

4. Autism Speaks, "National Housing and Residential Supports Survey."

5. Myers, Johnson, and Council on Children with Disabilities, "Management of Children with Autism Spectrum Disorders."

6. Autism Speaks, "National Housing and Residential Supports Survey."

7. Ibid.

8. American Academy of Pediatrics, Medical Home Initiatives for Children with Special Needs Project Advisory Committee, "The Medical Home," supplement, *Pediatrics* 113, no. S5 (2004): 1545–47; Cooley, W. C., "Redefining Primary Pediatric Care for Children with Special Health Care Needs: The Primary Care Medical Home," *Current Opinion in Pediatrics* 16 (2004): 689–92.

9. Myers, Johnson, and Council on Children with Disabilities, "Management of Children with Autism Spectrum Disorders."

10. Dawe, M., "Desperately Seeking Simplicity: How Young Adults with Cognitive Disabilities and Their Families Adopt Assistive Technologies," *Association for Computing Machinery Digital Library* (2006): 1143–52.

11. Huang, P., T. Kao, A. E. Curry, and D. R. Durbin, "Factors Associated with Driving in Teens with Autism Spectrum Disorders," *Journal of Developmental and Behavioral Pediatrics* 33, no. 1 (Jan. 2012): 70–74.

12. Ibid.

GLOSSARY OF TERMS AND ABBREVIATIONS

Abilify   An antipsychotic medication.

Antibiotic   A medication or substance that kills bacteria or slows their growth.

Antibody   A protein made by our immune system that attacks invading pathogens, allergens such as dust or foods, or even our own body tissues.

Antifungal   A medication or supplement that kills or slows the growth of yeast and fungi.

Antihistamines   Medications or supplements that reduce or block histamines, the chemicals that cause symptoms in an allergic reaction.

Antihypertensive   A medication that lowers blood pressure.

Antimicrobial (AM)   A medication or supplement that kills or slows the growth of microorganisms.

Antioxidant   A substance that prevents or slows oxidation (damage) of cells.

Antipsychotics   Psychiatric medications used for schizophrenia and bipolar disorder.

ASD   Autism spectrum disorder, a neurodevelopmental disorder characterized by varying degrees of social, communication, and behavioral difficulties.

Benzodiazepines   Tranquilizers.

Candidiasis   A Candida (yeast) infection.

Canker sore   An open, painful mouth ulcer.

Casomorphin   An opioid protein fragment formed when we digest dairy foods.

Celiac disease   Autoimmune disorder where eating gluten damages the small intestine.

Cellulase   Enzymes that break down cellulose.

Cellulose   A tough polysaccharide substance found in cell walls of plants.

Clostridia difficile Also known as C. diff, a gram-positive, spore-forming bacteria found in soil and nature.

Comprehensive psychological evaluation Also known as a "psych eval," an assessment that can diagnose emotional, developmental, and behavioral disorders, as well as emotional functioning.

Cradle cap Infantile seborrheic dermatitis, which causes scaly patches on the scalp.

Cytokines Proteins that act as molecular messengers between cells of the immune system to regulate the body's inflammatory responses.

DAN! Defeat Autism Now! A now-defunct program created in 1995 by the Autism Research Institute to treat underlying dysfunction of ASD.

Daytrana Stimulant ADHD medication patch.

Detoxification The removal of toxic substances from the body.

Developmental optometry An optometric specialty that corrects how a person processes visual information.

Die-off A term used to describe a mass death of fungi or bacteria, usually accompanied by a release of toxins.

Dyslexia A learning disorder that affects the way written and spoken words are recognized and processed.

Eczema Commonly called atopic dermatitis, an itchy rash usually on the face, the backs of the knees, wrists, hands, feet, and inner elbows. It can be associated with yeast infections in the GI tract.

Epsom salt A mineral containing hydrous magnesium sulphate. It is a home remedy to relieve muscle tension, cramping, and stress.

Failure to thrive (FTT) When a child isn't growing or developing normally, appears smaller and shorter than peers, and weighs less than the third percentile of standard growth charts.

Food sensitivity Not a true allergy, but a negative reaction after eating certain foods.

Floppy baby Also known as neonatal hypotonia, or low muscle tone.

GABA Gamma-aminobutyric acid, the main calming neurotransmitter made by our own body.

Genitourinary The organs of the urinary and reproductive systems.

Glutathione Our body's most important antioxidant, which neutralizes free radicals, among other important duties.

Gluteomorphin An opioid peptide that forms when we digest foods containing gluten.

Hyperbaric oxygen therapy (HBOT)   Medical treatment in a hard or soft-sided chamber with increased pressure and oxygen.

Hypothalamus   A structure in the brain.

IgE   Immunoglobulin E, a type of antibody associated with allergies.

IgG   Immunoglobulin G, a type of antibody associated with food sensitivities.

Keratosis pilaris   A skin condition with non-itchy bumps on the backs of the arms, thighs, buttocks, and cheeks.

Lactase   An enzyme that breaks down lactose.

Lortab   A painkiller.

Maldigestion   Problems with digesting food and absorbing nutrients.

Mast cell   A type of immune cell.

Melatonin   A hormone our body makes to control sleep/wake cycles.

Methylation   A metabolic process vital to life.

Methylphenidate   Stimulant ADHD medication.

Microbiome   The collection of microbes that live anywhere in our body.

Microglia   An immune defense cell in the brain and spinal cord.

MiraLAX   A laxative.

Mitochondria   Structures that generate the energy a cell needs.

Molluscum contagiosum   A viral skin infection that may be confused with the common wart.

Monocyte   A type of white blood cell.

Myelin basic protein   A protein that insulates nerves and brain cells.

Natural killer cell   A type of white blood cell.

Neopterin   A marker of activated cellular immunity.

Neurofeedback   A type of brain training.

Neuroinflammation   Brain inflammation.

Neuropeptides   Protein segments that can cross the blood-brain barrier into the brain.

Neurotensin   A peptide that is found in the central and peripheral nervous systems.

Neurotransmitters   Chemical messengers in the nervous system.

Nexium   An acid reflux medication.

Off-label use   When drugs are used for an unapproved indication.

Opioid A chemical that has opiate-like effects.

OT Occupational therapy addresses deficits in skills used to perform everyday activities

Oxalates The salts of oxalic acid that, when combined with metallic ions, form sharp hard crystals such as those found in kidney stones.

Oxidative stress Imbalance between free radicals and our body's antioxidant defenses, resulting in damage to tissues in the body.

Oxycontin A narcotic pain reliever.

Pathogen An infectious agent that causes disease or illness.

PECS Picture Exchange Communication System.

Pedia-Lax A pediatric line of constipation products.

Peptide A short chain of amino acids.

Perseveration Repeating words, phrases, or gestures.

Polypharmacy The use of four or more medications.

Prebiotic A food source for beneficial bacteria.

Prevacid A medication for acid reflux.

Proprionic acid A carboxylic acid produced by Clostridia difficile that, when injected into the brains of rats, produces "autistic behaviors" such as social impairment, hyperactivity, and perseveration, and changes such as neuroinflammation and glutathione depletion.

Proton pump inhibitor A class of medications for acid reflux.

Risperidone Generic for Risperdal, an antipsychotic.

Ritalin A stimulant ADHD medication.

Salicylate A type of organic acid found in plants.

Sensory diet Doing sensory activities throughout the day to maintain appropriate arousal states.

Sensory evaluation An evaluation of sensory-processing abilities by an occupational therapist.

Singulair A prescription asthma and allergic rhinitis medicine.

SLP Speech language pathologist.

Specific Carbohydrate Diet A diet free of grains, starches, and complex sugars.

ST Speech therapy.

Stereotypy Repetitive motions such as rocking or flapping the hands.

Stimming Stereotypy.

Stool softener A medication that softens the feces.

Strattera A nonstimulant ADHD medication.

Strep Shorthand for streptococcus bacteria.

Sulforaphanes Disease-fighting compounds found in plants, especially broccoli sprouts.

T-cell A type of lymphocyte in the immune system.

Thalamus A structure in the brain.

Th1 A type of T helper cell that is a part of the cell-mediated immune response associated with protecting us from viruses, fungi, and certain bacteria.

Th2 A type of T helper cell that is a part of the antibody-mediated immune response associated with allergies and asthma.

Tic Involuntary muscular contraction or vocalization.

Tourette disorder A neurological disorder characterized by involuntary muscular contractions and vocalizations.

Tubes Shorthand for a tympanostomy tube inserted into the eardrum.

Tympanostomy A procedure to insert a small tube into the eardrum to prevent buildup of fluid.

Vyvanse A stimulant ADHD medication.

Xylitol A sugar alcohol used to sweeten food and drinks.

Zyrtec An allergy medication.

HELPFUL RESOURCES

App: *The Un-Prescription for Autism*: An app by the author designed to schedule the protocols suggested in this book in a helpful calendar format. Available in the App Store.

Article: "Double Take: Developmental Optometry and Autism Spectrum Disorder" http://www.emaxhealth.com/12087/autism-and-optometry-double-take

Diets

- BodyEcology.com

- Feingold.org

- Gut and Psychology Syndrome (GAPS) Diet and book at doctor-natasha.com

- GFCFDiet.com

- Specific Carbohydrate Diet and book (for controlling yeast) at www.breaking theviciouscycle.info

- TACANow.org

Find a Doctor

- Medical Academy of Pediatric Special Needs (MAPS) maintains a clinician directory on its website: www.medmaps.org

- Elizabeth Mumper, MD, FAAP
  Rimland Center for Integrative Medicine
  2919 Confederate Avenue
  Lynchburg, VA 24501
  Phone: 434-528-9075
  www.rimlandcenter.com

- Monika Buerger, DC
  Eagle Canyon Wellness and Sensory Development Center
  1516 Midway Avenue
  Ammon, ID 83406
  208-346-7763
  www.EagleCanyonWellness.com

Laboratory Companies

- Alletess: foodallergy.com

- Doctor's Data: www.doctorsdata.com

- Genova Diagnostics: www.gdx.net

- Great Plains Laboratory: www.greatplainslaboratory.com

- NeuroScience: www.neurorelief.com

Liquid Extracts

- Candida Yeast Formula and Parasite Herbal Formula by KidsWellness: www.kidswellness.com

- Essential Fatty Acid Complex by Ecological Formulas. Available at: www.camformulas.com

- Herb Pharm, a large selection widely available in health stores and at: www.herb-pharm.com

- Kid's Super Daily D3 by Carlson Laboratories: www.carlsonlabs.com

- NutriBiotic Grapefruit Seed Extract: nutribiotic.com

- speak by SpeechNutrients: www.speechnutrients.com

Supplements

- 100% Aloe Vera by George's: www.warrenlabsaloe.com

- Enhansa by Lee Silsby Compounding Pharmacy

- Houston Enzymes has very high-quality enzyme formulations for every need. http://www.houston-enzymes.com

- Kirkman Labs has a full line of supplements, including Sac b, and that completely painless Vitamin D test I mentioned. www.kirkmangroup.com

- Klaire Labs/ProThera has a top line of probiotics, in addition to enzymes and a full line of supplements:
  Klaire Labs®
  A ProThera®, Inc. brand
  Available exclusively through licensed healthcare professionals.

- Nordic Naturals: https://www.nordicnaturals.com

Training
- MAPS offers twice-a-year conferences, under the guidance of Daniel Rossignol, MD, FAAFP, for scientific, evidence-based training designed "by clinicians for clinicians": www.medmaps.org

- Monika Buerger, DC, offers functional neurology training for health professionals: www.Intersect4Kids.com

Websites
- Autism.com, the website of the Autism Research Institute, has a vast amount of information, tips, and research.

- Autism360.org is "a unique tool which provides an accurate report that captures the details of your child's or your own individuality and offers treatment options that have worked for others with closely matching records."

- www.LoveAutismHealth.com is the author's website associated with her center, Autism Health!, Pllc. It contains helpful information for autism families, including "Fact or Fart?"—an online game to answer FAQs and help with troubleshooting.

- www.JanetLintala.com is the author's website for her speaking engagements and book.

- Saving Our Kids, Healing Our Planet (www.sokhop.com).

TESTIMONIALS FROM PARENTS

The phrase "I am different, not less" has become "I am more" in our home. —Kelli White, parent of Jordan Ray White (17), patient at Autism Health [Dr. Lintala's clinic]

It has been life changing for not just Isaac, but for our entire family. —Chastity B.

My daughter, Victoria, diagnosed with autism at the age of 4, had obvious issues with gluten and casein. Dr. Lintala and her staff provided me with a wealth of information on how controlling her intake of these "toxic" foods and beverages could potentially change her autistic symptoms. After a stringent amount of tests and the introduction of custom-designed supplements, many of her "behaviors" disappeared, and her speech and language was noticeably improved. . . . I was so impressed with the amount of information that I was provided from the center, and the support I received each and every time was overwhelming. By far the most educational and beneficial program geared toward autism that I have encountered. —Angel S., RN, MSN

My son's mental and physical health has greatly improved. —Kelly T.

Seth likes to joke with me now; before he didn't understand it. His communication skills have greatly improved. —Teresa B.

The protocols have made such an amazing change in Mason's life. He no longer head bangs, he is speaking more, and his communication has greatly improved. —Sharon D., retired schoolteacher

After providing Thomas Dr. Lintala's diet and nutrition plan, my 17-year-old son, who had no possibility of achieving basic life goals, now has endless goals far beyond basic ones. —Betty H.

Autism Health [Dr. Lintala's clinic] has provided treatment and support that has allowed many of my clients to optimize their learning and decrease behavioral issues that often impede the learning process. —Betsy A., preschool special needs teacher

He went from a thrashing and sleepless child to a calm all-night sleeper. —Robin E.

Zachary's behavior has dramatically changed and I give all the credit to Dr. Lintala's protocols for all his progress. —Theresa S.

My son potty trained at 11 years old and that was huge for me. —Melissa G.

I don't have to go to the school every day now. He is more focused and doesn't disrupt his classmates. —Anonymous

He is a new child!!! —Theresa T., foster mother

His speech has increased and he has fewer meltdowns since he has started the protocol. He also is eating more things since starting the enzymes. —Brenda T.

Hyperbaric oxygen therapy helped my son with his fogginess and concentration. —Chea B.

My son changed back to my sweet child that I always knew was in there. His appetite improved and his bowel movements improved greatly!! It took time and I couldn't have done this without Autism Health's [Dr. Lintala's clinic's] protocols. —Sara

After only a few months as Dr. Lintala's patient, my son James's digestive system is now normal. His handwriting, attention, and communication have improved dramatically. Dr. Lintala is truly a godsend to us. —James and Tammy W.

Two years ago our (now) six-year-old, nonverbal son was showing signs of stomach discomfort. He had severe diaper rash, draped his belly on furniture, and spent long nights dozing while sitting in a recliner. Within weeks of starting Dr. Lintala's protocol his whole behavior began to settle, the diaper rash cleared, and he actually slept through the night for the first time. —Lorrie S.

She is no longer getting sick, and some of her sensory issues have improved. She is calmer and sleeping better. Her overall color is better—we see pictures from before and after and it's amazing to see the change. —Sheila H., foster mother

After working with Autism Health [Dr. Lintala's clinic] my son is now able to communicate some of his wants and needs with others. He is also able to form more words, which helps with his learning skills. —Ida K.

INDEX